MAO'S
AMERICA

A SURVIVOR'S WARNING

XI VAN FLEET

CENTER
STREET
New York • Nashville

Center Street
Hachette Book Group
1290 Avenue of the Americas, New York, NY 10104
centerstreet.com
@CenterStreet/@CenterStreetBooks

Originally published in hardcover and ebook by Center Street in October 2023
First trade paperback edition: October 2024

Center Street is a division of Hachette Book Group, Inc. The Center Street
name and logo are registered trademarks of Hachette Book Group, Inc.

The publisher is not responsible for websites (or their content) that are not
owned by the publisher.

The Hachette Speakers Bureau provides a wide range of authors for speaking
events. To find out more, go to hachettespeakersbureau.com or email
HachetteSpeakers@hbgusa.com.

Center Street books may be purchased in bulk for business, educational, or
promotional use. For information, please contact your local bookseller
or the Hachette Book Group Special Markets Department at
special.markets@hbgusa.com.

All photos are from the author's collection.

Library of Congress Control Number: 2023020960

ISBNs: 978-1-5460-0631-2 (trade paperback), 978-1-5460-0632-9 (ebook)

Printed in the United States of America

LSC-C

Printing 2, 2024

To former Speaker of the House Newt Gingrich,
whose encouragement inspired me to write this book

To my husband, who has been the constant support
for my undertaking of writing this book

CONTENTS

FOREWORD

James Lindsay

March 2023

It was dark, and I was looking out the window of yet another jet. I was flying home from yet another trip, and we had maybe fifteen minutes more until we'd touch down. I pushed the button on the side of my phone and turned off its light and looked out the window. Streetlights, storefronts, porch lights, and headlamps blinked back up at me from a few thousand feet below. I was looking at the country that I love, my home, and I thought to myself: *This can't happen here.*

Like on most of my flights, I had been reading. In this case, I was reading *Thought Reform and the Psychology of Totalism: A Study of "Brainwashing" in China* by Robert Jay Lifton. In that book, published in the early 1960s, Lifton explored the psychological impacts of "Thought Reform" in the CCP-run brainwashing prisons in Mao Zedong's China; as with reading any close-up case study of any totalitarian project as it collides with the individual human, it was harrowing. *This can't happen here.*

But then it hit me, hard, as I looked down at the white, orange, blue, and yellow lights below me, dotting the nighttime landscape of Anywhere, USA. *This is already happening here.* It was instantaneous recognition followed by immediate grief and panic. *This is already happening here. This is diversity, equity, and inclusion training at work. This is social-emotional learning at school. This is already happening here.*

Mao proudly asserted that his revolution was based upon "Marxism-Leninism with Chinese characteristics," and in my reading of Lifton's book, I suddenly realized my intuition about what has been happening in America over the last decade, most visibly and tangibly since 2020, is the American cultural revolution: a Maoist cultural revolution with American characteristics. And I was right: *This can't happen here.* It has to be stopped.

The American cultural revolution is here and has progressed a long way toward its goals of destroying America from within to transform it into something based on some new mutation of Marxist theory. In early 2020, before virtually anyone knew who George Floyd was, I warned several senior officials that in my estimation, there would be a "Chinese-style cultural revolution" based on critical race theory kicking off in the United States within the next six months, but at the time, it just didn't seem plausible. I warned of an impending "anti-racist cultural revolution" through much of that year and used it to name the mayhem that erupted in the wake of the death of Floyd virtually immediately. I hoped someone would know how to stop it before it fully started.

How did I know? I'm not telling this story to puff myself up or make me look smart or special. It's far simpler than that, which is great news because it means anyone can do it. I got lucky, in a sense. It comes down to something very straightforward: I had spent most of the previous year reading about critical race theory in detail to understand what I had been seeing going on around me in our country over the previous decade, especially since 2015.

In the two and a half years since, I have taken the time to study many of Mao's tactics, strategies, and formulas, and his fingerprints are all over the American cultural revolution. I have also had the honor and pleasure of meeting brave voices within Chinese American communities who are speaking up and speaking out, telling their stories and raising the alarm: *This thing that's happening here; we know what it is! It's Maoism!* Among those voices I found Xi Van Fleet, who has written this admirable manuscript to tell her story of living through *two* cultural revolutions, one Chinese and one American, and to draw parallels between them. The evidence is undeniable. The theory, the practice, the strategies, the tools, and the results are all the same. The American cultural revolution is a Maoist Cultural Revolution with American characteristics. In these pages and in her speeches and interviews, Xi makes that fact abundantly clear. She also communicates viscerally what I felt on that plane that night: *This can't happen here.*

America is a special nation. It was a refuge for people like Xi from many other places around the world when Communists and other tyrants were robbing them of their freedoms and human dignity. It provided them liberty and opportunity like no other nation on earth could have done or ever has before. Now it's under extraordinary threat, and America may be repaid generously and saved from its own destruction because it stood through that crucial time as the beacon and promise of liberty in the world. People like Xi and millions of others came to this country in the hours of their darkest need, and they brought their stories with them. How it happened. What went wrong. What's coming if we don't wake up and stop it. Their stories are becoming our story, and that's a gift we should treasure.

It's my great honor to have been invited to write the foreword to this noble work that sounds one of the most important alarms that has ever rung in the world. May you find it as clarifying and encouraging as I did.

INTRODUCTION

The year 2020 was a watershed moment in American history. The outbreak of a pandemic brought ashore to us from the Chinese Communist Party (CCP) and the death of George Floyd created the perfect storm. This storm delivered a heavy blow to America, a blow so severe that America now appears to have been possibly changed forever.

Suddenly, many Americans, focused on working hard, raising their families, and minding their own business, awakened to the realization that they hardly recognized their own country anymore. Overnight, it seemed new realities were being forced upon them, challenging everything they believed to be true. From the progressives came the demand that one must comply with their cause to remake America by denouncing all its institutions, all its traditional values, and its very foundation. To do otherwise incurs being ostracized and demonized on social media, in schools, in workplaces, and even within families. To do otherwise, one is now simply labeled a *racist*. To do otherwise, one may lose their livelihood.

Many awoke only to find that they have become oppressors for being born white. Others found that they must now consider themselves hopelessly oppressed and incapable simply because they were born non-white. Many are bewildered that reality and common sense no longer mean anything. During the riots in the summer of 2020, viewers were told they were watching mostly peaceful protests while buildings were burning in the background. All of a sudden, no one is sure how to define a woman and everyone must now believe men can have babies. Parents were dumbfounded to see firsthand through Zoom classes what their children are being taught in public schools—that America is an unredeemable, racist country.

During the pandemic, average Americans found themselves less and less free to make choices for themselves and for their families. The government at every level now, from the school board to federal authorities, demands submission to tyrannical orders that often appear nonsensical and politically charged. Parents who speak out at school board meetings can now be labeled as domestic terrorists by the US Department of Justice. Americans are now told to accept a new reality where the police have become villains and criminals have become victims who are allowed to roam freely in our cities and communities, terrorizing the citizens.

Hardworking, tax-paying Americans have found themselves strangers in their own country. What is happening? Why? For what purpose?

But wait…I have seen all of this before.

Like most Americans, I also felt like I was hit by a storm. Unlike most Americans, this storm hit me once before, more than fifty years ago, when I was only seven years old, just starting school in China.

The storm was the Great Proletarian Cultural Revolution launched by Mao Zedong, the Communist dictator who ruled over China from 1949 to 1976. And it lasted ten years, covering most of my school years.

In my memory, it also appeared to happen overnight, just like it did here in America in 2020!

Overnight, we were told the country we lived in was rotten to the core and needed to be dismantled. Instead of looking for racists, we were ordered to look for "counterrevolutionaries." Just like the term *racist* now has an ever-changing, fluid definition, such was the term "counterrevolutionary." The term was applied to anyone Mao did not like, anyone we thought Mao would not like, anyone who dared to question, and anyone who was not enthusiastically participating in the Cultural Revolution. Everyone frantically joined the ranks of the revolutionaries. To be left out meant ending up an enemy of Mao.

People turned against each other in search of enemies and in defense of Mao. Friends turned against friends, neighbors against neighbors, coworkers against coworkers, and family members turned against each other. As children, we were taught to report on family members, including our parents.

Cancel culture ensued, and on its path anything that was not pure Maoist—including our Chinese heritage—was literally destroyed. Statues were toppled by mobs. Books and art were burned. In the course of the Chinese Cultural Revolution, artifacts, symbols, traditions, and customs of 3,000 years of Chinese civilization were removed from our daily lives.

By the death of Mao in 1976, up to twenty million lives were lost, and China as we once knew it was burned to the ground by the flames of the Revolution.

Back to 2020 in America again, this storm not only shocked me, but also enraged me. But instead of crying on the couch, I took action. I did so because I know full well how America, my beloved adopted country, could also be burned to the ground like China was if we don't stop it.

Rage and a burning desire for action made me abandon the Chinese wisdom that my parents and Chinese culture have drilled into me: *The bird who sticks its head out first gets shot.* I decided to stick out my head and take the shot. America has been my home for over three decades, where I have been afforded the freedom and prosperity fought for and defended by generations of Americans. Now it is my turn. For the first time I took the giant step and joined the fight in defense of our children, and in defense of America. I went to a school board meeting with hundreds of concerned parents in my hometown of Loudoun County, Virginia, to deliver a one-minute comment. In those sixty seconds, I drew the parallel between critical race theory (CRT) and the Chinese Cultural Revolution, and warned the audience that CRT *is* Marxism.

Loudoun County is now known across the country for the parent revolt against CRT and the tyrannical order of school COVID shutdowns. I found myself in the midst of this new revolution.

The video of my speech went viral. After my first appearance on Fox News, invitations poured in, asking me for interviews and speeches.

Through speaking at political and educational events, as well as online feedback from my interviews, I realized that most Americans do not know much, if anything at all, about the Chinese Cultural Revolution, Communist China, Communism, or cultural Marxism in general. That explains why so few have recognized that the root of today's "woke revolution," not to mention its ultimate goal, is Marxism followed by Communism.

So many people have encouraged me to write a book so that my message can reach more Americans. Even with all the media coverage and speaking opportunities, I simply could not tell the whole story that a book can. There are few, if any, such books available now at a time when they are so badly needed. It was during a podcast interview with former Speaker of the House Newt Gingrich that he urged me to write a book. I became convinced that I should take up this challenge.

In this book I tell the tale of two cultural revolutions: one driven by Mao and the Chinese Communist Party (CCP) and the one that is unfolding in today's America. Using my personal experience and extensive historic research, the book demonstrates the stunning similarities of these two revolutions. It guides readers to see that:

- Both revolutions use Marxist tactics of division, indoctrination, deception, coercion, cancelation, subversion, and violence.
- Both revolutions aim to destroy the foundation of traditional culture to replace it with Marxist ideologies.
- Both revolutions weaponize youth, using them as their means to an end.

- Both revolutions share the same goal of achieving absolute power at the expense of the people.
- Both revolutions lead to the same ending: loss of freedom and totalitarian rule.

The horrific historic events and shocking tales that are recounted in this book will hit it home to readers that history is being repeated here today.

This book also tells my personal story—as a child growing up under Communist rule, as an immigrant who learned to understand and believe in American exceptionalism, and as a proud citizen who made the decision to fight against the rising authoritarianism in America—and how I overcame fear and reluctance to get involved in the conservative movement to save America.

This book intends to alarm you, enrage you, pull you off of the couch, push you into action, and inspire you to join the fight for the survival of America.

CHAPTER 1

Leaving the Kitchen Table

never expected any of this. Nor is there any way possible I could have planned for it. All I knew before I headed out that afternoon in June 2021 to attend a school board meeting, one for which I had signed up to speak, was that I had something important to say and I would be limited to two minutes to say it. I was on the clock and my time had come.

What brought me out of hiding—as a typically quiet Asian American—and eventually into the national spotlight was my local school district's insistence on promoting and practicing critical race theory (CRT) in the classrooms in Loudoun County,

Virginia, where I live. This has been going on for several years in schools throughout much of America.

CRT is a Marxist ideology built on lies and a false narrative. It preaches a dogma that is pushed forward by Marxist-driven organizations and forces such as Black Lives Matter (BLM) and cancel culture, working together to transform America into a Marxist state. It's happening in plain sight, yet many people don't see it. I do. How can I not see it? I witnessed Communism's tyranny and violence when I was growing up in China. This was during the Mao Zedong–led Cultural Revolution that swept through the country between 1966 and 1976. This Cultural Revolution led to the total destruction of Chinese society and traditional Chinese civilization. Never in my wildest dreams did I think I would live to see a repeat of this in America, but that is where we are headed— and that includes Loudoun County, Virginia, where I now live.

America has been home for me for almost forty years, one that I love so much since leaving my native China to come here at age twenty-six. After personally experiencing the shackles of Communism and the human atrocities that go along with a Communist regime, I am heartbroken and terrified to see not only the signs, but the actual totalitarianism happening right here in the United States of America.

I recognized the ideology of CRT as a tool meant to lead America away from individual freedom and liberty to a dark and menacing way of life that is familiar to me. It was against this backdrop that I realized my life was about to change. On June 8, 2021, during the public comment portion of the Loudoun County school board meeting in Ashburn, Virginia, I was determined to stand up and speak out against the tenets of CRT that were being used in our schools to indoctrinate our children and sow the seeds of Communism in America. For a full year prior, a divide had grown between the school board and the parents. The board had grown nontransparent and openly hostile to parents. But none of this stopped the many parents from showing up week after week to fight for their kids and their country.

On that Tuesday afternoon, when I arrived at the offices of administration where the school board held its regular meetings, I was surprised to learn that Brenda Sheridan, the chairwoman of the school board, reduced the speakers' time for their statements from the original two minutes to just one minute!

I had carefully written my speech and rehearsed it several times, timing it to make sure I could get through it in under two minutes. I hurriedly entered the large boardroom taking a seat in the third row behind the speaker's podium, among hundreds of parents and community members who were also there to speak or just to listen. I sat down with urgency to cut my prepared statement in half, as I was informed that Ms. Sheridan seemed to take pleasure in slamming her hand down on the loud buzzer when the timer ticked down from sixty seconds to zero, and unceremoniously cut off your mic while telling you to "yield the mic."

Cutting a speech in half and having it still be meaningful is difficult for most people, but it was even more difficult for me. English is not my native language. I was about to make a public speech for the first time, and it would be on a subject that was emotionally taxing for me even without a mic in front of me. Thoughts about the Cultural Revolution mixed with present-day America were a jumble inside my head, and I had to again sort them out, cutting it all down in size to keep it to no more than one minute. Nervousness doesn't quite describe what I felt…and I didn't have a pen. Thanks to the supportive parents around me, who would soon become my friends and partners in this fight, I was given a pen and encouragement. I continued my frantic efforts to edit my planned statement before my name was called by Ms. Sheridan from the school board dais.

When it was finally my turn to step to the mic and speak, I took a deep breath and then delivered my swiftly revised presentation in just under a minute, all the while wearing a COVID mask in accordance with local protocols. I was actually thankful for that mask—oddly, it served as my security blanket.

I made it through my presentation with a few seconds to spare:

I've been very alarmed by what's been going on in our schools. You are now teaching and training our students to be social justice warriors and to loathe our country and its history. Growing up in Mao's China, all this seems very familiar. The Communist regime used the same critical theory to divide the people. The only difference is that they used class instead of race. During the Cultural Revolution, I witnessed students and teachers turn against each other. We changed school names to be politically correct. We were taught to denounce our heritage. The Red Guards destroyed anything that was not Communist—old statues, books, and anything else. We were also encouraged to report on each other just like the student equity ambassador program and the bias reporting system [in Loudoun schools]. This is indeed the American version of the Chinese Cultural Revolution. Critical race theory has its roots in cultural Marxism. It should have no place in our schools.

When I ended my statement, I returned to my seat briefly, then walked out of the meeting room and exited the building. I had to hurry back to work to make up the time that I took for the meeting. Ian Prior, a Loudoun County public school dad, was among those parents and community members supportive of what I had said. He later told Fox News that my brief speech "should serve as a stark warning," adding, "I think for a while now, school systems have really put this stuff in the schools right under our very noses, and we just weren't aware."[1] Most of the parents, including myself, had blindly trusted our children to the system, believing that our schools educate not indoctrinate the children.

Walking out of the meeting, I was pleased with my presentation. I had briefly stumbled over my word choices in a few places, but the important thing is that I spoke with knowledge and conviction. I didn't freeze up and I had covered everything I wanted to say without missing any key points.

What I didn't realize then was that my stark warning had a lasting effect on many people in that boardroom, and so many others across the country who would later hear my story. For the first time, CRT was compared to Mao's Cultural Revolution by someone who actually lived through it. A new dimension was added to the discussion and a new tool was created for the fight against American Marxism.

* * *

Going in front of the school board had not been an impulsive decision. I didn't just wake up one morning a week before the school board meeting and decide I would give the board members a piece of my mind concerning CRT. Getting the courage to get up and speak in public, regardless of the topic, or the size and makeup of the audience, was a huge leap for me. I look back now and see how it had begun almost exactly a year earlier in the wake of the death of George Floyd, a Black man, at the hands of a white police officer in Minneapolis, Minnesota, on May 25, 2020.

My transformation from reclusive political observer to outspoken political activist occurred in the immediate aftermath of Floyd's death. Within days of his tragic death, George Floyd was hailed as a "martyr" and hero despite having a reportedly lengthy criminal past that included numerous arrests and multiple felony convictions. Soon he was being remembered as a hero.

Protestors across America gathered to honor Floyd by condemning racial injustice and police brutality, calling for defunding the police. However, this so-called protest "movement" quickly grew into something sinister and destructive—a series of violent, yet apparently well-orchestrated riots (most media still categorized them as "peaceful protests") that touched—and, in some cases, torched—many major cities.

Across parts of America, police cars were vandalized; stores were looted; law-enforcement officers were shot and wounded; businesses were set ablaze; entire city blocks in cities such as Seattle were cordoned off and claimed as protest "autonomous zones" by armed rioters.

Watching this chaos and violence unfold day after day on television reminded me of the chaos, violence, and horror of China's Cultural Revolution that I had witnessed as a schoolgirl.

What's really scary is the striking similarity between China's Cultural Revolution and what has happened and is continuing to happen here in America. I know what it is that is happening here because I've seen this on both fronts: far-left progressive forces, using weapons such as CRT, woke-ism, BLM, and cancel culture, in order to root out conservatives and any resistance to their radical agenda. If we speak out, we risk being ostracized and losing our place in this society. Free speech now is only allowed for the loud progressive left. Our First Amendment rights are under attack. Our Second Amendment rights are under attack. Our freedom is under attack. Our country is under attack.

Watching the Floyd-inspired riots in 2020 and seeing the parallels to China's Cultural Revolution was an epiphany for me. Enough is enough. I felt a personal urgency to get involved politically and to do my part in my small slice of this world, in order to help keep America from going over a cliff. It was hitting home, too, for Chinese American parents with school-aged children. They were now being scorned by their sons and daughters whose confrontational attitude and unprecedented disrespect went well beyond the usual teenage angst and rebellion. Chalk this up to the promotion of CRT in schools, where the teachings are designed to violate and disrespect the sanctity of family and usurp parental values. Many students now questioned their parents' attitudes about race and oppression, accusing them of being racists.

What I had seen in 2020, as well as what I had recalled from years earlier, remained so vivid for me that I was determined to not let people dismiss this as not happening, as unreal. It was a full-blown Marxist revolution, American style. I also read online on WeChat, a Chinese social media similar to Facebook, how many Chinese people in China were laughing at what was going on in the US, calling it the "American cultural revolution." Those who laugh at us would love to see the downfall of America.

* * *

Until the rapid spread of CRT and the 2020 riots, my interest in politics had been a private thing—mostly conversations at the kitchen table or on the phone, after work, with like-minded friends. Then, one night in particular, I came across a Fox News segment featuring Dan Bongino, a popular television news commentator, political influencer, and radio and podcast host. Mr. Bongino spoke about the importance of getting involved politically, starting at the local level—encouraging viewers to use their voices to make a difference. That's possible in a country where a majority of Americans still cherish and choose to exercise free speech. I felt he was speaking directly to me about what I needed to do. Getting out into the "public square" and becoming politically active would mean a big change for me, though. It is intimidating for most, but for me, even more so. It would mean coming out of my shell personally and revealing myself politically. Taking Bongino's pep talk to heart, I stepped away from my kitchen table and out from behind my cell phone, and into the action. I joined the Loudoun County Republican Committee (LCRC).

In joining the LCRC, I was mostly interested in the issues of election integrity and stopping the spread of Communist ideology in the United States, of which CRT is only a part. Soon after joining the LCRC, I was appointed as a precinct captain. That suited me because of my strong interest in election integrity. I now had a role handing out sample ballots, which put me in a position to help educate and urge voters to vote for conservative candidates.

Eager for even more action, I also eventually joined the Loudoun County Republican Women's Club, and quickly became friends with its members. They were warm and attentive, encouraging me to share stories from my experiences in Mao's China. They told me I should consider expressing my thoughts and opinions at local school board meetings, that I had important things to say that the school board needed to hear and take seriously.

"But I don't have children in school anymore," I said.

They told me it didn't matter, that as a taxpayer I still had a right and maybe even an obligation to speak out about it. Emboldened by such support, I saw it as a chance for me to grow, to become bolder in standing up for my beliefs and country—this was no longer just about me.

"What do I say?" I asked.

"Whatever you want to say," was the answer I received.

That's how I got onto my fast track, choosing to start off with calling out CRT in Loudoun County schools.

Before I even made the decision, battalions of conservatives and even moderate Democrats had been joining together to stop tyrannical school board policies and indoctrination by going to school board meeting to voice their concerns and objections. The progressives were not happy about the pushback.

In early 2021, a secret Facebook group called "Anti-Racist Parents of Loudoun County" was formed, which included six of nine board members and over six hundred teachers and parents. Their goal, as one group member put it, was to "combat anti–critical race theory advocates and websites…to 'gather information' on critics of the controversial race-based education platform, to 'infiltrate' their groups and sought 'hackers who can either shut down their websites or redirect them.'"[2] This radical group made a list of outspoken parents the group aimed to silence. The parents were labeled as "racist" for daring to challenge the school board. One of those on the list is Jessica Mendez, mother of two girls. She told me that someone from the group sent letters to her employer and reported her as a racist.

To the dismay of the progressives, these brave parents did not back off. Instead, they launched a movement known as Fight for Schools, led by Ian Prior, to fight back and recall those radical school board members. The movement had already generated lots of media attention. That explains why my speech to the school board would go viral as part of a larger movement.

Our prominent role in countering the far left's activism infiltrating our public schools had resonated throughout the state, the country, and even the entire Western world. Here in Virginia, it played a major role in turning the state red and helping to influence the victory by Republican Glenn Youngkin in Virginia's 2021 gubernatorial race. This was a major upset for the Democratic Party and sent a message to parents across the country to be brave, strong, and involved, because their voices matter.

* * *

On the morning of the day after my school board appearance, I got a call from a Fox News reporter who had heard my public comment and wanted to interview me for a story. At first, I wasn't sure I wanted to do the interview. I feared that I might say things that may be politically liable or could end up hurting me or my family. I was also concerned about the exposure, about stepping into the national spotlight. Remember, this was less than twenty-four hours after I had just finished public speaking for the first time in my life, and that meeting was in front of a local audience of hundreds, not the millions who read Fox News. Doing the interview would mean stepping out of the safety and comfort of my private life.

Am I ready for this?

Apparently, I was, because I agreed to do the interview, even while realizing that once words came out of my mouth, there would be no retrieving them. As they say, you can't un-ring a bell! You could hear the hesitation in my voice when I told the reporter writing the story for Fox News Digital, "I can't really just say what I mean, even though the other side can say whatever." My point was: The far left can speak out without consequences. That's not always the case for people expressing conservative viewpoints.

I then went on to tell the reporter: "To me, and to a lot of Chinese, it is heartbreaking that we escaped communism and now we experience communism here…I just want Americans to know that their privilege is to be here living in America, that is just the biggest privilege. I do not think a lot of people understand. They are thinking they are doing the right thing, 'be against racism' sounds really good. But they are basically breaking the system that is against racism."[3]

That piece on Fox News Digital was trending. People were paying attention. People were interested in my experience and wanted to hear what I had to say.

A day later, after the article was published, I got another text message from the network, this time from a producer working on Sean Hannity's show on Fox News. The producer invited me to be interviewed on *Hannity*—that night! Once again, it was decision time, and it would be an even bigger step than my earlier article interview. *Is this really happening?* As they say, it all happened so fast.

Later that afternoon, I was seated in a mobile TV "studio van" that had been dispatched to my home. As the earpiece was placed snuggly in my ear and I was doing the sound check, just minutes away from my airtime with Sean Hannity via a satellite feed from the van, it hit me that I was about to go face-to-face with millions of viewers. I stared into the black hole of the camera's eye. While the screen was a black, vacant space, I focused my eyes on the bright pin light by the lens. I was now keenly aware that America was watching…and I was ready.

Or was I? I was once again nervous and worried that I could possibly freeze up during the interview. I was having an entire dialogue with myself inside my head. Hannity would be speaking to me any minute. *What if I make a fool of myself in front of the entire nation?* Television viewers would be tuned in, in seconds: *What if they wonder why this unknown Chinese woman is stepping into the national spotlight, a total novice?* I thought: *Do I look nervous? How do I look? Should I smile? What if he asks questions and I do not have the answers?*

Then I heard that familiar voice setting up our segment for his audience. And then I heard him speaking to me! Hannity started by asking me what had happened to me back in China. He mentioned how I was six years old when the Cultural Revolution started, and then he asked me to explain what I had seen and experienced. Just like at that June 8 school board meeting, I knew that I had very little time to make my key points. I went straight into why this inexperienced Chinese woman was there speaking on the topic of schools and CRT, expanding on what I had told the school board. Hannity was kind enough to let me run with it.

When I was finished with my segment, which also included former US congressman Jason Chaffetz sharing airtime with me, I felt good about what I had said and how I had come across. It felt like I was doing God's will. I'm not religious, but I believe there's something greater than me guiding my way. Afterward, when I watched the replay of myself on the segment, I was like, "Oh, my

God!" It's really difficult seeing yourself on TV. You can't help but be your own worst critic. All in all, once I got past my initial reaction to seeing myself, I felt quite good about how I had done, and most importantly, I believe the viewers received my most important points in the way that I had hoped.

Once my appearance on *Hannity* was posted on YouTube and I was able to view it, all of my worries washed away. More than six thousand comments from viewers had been posted and they were overwhelmingly positive. What really pleased me was seeing reactions from people who have lived under Communism in countries such as China, Vietnam, Cuba, Poland, Romania, Russia, and Serbia. They shared their own stories about their families and what they had seen and experienced, saying that I had been absolutely right in relating my experiences growing up in Communist China to what's going on in America. That was important to me because it validated my story and solidified that what I was doing was not just right, but vital.

My appearance on *Hannity* set other things in motion for me. Soon I was taking requests from not only other media outlets but also various organizations and political action committees wanting me to share my story and perspectives. The next big thing I was invited to was the Conservative Political Action Conference (CPAC) 2021 America Uncanceled event in Dallas. It was live, with thousands of conservatives in attendance. I was on a panel with three attorneys—two of them had worked for the Trump administration and one had worked for President George W. Bush. I was worried afterward that I didn't do very well, considering my lack of previous experience speaking before large crowds. But I managed to say the most important thing that needed to be said: the Communist infiltration in America is complete; it is absolutely everywhere. I also said we are in a war, a war of life and death for our country. We received a standing ovation afterward. It was very moving. I must have touched so many by sharing my story, as many came up to me after I spoke, some even asking to give me a hug. That further bolstered my confidence.

The next big event for me was a Heritage Action Sentinels conference held in November 2021 in Orlando, Florida. After I gave my speech, people told me it brought tears to their eyes. It was basically the same message I had been proclaiming elsewhere, about Communism and how it has already taken root here in America. Around that time, I also did interviews with Glenn Beck and Newt Gingrich, among others. During my interview with the former Speaker, he said to me, "You have to write a book. When you finish that book, we're going to have to have another interview." I took his words to heart.

I've had similar experiences and reactions from other interviews and appearances I've been involved with. That includes one of the best in-depth interviews I've had, which was with Jan Jekielek, host of *American Thought Leaders*, a program produced by the *Epoch Times*. Other similar speaking or interview opportunities for me have included speaking with Moms for America in front of the National School Boards Association, as well as speaking out against co-parenting with the government for the Independent Women's Forum in front of the Capitol. I appeared on a panel in Dr. Ben Carson's anti-CRT rally in Loudoun County and did many other interviews on Fox News and Newsmax. I also received recognition from Mark Levin, the conservative radio host and bestselling author, who played a segment of my school board speech on his radio show.

Next came Twitter.

It is said that one of the fastest ways to spread information is through word of mouth. In order to continue sharing my story and warning of the dangers of Communism in our country and to encourage people to step off the sidelines and into this fight, I began to ramp up my social media activity. So, I took my battle to Twitter, where I am able to engage with people from both sides.

Before I became an activist, my only social media footprint was on Instagram where I would share my photos. (What many people don't know about me is that I am an amateur, but serious, photographer. Even with my pictures on Instagram, I was never an influencer.) Stepping up my social media game in the political arena has been quite the experience, and I am still feeling out the best way to present myself and my messaging. It is quite the roller-coaster ride for me. I was quite surprised when one of my tweets received about two million views. It's a high-wire act for me at times and can be nerve-racking, holding my breath as I read comments. When I see that my message is resonating with users, it can be quite exciting and gives me so much hope that together we can save our country.

One of my first engagements on Twitter was memorable. It was with a woman—obviously a liberal—who also lived in Loudoun County. I had posted about the Pledge of Allegiance and she responded by claiming people were being "forced to pledge to the American flag."

Are you calling this oppression? For real?

"I don't know about you," I wrote back, "but I lived under Communism, and that is REAL oppression. I can't say much about why you hate America this much, but we are going to teach OUR children to love this country because this is the best country in the world."

She did not respond.

I did not expect that I also would eventually engage in a fierce Twitter exchange with Nikole Hannah-Jones, author of the infamous 1619 Project. On February 26, 2023, I responded to a tweet from Hannah-Jones that condemned "the narrative of American Exceptionalism." I replied on Twitter, "Yourself and I, an immigrant from China with 200 borrowed dollars in my pocket when I arrived more than 30 yrs ago, are the proof of American Exceptionalism." She then demanded that I be specific. So I replied: "Natural rights is unique to American founding. Bc of it we were able to abolish slavery, Jim Crow, anti-Chinese laws...to allow individuals to succeed. What is not unique to America is slavery, which still exists today. Ppl fighting for human rights in China are jailed by CCP." A crowd of Twitter users joined the debate. It was a marvelous sight to behold. Twitter as a platform allows me to directly challenge Hannah-Jones when the left-controlled mainstream media only cheers her on. To my surprise, the conservative media widely reported the story the next day. More TV and radio interviews followed. My message was really getting out. I loved it.

Many people with whom I have interacted via social media have been good sources of encouragement for me. I need such support in a world where ideas and words are all we have, when in any other setting, fists, swords, or pistols would possibly be used. One friendly Twitter follower once said something really touching to me, writing: "Please continue to shout on the rooftop. You need to tell us, you know, what we're dealing with here, with your own experience."

That's the kind of support that tells me my voice has become a powerful influence in the fight against American Marxists. I am now totally committed to this mission, and you will definitely hear more from me in public forums.

When I think about how far I have come since this journey began, it shocks me to see all I am doing that I couldn't even imagine doing had I not taken the chance. I hope that when people read my story, they will become inspired and maybe believe in themselves enough to speak out and step up in the fight for America.

First, though, let me take you back to the China of the 1960s and 1970s, and tell you about what I saw and experienced as a schoolgirl during the turbulent, decade-long Cultural Revolution. As I take you on this journey, I will point out the eerie parallels between what took place then and what is happening now across America.

CHAPTER 2

Growing Up in Mao's China

When I see sickles on Communist flags, I often think about my poor little fingers.

After entering the fifth grade at the age of ten in the midst of the Cultural Revolution, we were sent to the countryside for a month to live with the peasants, where we helped with what was called "double-task season." This included harvesting early-season rice and planting the rice shoots for the later summer season. This wasn't just some simple field trip. It was the real deal. Mao's orders.

I used a sickle for the first time to cut the rice stalks, and, like so many of my classmates, I cut my fingers many times. One student almost severed her little finger.

Let me back up some. My young life growing up in China was divided into two distinct parts: life before the Cultural Revolution and life after. It was like day and night, the calm before the chaos.

I was six going on seven when the Cultural Revolution started in 1966. It was a sudden thing, or at least it seemed that way to my almost-seven-year-old self. I don't recall much about life during the time prior to the start of the Cultural Revolution, only that it was peaceful and uneventful for me, in the way that it should be for children. The Cultural Revolution was a political campaign launched by Mao Zedong, China's supreme ruler, with the goal of rooting out all capitalist/bourgeois elements in the Chinese

The author (far right) with friends and neighbors in China in April 1969

Communist Party (CCP) and all levels of the government in order to prevent the derailment of Chinese socialism. It was a campaign of all campaigns that turned China upside down.

I was born to parents who belonged to the revolutionary *cadre* class, which was made up of CCP bureaucrats similar to civil service employees in America. Both had joined the Communist Revolution as progressive and idealistic youths who shared the vision projected by the Chinese Communist Party—to "liberate the oppressed from the oppression of the oppressors." We lived in the city of Chengdu in the Sichuan province. Because my parents were cadres, we were considered a privileged class. We were given the privilege of sharing a bathroom with four families, while many had to share a community outhouse that served an entire building of residents. Our five-person family was given the privilege of sharing one and a half rooms, while many others were forced

The author in Tiananmen Square in November 1986 after obtaining her US visa

to share a single room as multigenerational families. The shared kitchen was one room that each of the families occupied, a tiny space for a coal stove and a little table. That was my home until age sixteen, when I was sent to live in the countryside, where I would essentially work as a peasant.

My greatest privilege growing up was that I was spared the hunger and starvation that many of my fellow countrymen suffered. I was considered well fed even though we only had the very basics. As a little girl, I had a constant yearning for sweets. One day, I noticed a container of what appeared to be white sugar on the kitchen shelf. I couldn't believe my eyes! When there was no one around, I got hold of a chair, climbed on it, and grabbed that container right off the shelf! I eagerly put a heaping spoonful of it into my mouth. Imagine my surprise when I found out that what I had taken for sugar was actually salt! To me, this little incident from my youth seems so symbolic of Communism itself—deprivation and deception, which now it seems so many young Americans cannot comprehend.

Since the work of both of my parents required them to be away from home for long periods of time, they enrolled me in the boarding option at my school, where I lived six days out of the week. Being a boarding student was like living in an orphanage. Again, I found myself more fortunate than so many others. There was a teacher at my school who really cared about me. The students called her Teacher Huang. She was my saving grace. She was a young woman and a new teacher. In fact, my class was the first class she taught at the school. She really took a liking to me. The feeling was mutual. She was like a surrogate mother who took it upon herself to look out for me. I don't remember much about being in class or what was being taught, but I do remember my time with her.

On Sundays, when my parents were unable to come and take me home, Teacher Huang and her newly wedded husband would take me to the zoo or to parks. Those are the good memories that stand out for me before everything changed so quickly and so violently with the storm that would be known as the Cultural Revolution.

It was spring of 1966—for me, the second semester of first grade—when the Revolution started, and schools were immediately affected. One of my earliest and most vivid memories of the Cultural Revolution was the sudden appearance of giant posters in the school cafeteria (the only indoor space with high wall space for posters), denouncing teachers and school administrators. They were called "big-character posters," characterized by large lettering and cartoon-like depictions that were drawn so big they could be seen and read from a distance. By design, they were made large enough to intimidate and strike fear into people, and they were effective. They were *the* social media back then. Just like today's social media, anyone could post a poster—anyone except those who were the target of the Revolution, to be more precise.

How would I describe what I saw and felt? Chaos, frenzied commotion, fear, and bewilderment. *What was happening?!*

I was too young to fully understand the content of the posters, but I could tell they were critical of the school's administrators and teachers. I remember one poster with eye-catching drawings attacking a certain female teacher for dressing nicely and wearing heels. She was being condemned and admonished for being "bourgeois," the people despised and openly disparaged by Mao.

Soon afterward, the attacks escalated. One day, I saw a group of older students follow this teacher and call her names. They eventually surrounded her and started to spit on her. Before long, she was covered in spit from head to toe.

I also remember another teacher from my school, and her husband, who had adopted a daughter because they were unable to have children of their own. For that, she was accused of oppressing and exploiting a helpless orphan child. The older students raided her home—it was just a single room in a faculty dorm where teachers were housed. Nothing was sacred—not a person's personal belongings, nor their homes.

After the raid on the teacher's home, I remember seeing their adopted daughter at the back corner of the building in an area that had been reconfigured into a communal kitchen. The girl, who was about ten years old, was in a squatting position on the floor and crying uncontrollably, her head buried between her arms and legs. Her mom had been taken away by the students for a *struggle session* (public shaming). I was really confused. The students claimed to defend this little girl against her oppressive parents, but they made her cry. During my boarding time at the school, I had seen a lot of this teacher's daughter after school on campus, and she seemed to be a happy girl, loved by her parents. What was going on?

One day, I walked into the classroom and saw a message on the blackboard: No classes for three days. It had been written there by my teacher, who obviously did not know those three days would turn into almost two years. There was no official school announcement about the closure. The fact is, there was no one running the school, as all the school administrators were ousted from their positions.

No one was prepared for it. Everyone was shocked. Like I said, day and night. One day it was school learning as usual; the next day all hell was breaking loose. I think me telling my parents that night about what was going on at school is how they found out about it. I don't remember their reaction. Probably not much, because both of them were busy dealing with the hell that was breaking loose in their workplaces as well. It was through some older kids that I eventually learned that school would be closed indefinitely. In fact, it wouldn't be until late 1967 that Mao's Cultural Revolution Committee issued an order for schools to reopen with the slogan "Carry on the revolution in the classroom."

There was no school and no parental supervision, as the parents were caught up in the Cultural Revolution at work. That meant studying the latest instruction from Mao or the Central Cultural Revolution Committee, participating in self-criticism to see whether we were in line with the instruction, and holding struggle sessions for those found to be out of line with the Party on any given day. As children, we were free to roam around outside. It afforded me a front-row seat for the Cultural Revolution as it played out on the streets. I saw so many "struggle sessions," a form of public trials that intended to brutally shame and denounce the targeted individuals, and parades of trucks full of people who were deemed enemies of the people, with their sins and crimes written on a big sign they had to wear over their chests and a tall paper cone hat on their heads. The signs included their names written in large characters with lines crossing them out, as if to symbolize the very existence of these men had been canceled. All I knew was that they must have been really bad people. Why else were the Red Guards calling them out in the open for everyone to see and denounce? I have the entire Chapter 6 devoted to this topic of the Red Guards. In short, they were the indoctrinated and mobilized youths who vowed to carry out the Cultural Revolution by loyally following Mao's orders.

One day, I was outside watching a rally with a friend of mine when a line of trucks came by with men in the back, all of whom wore those large signs and tall cone hats. As fate would have it, one of the men on the truck happened to be my friend's father. On his signboard was his name, crossed out and replaced with the phrase "little reptile," which meant he was a follower of a denounced Party leader. My friend started crying upon seeing her father disparaged and humiliated like that. At that moment, it hit me that it could just as well have been *my* father, because my father was a low-ranking cadre just like my friend's father. I prayed that my father would not do anything wrong to be caught and paraded, too.

What I witnessed in Chengdu was happening all over China. The Red Guards would run down whole streets. Practically no one was off-limits from Red Guard persecution—even Li Jingquan, the governor of the Sichuan province, was subjected to a struggle session, which I witnessed.

Eventually, the Red Guards started fighting among themselves because of factional disputes, with each side asserting that they were the only true representative of Maoist thought. The violence escalated to something that looked like a civil war. One day, a stray bullet struck just below our window when we were having dinner. If it had been just a little bit higher, it would have entered our home and one of us might have been badly injured, or worse. It was at that time we started to see posters everywhere on the streets with photos of the dead, allegedly killed by one Red Guard faction or another. I remember especially well one such poster with photos of a mutilated body with eyes gouged out and the body cut open. I had nightmares because of it for a long time.

One day, we heard loud music coming from a distance. The music was a Chinese funeral march and it sounded awful and scary. We all stopped what we were doing and started running toward the sound of the ominous music. Information was passed back through the throngs of people, letting us know that it was a corpse parade. The corpse parade was designed to gain public sympathy for one faction of the Red Guard over another by demonstrating themselves as victims of a competing cruel and inhuman faction. Just as I got close enough, I was overcome with fear and suddenly stopped. I realized that if I continued forward, I would never be able to unsee what I was going to see. Yet, my imagination filled in the horrific scene that I did not see, and I was haunted by endless nightmares. Sadly, my uncle died of cancer in a hospital during that time. Because the Red Guards were ransacking hospital morgues for bodies and claiming them as murdered comrades to boost the size of their corpse parade, my mother had to help my aunt arrange to have his body cremated as fast as possible.

Those were chaotic times, not just on the streets, but at home, too. With both of my parents absent from home so much, I was given the job of taking care of my sister, three years younger than me. That's when I became her "mother," taking care of her and myself most of the time until after 1969, when things quieted down somewhat. Meanwhile, my little brother was placed in the care of a couple.

When schools were finally reopened at the end of 1967, I was classified as a first-semester fourth grader, as if no one even noticed we missed so much school time. (I am reminded of this today as American children suffer after being deprived of their education, not by COVID, but by the bad COVID school closure policies mandated by most state governments in 2020.)

The school I returned to was no longer the school I attended before the Cultural Revolution. Old textbooks were now banned, but no new textbooks had been procured yet to replace them. The only new textbook provided was a collection of Mao's quotations, commonly known as *The Little Red Book*. All academic study was replaced by reading Mao's *Little Red Book*. We not only recited Mao's quotations, we also sang songs that were composed of his quotes.

All academics and any type of learning were replaced exclusively with Mao's ideology. I must admit, I was among the many students who were buying in to it. What choice did we have? I certainly didn't know any better. However, there is one of Mao's quotations I did question: "Whatever the enemy opposes, we shall support. Whatever the enemy supports, we shall oppose." I couldn't help thinking to myself, "What if our enemy loves candy; am I supposed to hate it?" My doubts would live inside my own head, never escaping through my lips for anyone to hear.

In allowing schools to reopen, Mao proclaimed that restoring teaching in schools would mean that we could continue the Cultural Revolution in school, but this time through classroom "study" of his book. I pretty much remember most of the quotations, and I can still sing those songs, as well as recite Mao's poetry. I especially enjoyed one easy line in one of Mao's poems: "Farting not allowed."

Studying and reciting Mao's quotation and poems was mostly what we did in class, day after day. I couldn't help but remember them. After a while, I just couldn't get that stuff out of my head. It even got competitive between parents, on how well their children were able to recite the quotations and poems. One day, my father came home and said his colleague's daughter, who was younger than me, could recite all of Mao's poems flawlessly. He said to me, "You need to work harder."

In addition to studying Mao's words, we would have classroom criticism and self-criticism sessions, a softer version of struggle sessions, that involved students interacting with each other using the quotes we had learned from Mao's book. Criticism included criticizing individual students who did not talk or behave in the "right" way. Self-criticism included criticizing oneself for not living up to Mao's teaching. This was called *huo xue hua yong*, or "apply as you learn." More than once, I was selected to represent my class at the end of a semester as the exemplary activist who studied and applied Mao Zedong Thought—Mao's version of Marxist theory.

You may wonder what kind of criticisms I received from my classmates and my teacher. One of the reoccurring criticisms was that I was too proud and too self-assured. This went against Mao's teaching to be modest and humble. Self-esteem was a bad thing. For convenience, I also used it for self-criticism. Otherwise, I had to find something else to criticize myself about. After a while, the study sessions became predictable and repetitive.

Later, improved versions of math textbooks were made available to us. The new textbooks were not much different from Mao's *Little Red Book*. New textbooks were actually the *Little Red Book* reincarnated in math, reading, and all other subjects. Our education was greatly stymied, limiting us to become obedient, Mao-inspired robots.

During my ten years of "schooling," we didn't learn much. The one thing we were required by Mao to do was spend a month during each school semester taking part in a program known as "Learn from Workers, Peasants, and Soldiers." I worked in the fields harvesting rice. I also labored in a silk factory, as well as a food-canning factory. For one factory-work assignment, we used a hammer to crush coal waste to salvage the unburned parts for reuse—of course, without any protective gear. Once while hammering, a tiny shard flew into my eye, causing sharp pain. When I finally managed to locate the factory clinic, I had to wait for the doctor to finish his chat with his friend before attending to me, all the while trembling with pain. This was my experience with the hammer to complement my experience with the sickle. Both brutal! For military trainings, I took part in target shooting and long-distance hiking. We even dug trenches on the school campus to defend ourselves from possible Russian revisionist-imperial invasions. The trench we dug ran along a wall that encircled our playground. I always wondered where we could retreat when the Russians actually showed up in front of our trenches.

Another important activity we had was known as "Remember the bitterness of the past; appreciate the sweetness of today," or "Remember the Bitterness" for short. We would gather edible weeds and use them to make buns with rough corn flour and listen to elder workers telling us stories of their suffering in the old days before the "liberation" by the CCP. Eating these buns was meant to remind us of the "bitterness of the past" to ensure that we were grateful to Mao for the happy life he allowed us to live. As you can imagine, the buns tasted pretty bad. Students from poor families would, however, eagerly eat them to fill their hungry bellies.

It wasn't until 1974, when Mao allowed Deng Xiaoping to return to a position of influence as the first vice-premier, that we were able to resume learning real academic subjects. But that would last only for a short time. During the brief period when the door was reopened to authentic academic learning, a feeling, so foreign to us, began to blossom within us. It was the feeling of hope. We never had occasion to even imagine that we would be given the opportunity to take entrance exams for college. My friends and I were so excited and spent time talking about something we never talked about before—what we wanted to be when we grew up. By then I was fifteen years old. A year later, Mao deemed Deng a "rightist"—someone who wanted to reverse the "progress" of the Cultural Revolution—and in 1975 Deng's policies were reversed before Mao eventually removed him from power. That summer, I graduated high school.

After Deng was purged, so were our dreams. In my last year of high school, the hope of going to college was dashed. Instead, we faced the dreadful fate of being sent back to the countryside as part of the "Up to the Mountains and Down to the Countryside Movement."

The movement was launched two years after the start of the Cultural Revolution. It mandated about sixteen million urban youths resettle in rural areas, some in remote areas, to work in uncultivated regions to create new farmland. For the majority of urban youths, it would be for a lot longer than a month—possibly a life sentence.

This huge campaign lasted until 1978, two years after Mao's death in 1976. I endured laboring in the countryside for three long years (1975–1978). The time we spent "learning" side by side with the peasants in the fields was called "reeducation." The work was hard labor under primitive conditions, including working with manure—both animal and human feces, mixed with straw ashes—and spreading it around the fields as fertilizer without the benefit of any protection from the filth and stench. By the end of the day, no matter how much I washed my hands, I could not get the smell out of them. I ended up making "gloves" by wrapping my hands in thick towels to keep the stench off my hands, which made me gag while I ate my dinner.

The peasants who were born in the countryside lived there forever. They spent their days working the fields from sunup to sundown. At least when they finally made the trek home in the evening, the meals were prepared by family elders. But for the "sent-down" youths, cooking dinner was more than a chore after a day's hard labor. Often, we had to worry about getting enough twigs as fuel for cooking dinner, leaving us sometimes with only half-cooked rice, flavored with nothing but salt. From time to time, I would get lucky and find in the field an eel or giant frog to cook.

Each year, the commune where we lived and worked would choose the most exemplary "sent-down" youths. One of my friends was lucky enough to be one of them. I must admit that I was a little jealous, telling myself that I was not made to endure hardship. The phrase we used to describe this type of personal constitution was "eating bitterness spirit." I was great at many things like studying and applying Mao's Thought in school. Why was I not able to be the best at the backbreaking work in the countryside? I silently berated myself for being too bourgeois, for lacking the real revolutionary quality that my friend possessed.

Upon my father's repeated urgings to submit an application for membership with the Communist Party, I finally did so. While I knew that being a Party member might help me qualify for opportunities to go back to the city, I was apprehensive, because I knew the only way I could prove myself would be to double down on my efforts in the area where I was weakest—in the area of "eating hardships."

Being accepted into the Communist Party as a member was considered an honor and a privilege. Only a good prospective would receive a response from the Party leader to start the long trial process that included a request for an explanation for motivation, detailed bio, and a plan of action. Unfortunately for me, the Party leader apparently believed that I was not a good worker and did not even bother to give me a response.

Since the sent-down youths were assigned to different production teams and scattered over a large area, market day (when people from surrounding villages came to town to trade) was the best opportunity for us to meet and reconnect. On one particular day, the boys I had met were very open with me about what was going on outside of our little isolated world. As we went deeper into our conversation, they told me that they secretly listened to BBC (British Broadcasting Corporation) and VOA (Voice of America) through a shortwave radio that they kept hidden. This was almost too much for me to handle, because this was an offense that could result in imprisonment or even execution in the early days of the Cultural Revolution, and I, at that time, was a loyal believer!

I was so paralyzed with fear that I didn't remember any of the information they told me! When I got back and settled in for the night, I took out my diary and furiously wrote down that these boys were headed down a very dangerous path. How could they not be following the direction Mao and the Party had laid out for us?

It is usually good to keep a diary in order to keep your memories alive and to help you through difficult times. This was not why I was keeping a diary. My father, who was a professional writer at a local Propaganda Department for the Party, advised me to keep a diary so that I would continue improving my writing skills. He said that when I returned home, he would check my writing and we would work on the errors. In one of my diary entries, I documented a political statement someone made that I felt was not politically correct and qualified as a counterrevolutionary remark.

Upon reading this entry, my father had a look on his face I had not seen before. He had a serious expression as he looked deeply into my eyes. He asked me very pointedly, "Why did you write this down? Do you plan on reporting him?" He warned me: "Don't do it again." Like many parents, my father never discussed politics with us. I had no idea how he felt on these matters. The reason for this is very likely because many children were indoctrinated to report their own parents, and many of those parents were jailed or even executed! The fact that my father said these candid words to me was an absolute shock. For the first time, I got an inner glimpse of my father's political views. I thought he was a loyal Party member, but in fact, he did hold dissenting views.

Apart from the harsh peasant life, the worst part of being sent to the countryside was the dampening of any hope I would one day return to the city. I had already given up my dreams of a college degree and a good career. All I wanted was to be able to leave the countryside and its primitive conditions. I would be happy to get ANY job as long as I could go back to my city, Chengdu.

I must admit, one of the best things about being stuck in the countryside was that we had access to banned books. During the Cultural Revolution, books were banned and burned. Libraries were closed. But some books did survive. When I was in middle school, after the fever of the Red Guards quieted down, books that had survived the purge began to be circulated among the kids. I never knew who originally owned these books or where they were coming from, but it didn't matter to me as long as I got my hands on them. I was so grateful to escape from my bleak world into another world living within the pages of those books. I read books like *One Thousand and One Nights*, Hans Christian Andersen's Fairy Tales, *Robinson Crusoe, Gulliver's Travels*, and the Chinese classics *Journey to the West* and *Romance of the Three Kingdoms*. As soon as I finished a book, I was sure to pass it on to another kid so that they, too, could learn, escape, imagine, or laugh.

Fortunately, one of the sent-down youths had a lot of books. His father had been a librarian who took a lot of the books home before the library collection was destroyed. From him, I was able to get my hands on some great classic French, English, and Russian novels, and *The Rise and Fall of the Third Reich*. I remember being shocked by the Nazi atrocities and felt blessed that I did not live in Nazi Germany, while oblivious to the extreme oppression I was living under. Oppression was my normal.

While facing harsh reality, I occasionally still let myself dream of doing bigger things with my life. I had a dream of one day being able to work as an interpreter for Chinese delegates to Albania. Why Albania? Because it is one of the most exotic countries among the three allies China had at that time: Albania, North Korea, and North Vietnam.

My reeducation in the countryside did teach me something. For the first time, I had real-world knowledge that socialism was totally ineffective. In the commune, the land was "collectively" owned, which really meant that no one owned any land. Peasants and the sent-down youths worked to earn "work points," which were exchanged for produce during harvest times. There were two ways to earn work points: one measured by time, the other by result. Each morning, we would gather at our team meeting place where we would receive our daily work instructions. If the work assignment was to harvest potatoes, for example, one would get the work points by the weight of potatoes one had harvested. This inspired people to be competitive and work as hard as possible at getting the most potatoes. However, if our work was, for example, weeding, no one felt competitive or inspired to put in hard work. We would spend the day being lazy and gossiping among ourselves. Why would this be? Because there was no incentive. We would not get more or less points than anyone else on our team, so why expel the energy for nothing in return? The production team leader spent his days urging us to get back to work. You see, in a socialist society, if you get the same rewards as everyone else no matter how hard or how little you work, why be the one who does extra work?

Mao died in 1976, and that marked the end of his Cultural Revolution. I had no idea at the time what that would ultimately mean to me and my life. I did not expect anything would change. I did not know any other way but Mao's way for us to live. All I heard from the media was that we would forever follow the direction that Mao had laid out for us. Thank God, that turned out not to be the case. In 1977, Deng Xiaoping again seized power and opened up China to the West, called an end to the Cultural Revolution, and focused on improving the economy in China. Within a year, colleges and universities were open to those who could pass entrance examinations. I was so excited; now, I could simply take exams to be qualified for college. Once again, I believed it was possible for my dreams to come true. I had real hope.

China's reinstitution of the college entrance exam was a historical event, because it opened up educational opportunities for millions of youths who had been denied such access during the decade-long Cultural Revolution, which also meant I had to compete not just with my class of 1975, but with millions of students from the classes of 1966 to 1977!

I hadn't learned much during my ten years of "schooling." Knowing Mao's *Little Red Book* front to back did me no good. Plus, I had forgotten what little academics I had learned, thanks to those years working as a peasant in the countryside. I failed the examination. I was given the opportunity to go to a vocational pharmacy school. I turned it down.

I was determined to pass that test the next time it was offered, which would be 1978. I had to. My future depended on it. Passing that test would be the only way that I would get out of the countryside. This was also the year that the Party stopped forcing high school graduates to go to the countryside. I would not be left behind! I mustered all of my confidence and went to have a conversation with the Party leader of my production team. I am so glad I did, because the Party leader gave me permission to return to Chengdu to prepare for the college entrance exam once I had worked all the required hours for the season. I was so excited. I worked hard that season, mostly on digging irrigation channels, so that my Party leader would give me a good recommendation, should he be asked.

Through a connection, a friend of my parents, I was able to get a standby seat (not an official seat) for an examination preparation class in one of Chengdu's best high schools. While I was only nineteen when I entered the high school to take the preparation class, everyone else was just sixteen or seventeen years old. I felt like I stuck out like a sore thumb among all the fresh smiling faces that never knew a day's work in the countryside. By this time, I had spent three long years working in the fields. That's also three long years of learning loss. I was committed to not wasting this opportunity to launch my life, so I studied day and night for three straight months.

The preparation class came to an end, and I had done all the studying a person can possibly do. It was time to go back to the county township of my commune to take the examination. The couple of months it took to find out if I had passed or failed dragged on. I felt butterflies in my stomach around the clock. Then, finally, my mother received my notice of acceptance at her work unit. My mom hopped on her bike and pedaled her shaking legs as fast as she could to get home to deliver the news. It was just three years earlier in 1975 that she was on her bike, legs shaking, mind racing, as she pedaled home after changing my residence registration (*hu kou*) from urban to rural to send me to the countryside for what would be a miserable experience for me. On that ride, her eyes filled with tears and her heart was filled with despair; this time, her eyes glistened with excitement and her heart was full of pure joy.

It was happening. I was going to college to study English. All those years of my hopes being dashed were over. At the age of nineteen, I was going to college and was excited about my future. I had no idea this would lead me to something that I did not imagine even in my wildest dreams: a new life in America.

CHAPTER 3

Land of the Free

Bags packed and goodbyes said, I left my home in Chengdu for the long trip to my college in Chongqing. It was an all-night train ride to get there, and I had a feeling of adventure. I was no longer a young girl confined to a world where hope was a foreign concept (literally). What I did have was hope and a dream that my destination would give me the opportunity to change my life.

Upon arrival, I was greeted with total chaos. Our dorms were not ready. Years of destruction of the Cultural Revolution and neglect in educational institutions had left most colleges and universities struggling. We were told that we would have to sleep on the floor in our classroom for a few weeks. That didn't dampen my spirit—I had slept in much worse. Those years banished to dirty and primitive conditions in the countryside had prepared me for almost anything. While other students complained, I smiled the whole time. I was filled with gratitude for my new situation because I was in a much better place.

The dorms we eventually moved into were offices that were converted into living spaces by simply setting up bunk beds. I shared a room with three other girls. The room was small, and in the middle of it was a laundry line for us to dry our clothes. Our classroom was just next door. The whole floor, including two wings, shared one restroom. There was a communal shower for the entire college, and it opened once a week. Thinking back, it was a pretty wild situation that many young Chinese college students today would have a hard time believing.

The quality of education we received was well below what I had anticipated. The textbooks we used were the standard college English textbooks by Professor Xu Guozhang. They did not really teach English, but rather presented more of the same CCP-approved Communist narratives that I had seen in secondary school. Most college professors in China had learned English from these same textbooks. Many of the professors were "worker-peasant-soldier" college graduates who had been admitted into college between 1970 and 1976, toward the end of the Cultural Revolution. They had gotten there based on recommendations by Party leaders rather than admitted for academic excellence and achievement, which most lacked.

Learning English in college meant starting with the ABCs. Literally! Few of us had been properly taught English in secondary school. The assigned textbooks were pretty much all we had. The college had no library where students could find real English books and reading materials by native English speakers. During summer vacations, I would go to the "English-speaking corner" located just outside the only hotel in Chengdu for foreigners. There we could always meet foreigners willing to talk to us in English. I remember greeting them not with "How are you?" but rather, "Have you eaten?"—the standard Chinese greeting at the time (it must be that having food was on everyone's mind). Their puzzled looks made me realize that my English textbooks did not teach us *real* English, but "Chinglish" with CCP characteristics.

Things did eventually improve, fortunately. Although the college was still pushing the CPP narrative, they began to offer an extensive reading class. This was a course where we read original English literature, such as *The Adventures of Tom Sawyer*, which I loved. It was so captivating and funny. Also, we could openly listen to English learning programs that were broadcast on BBC or VOA. The world was starting to open up for me.

More and more, what had been off-limits to us became acceptable. We finally had access to a small special library of pirated copies of original English works (yes, the CCP had been stealing intellectual property for a long time). Things got even better when we started getting English teachers from English-speaking countries. The first group came from Canada to teach only professors and later graduate students, so that left me out. Still, having foreigners on campus made us feel as though we were finally open to the West.

Four years in college flew by. At the end of my time there, we got to see undubbed foreign films such as adaptations of Charles Dickens's *Great Expectations* and *Oliver Twist*. Even with four years of English instruction, though, the only words I understood from *Oliver Twist* were, "I want some more." Around the same time, an hour-long English TV program called *Wild Kingdom* with Chinese captioning was available for viewing every Sunday at 1:00 p.m. It was just what I needed. I could listen to English while getting help from the Chinese subtitles. There were no TVs for students; fortunately for me, a kind professor couple allowed me to watch the show on their newly acquired tiny black-and-white TV. I never missed an episode.

Those movies, TV shows, and books, along with BBC and VOA radio stations, were windows to the rest of the world for me. I ached for more. So much for my dream of going to Albania; all I wanted was to see the Western world with my own eyes!

In 1982, I graduated college. Instead of a commencement ceremony, we graduates had to wait through an agonizing meeting in which the college administrator read aloud the work assignment for each individual graduate. In the Communist China I grew up in, it was the Party who made every decision for us, including jobs. We did not get to choose our own career; we were given one. I was thrilled to find out that I would be returning to my hometown, Chengdu, with an assignment to work at a teacher-training college. Other graduates were not as fortunate. Some graduates were given awful assignments and they burst into curses and tears. One girl was sent to work in Lhasa, Tibet, which was like a sentence of exile back then.

Two years later, in 1984, the college where I was teaching started to receive volunteer teachers from America. They came to China to teach English during the summer. I worked as an interpreter for them, and it was like I had entered a new world; I was no longer seeing it only on film or in TV shows. I was able to ask these visiting teachers all sorts of questions about America, and, in turn, tell them everything they wanted to know about China or myself.

One conversation I had with a Chinese-American woman who had immigrated to the United States from Southeast Asia had a profound and lasting effect on me. She told me that America was the best country in the world for immigrants, where they were welcomed and treated fairly. Another woman I met quickly became a friend. Her name was Pat Nave, from Kentucky. Pat and I talked a lot about life and education in America. She wanted to help bring me to America to pursue a graduate education in Kentucky. Things were starting to fall into place for me, and hope started to look more tangible.

It was sad for me to see those American teachers leave at the end of the summer. They had changed my outlook on life. I was optimistic that Pat would follow up on her promise. I didn't have to wait long. True to her word, Pat sent me a letter telling me she had begun the process of securing a college assistantship for me, while also cautioning me that the process was neither simple nor quick. She wasn't kidding. It took a year's worth of paperwork with long waits in between correspondence before the day finally arrived when I received an offer letter from Western Kentucky University. Things had now been set in motion for me to leave China, destination: Kentucky.

I was not simply waiting for Pat to do all the work. To qualify, I had to take—and pass—the Test of English as a Foreign Language exam, known as TOEFL. This was the real test; nothing like those I took in college. Preparing for the test required arduous work. In the process, I realized my English sufficiency was seriously questionable. Listening was always the most challenging part. But even reading was not easy, especially in the area of understanding connotations, meaning I could understand every word of a sentence but could not understand what it tried to convey. I remember one reading question asked us to determine whether the tone was positive or critical in a description of American tourists in Mexico buying Mexican hats as souvenirs. I had no idea whether the author was simply describing or mocking those tourists. I had never traveled as a tourist nor had I ever seen tourist souvenirs. In addition, paying for the test was not easy, either. I no longer remember the exact test fee I paid, only that it was more than my meager ¥50 monthly salary. Plus, I had to travel back to Chongqing to take the test; that involved a fair amount of travel expenses as well. I managed to get there and pass the test.

To secure my Chinese passport, I had to go through layers of red tape and make promises to my college administration that I intended to come back to serve the motherland after I completed my studies in America.

When all the paperwork arrived from Pat, I was ready to apply for my student visa. Getting my student visa was a more difficult task. All the work Pat and I had done would be for nothing if the visa was not granted to me.

It was in spring 1986 that I went to the American consulate in Chengdu with all the necessary papers in hand and a lot of prayers to apply for my visa, only to be promptly rejected.

The visa officer was a woman originally from Taiwan. When it was my turn, I handed her my application. She then interrogated me with questions while making notes on my papers as I talked. When she was finished grilling me, she took my papers, held them up in front of me, and tore them in half, telling me that my visa application was denied. She announced her decision to me not in English, but in Chinese. Rubbing it in.

I felt cheated.

But I refused to let her kill my dream. I came this far and I was not about to give up!

I decided I would go to Beijing to try the application process there. In November, I rode a train for two days to Beijing, hoping I would have luck this time. I reasoned that by going to Beijing, they would have no record of my rejected application in Chengdu, so I could reapply quickly. Remember, the computerized, digital access to data we have in 2023 didn't exist in the 1980s.

It was the day after Thanksgiving 1986 that I got to the American embassy in Beijing. I arrived very early, but there was already a long line outside, and it was an extremely cold day. When I finally got to the front gate, my hands were so frozen that I could not even hold a pen to sign the registration paper to be allowed in. After a long wait inside, my name was called. I nervously approached the window, where I was greeted by a visa officer, a smiling young man. He quickly scanned my papers and told me to come back in seven days to pick up my student visa. I was stunned. I was so excited that I almost ran out of the office, fearing that the visa officer would stop me and tell me that it was all a mistake. I often think about that visa officer. I am so thankful that he opened the door and let me come to America by issuing me the US visa.

When word spread that I was going to America, all my family and friends regarded me as the luckiest person on earth. It was as if I had won the lottery. It was true. I did win a lottery that would change my life forever.

One more challenge awaited me before I could be on my way to America: money for my flight there. One of my uncles stepped up to help me out. He had a business connection with people in Hong Kong who helped him buy the ticket with US dollars. Without my uncle's help, it would have been very difficult for me to afford the astronomical amount of money needed for the ticket using Chinese yuan. I promised to pay it back later. And I did.

My mom accompanied me to Guangzhou to see me off. I would never forget the moment I crossed the border to enter into Hong Kong and left China behind me. It felt like a heavy chain being lifted off my back, like a prisoner being set free.

Boarding the United Airlines flight, I was greeted with a huge smile from an airline steward; I had never in my whole life seen a smile so big, so carefree, and so welcoming. I knew that all would be fine for me.

* * *

To describe my first impressions, I don't even know where to start. Everything was new. Everything was exciting. Everything was good.

One thing that stood out immediately was the openness in America. Lots of open space; it felt like I was on another planet. For someone who had grown up in a country that is seemingly packed with people everywhere, it's stunning.

It hit me quickly that there were choices, choices, and more choices for just about everything. I was amazed by the choice of food brands in grocery stores, any given commercial item, even college courses. Choice was something I did not have growing up in China. Now I had to learn to make choices. Oftentimes it seemed too overwhelming, and sometimes even paralyzing.

One thing I noticed right away was that there was a lot of bad news on TV. In China, all news was good news, no matter how it contradicted the reality that everyone could see. I was so used to it that the contrast in America was startling.

The college experience was different, too. The whole way of learning was new to me. In China, we were told to read this and memorize that. We memorized who, what, when, where, and how, and then we spit it back out in tests. Now, learning required thinking. That was challenging. I had to learn to think and form my own opinions. Up to that point, my opinion was totally based on the opinion of the Party.

The first semester was difficult for me. I took an English literature class in which we were asked to write a paper critiquing a work by a chosen author. I picked Daniel Defoe. In China, I had read a translation of his book *Robinson Crusoe*. So, I said to myself, "I'm going to find a lesser-known book by Defoe, and I'm sure there will only be a few critiques that I have to read." Instead, I found about thirty written critiques in the library—much more research than I had planned for. I couldn't grasp why there was such a diversity of critiques and opinions about one of Defoe's minor works. Why did Americans have so many opinions? I wondered.

* * *

It turns out that my future husband was in two of the first three classes I took.

One day in the school library, I got lost trying to find a certain book for my reading. Mark couldn't help but notice I was having a navigational problem. He helped me out and then we started talking. Sometime later, he helped me with a paper I was struggling to write. But that's all it was at the time—two new members of a friend zone.

As we got to know each other more, I got to meet some of his family, most of whom were living in the area of Bowling Green, Kentucky. The very first one I met was his paternal grandmother, a woman who had met few foreigners, if any. I was nervous about it and wondered if she wouldn't think well of me because of my race. He told me not to worry about meeting his grandmother, that she was quite nice. She was, and I was impressed by how she treated me like I wasn't different after all. In China, people look at someone who is different from them with a rude curiosity, often staring at them, sometimes even surrounding them as if they were in a zoo. I never experienced any of that in America, and definitely not with anyone in Mark's family. Eventually, I met all his cousins— he had a lot of cousins—and aunts and uncles. I met all of them before I met Mark's parents, because they lived a good distance away, and then they came to visit. It was the same thing with them; they accepted me just like his grandmother and his other relatives already had.

After getting my MA in English at Western Kentucky University, I moved to another university in Florida for a graduate program in adult education. I didn't really know what else to do; I had to stay in school to hold on to my student status for the sake of my visa. Meanwhile, Mark was in Europe teaching English.

* * *

I might have left CCP China, but it took years for the CCP mindset to leave me. Seeing all the open land and forests, I couldn't grasp how land ownership works. I remember asking Mark, "Who owns all this?" and his answer was, "I don't know. People own it." But wait—in China we were also told that the people owned everything and that the people were the masters of China. I soon figured out the difference. "People" in CCP vocabulary means *the state*. "People" in America means individuals. Gazing at all this privately owned land, I was reminded of the freedom there is in America, and I soaked it up.

It took a long time to "detox" myself from all that was inside my head, courtesy of the CCP. Another thing that always baffled me was that Mark would stop at a stop sign even when there was clearly no one else around. When asked, he told me it was the law and we should all follow it. I started to appreciate that in America people do follow the law, big and small. People in America are citizens, the real "masters" of their country; one of the reasons why America is so great. Sadly, it is no longer the case. Lawlessness has increasingly become the norm.

Then there was the simple act of politely holding the door open for someone. In China, the CCP had managed to kill kindness and courtesy and everyone was out for themselves. A common scene I grew up with was fighting to get on busses where only the fittest had the chance and the old, weak, and young were left behind. When I was out with Mark, he would see me not holding open the door for others behind me. He said, "You're basically hitting people behind you with the door by not holding it for them. That's not polite."

I could go on for a whole chapter on this topic.

There is a lot of discussion these days about immigrant assimilation and what it is supposed to be. Some are even against it. To me, assimilation meant learning and adapting to American values. It is these values that made America that place I so desperately wanted to come. How could I not want to assimilate? It also meant that I would have to detox from the CCP indoctrination in me.

Mark and I got married in 1990. It was a simple ceremony. We had little money between us, so his parents paid for everything. My mother-in-law bought a white linen dress for me as my wedding gown. We held the service in the backyard of his uncle's house in the country, the one in which his mother had grown up. We couldn't afford a photographer, but family members took a lot of photos. I had never been taught I was a princess and never had dreams, like most young girls in America, of my perfect wedding, but I loved everything about our simple country wedding.

We lived in Florida for about a year after we got married. We had very little savings. I had $2,500 in my savings account. That money came from every penny I had made and every penny not spent while painting college dorms, babysitting, house cleaning, living rent free as a companion to an elderly woman with Alzheimer's, bussing tables in a Chinese restaurant, waitressing, even being an entrepreneur sewing hair bands to sell to the department staff where I worked as a student assistant.

We were able to rent a one-bedroom apartment. We acquired most of our furniture by retrieving it from the apartment complex's dumpster. No joke!

In 1991, we moved to northern Virginia where Mark's parents lived, since it was where we thought the jobs were. We lived in their basement for a couple of years before we could save enough money to have a place of our own.

It was a struggle for us because we were both overeducated and underemployed. I worked in a department store and did other odd jobs, while Mark was applying for positions, but his master's degree in German wasn't a good fit for the jobs he was seeking. At times I would think, "Really? This is the land of opportunity? I don't see anything for me." I had made it this far—I had come to this country, gotten my degree, gotten married, but there was nothing (workwise) for me.

I remember looking through the *Washington Post*'s job pages line by line every week to look for any possible jobs to apply for. I seldom heard back from the applications I sent out. At one point, my father-in-law heard from a friend about a contractor who had an opening for some type of assistant. I went and interviewed for the job. The only thing I knew about it was that they did some work for the federal government. The job involved answering phones and transferring calls. The interviewer repeated the acronym "DOD" during the interview. At one point, I finally mustered up the courage to ask what DOD (Department of Defense) actually meant. I could see from her face in that moment that she thought I was an idiot. And at that moment, I thought so, too. That crushed my almost nonexistent confidence.

But I refused to just feel sorry for myself. I decided that I had to do something else.

At age thirty-two, I decided to go back to school, this time to get a degree in library science, believing that would help me get on a career path. That took me to Catholic University of America in Washington, DC. I was fortunate to obtain an assistantship that allowed me to work in the university library in exchange for free tuition. We were still living with my in-laws. Every day, I commuted from a Virginia suburb to DC to work during the day and take classes in the evening. My hard work paid off. I was thrilled that I was offered a professional job before I even graduated. I became a special librarian working to index publications and manage a photo collection for a major news magazine. I was so happy to be on a career path, which has given me much satisfaction.

The same year I got my first professional job was the year I became an American citizen. Yes, I've been a US citizen for more than thirty years.

Meanwhile, Mark became a software engineer after taking evening classes. Finally, we both had real jobs that put us on a path to success. It is often said that America is a land of opportunity; what many people refuse to acknowledge is that while the opportunity is there, you still have to work and strive for it. Opportunity is not a government handout.

Soon after, we were able to buy our very first house. In 1996, we welcomed our son.

To me, this was the beginning of the realization of my American dream: We finally became proud homeowners and part of the middle class. I always say American dreams come in all sizes. My dream might be too small for some people. But it is my dream and I made it happen. In that, I took great pride.

* * *

I suppose it was inevitable. My experience in America was not without encounters with racism. It started not long after I had arrived in America. When Mark and I were still dating, he would tell me about times he had spotted people behind my back, using their fingers to push up the outsides of their eyes to mimic Asian eyes. There were a lot of incidents like this, especially in areas that were less cosmopolitan.

There was also the time in the mid-1990s when I was in New York City's Chinatown visiting with Chinese friends, when a Black man on the street yelled at us, "You dirty Chinese," as we walked by. There had to be irony in that—my first open racism encounter was with an African American.

Of course, there were also some with white Americans. One day, Mark and I were driving in Pennsylvania when we got a flat tire. We pulled off to the side of the road, and Mark called road service because we didn't have a spare tire. I was close enough to the phone to hear both ends of the conversation, with the guy on the other end sounding very friendly and chatty, assuring us, "We'll be right there, don't you worry!"

It wasn't long before we saw the driver in his truck approaching us on the other side of the road. They (his wife was with him) waved at us—still very friendly—and said they would be right over, after a U-turn. As soon as they pulled up, stopped, and saw us up close, the friendly banter and smiles came to a screeching halt. No longer speaking, they quickly went to work, removing the flat tire, putting on a new one, and then completing the work silently. They got back into their truck and drove away. I looked at Mark and said, "I think it's me, don't you?"

"I think so, too."

Apparently, they did not like the sight of a Chinese woman coupled with a white man.

Incidents like this bothered me, of course. But I never dwell on them much. Mark revealed to me many instances of subtle racism toward me when interacting with other people that I was not able to see. But that's okay that I didn't see it. I was never looking for it. I had not come from a gentle place. During my twenty-six years in China, I had witnessed people being brutalized by the government and by each other. As an elementary schoolgirl, on the way to school, I once saw a dead baby dumped next to a pile of trash. I also witnessed an angry crowd beat a young thief to the point of near death. There was also the time as a young girl when I had a bike accident while riding through a small construction site on the street. Some of my skin around my knee had been scraped off, and despite my obvious distress and the blood on my leg, the construction workers cheered. These are my reference points, which always helped me put things in perspective and made me more forgiving.

However, two incidents in particular involving racism stand out for me and shook me to my core: My American identity was challenged because of my race. The first was another incident involving a different visa officer at the American consulate in Chengdu. On this occasion, I was there with my mother helping her get a visa to come to the United States with me. I had gone to China for my father's funeral and was trying to bring my mom back with me for a short visit to have some recovery time. The visa officer, a middle-aged woman, would not allow me to speak for my mother, who knew hardly any English. "Which one of you is applying?" the woman asked.

I spoke up and said, "It's my mother." She said she wouldn't speak to anyone but the applicant. I tried to explain the situation when she abruptly closed the window, and that was that. No other way to explain what had just happened. I could not see her treating any American citizen that way—I mean any easily identifiable American, white, Black, or brown. I was firmly convinced that she did not think I was an American citizen because of my race. I was being rudely singled out because of my *Chinese-ness*.

The second incident occurred at a Walmart in Virginia. I was in a long checkout line, almost to the cashier, with only two or three items in my hands. I was in a hurry because I had already been in line a long time, and my husband and our son were waiting for me in the car. I was approached by two white women who were together and had only a couple items. They asked if they could cut in front of me because they were in a hurry. Bad timing. I told them, "I'm sorry, but no," that I, too, had just a few items and was also in a hurry.

One of them said to the other, talking about me, "She's not an American. An American would let us go in front of them." I was now shaking, hearing that. I had no good argument to counter with, and my voice was trembling as I said, "I *am* an American!"

I could have come to the conclusion that because I was discriminated against as an Asian, America is a racist country. But I chose not to. Not because I chose to believe racism does not exist in America, but because for every explicit or implicit racist encounter I had, I have had thousands more encounters with Americans of all skin colors and all walks of life that were not only positive, but also beautiful.

* * *

Ever since becoming an American citizen, I have been sure to vote at every opportunity, despite for the longest time not having much of an understanding of politics. Whenever I watched a debate, I thought both sides sounded reasonable; I couldn't argue with either. I didn't make the effort to learn more about politics and candidates. Instead, I spent my free time pursuing my hobbies—art, photography, traveling, gardening, and reading about history.

It all started to change for me one day in 2008. My husband was watching one of the primary Republican presidential debates, while I was occupied with chores, not paying much attention. I could hear the voices, but I wasn't listening—there was no difference. They all sounded the same to me.

One candidate, however, suddenly grabbed my attention. He didn't sound like any of the other candidates. He was speaking about issues head-on, very matter of fact about them; nothing he said seemed to be polished sound bites or political doublespeak. For the first time, I was hearing something political that didn't sound political; it made real sense to me. I'm talking about then-congressman Ron Paul. I stopped what I was doing and watched the rest of the debate. After that, I started to pay close attention to him and whatever he had to say. He spoke like someone determined to tell Americans things we didn't want to hear but needed to hear. I soon bought and read his book *End the Fed*.

I did not turn into a libertarian. However, this marked the beginning of my devoted interest in politics, and it has intensified as time has passed. Since then, I've read many books on American politics and followed many conservative commentators. By the 2016 elections, I had formed a conservative political view clearly my own.

* * *

Until the last decade or so, I had not given much thought to the premise that freedom "is never more than one generation away from extinction." I never entertained the idea that Marxism could take such a prominent place in America.

I trace my first encounter of woke-ism in the form of political correctness back to 1990, when I took a special-education course in Florida. Our professor told us about a bill that had just been passed for people with disabilities (the Americans with Disabilities Act) and that we needed to be respectful in how we chose our words when speaking about individuals with disabilities. For example, we should not say "blind"; the preferred phrase was now "vision impaired." Nor should we say "crippled" going forward; the fashionable new word was "handicapped." That has since evolved into "disabled" and now "differently abled."

Back then, I thought, "Wow! Americans are so nice; they want to be respectful." Now I know better. The real intention is not about respect. This was just an early form of language manipulation to control people. If you can orchestrate the words people use and how they use them, you can control their speech and therefore their thoughts.

Another watershed moment for me in the world of political correctness came in 2003, when Senate minority leader Trent Lott was forced to resign. I did not know all the details at the time, only that he had praised Senator Strom Thurmond, who was deemed a segregationist and racist. I remember telling myself that it sounded like the Cultural Revolution, when one wrong word could ruin an individual. But I did not give it much thought and quickly forgot about the whole thing.

In 2000, I transitioned to a new position working for a nonprofit organization. Around 2012, I was invited to be a member of the newly formed Diversity & Inclusion (D&I) Council. Not knowing too much about what this was all about, I gladly said yes. The council members consisted of employees of different ethnicities.

I thought, if I could be part of something that would help all employees learn to appreciate one another's differences and work together, why not? Soon I found out the intent of the council was different than my assumptions.

The intention of the D&I council leader, as it turned out, was to introduce CRT into the company, although we did not know the term back then. My company was multiethnic and multicultural, with more than half of the employees being women, including leadership, and whose CEO was an African American when I joined. Obviously, this was not good enough. The council aimed to raise the staff's consciousness of systemic racism. Soon, outside speakers were brought in to give talks on topics such as microaggressions. Emails were distributed containing articles on racial issues from left-leaning media like *HuffPost*. I felt there was a political agenda being pushed. I eventually quit the council.

Also during this time, I started to hear from my son, still in high school, about things like race versus power, transgenderism, and the evil of American imperialism. After he started college, I learned more from him of what was taught in higher education, like intersectionality, white privilege, social justice…

Now, I could see it happening all around me, from my home to my workplace to the larger society. The macro and micro worlds had merged. The woke revolution was taking over my life. It was taking over America!

Finally came the last straw. With the death of George Floyd and the Black Lives Matter protests sweeping the nation in 2020, my company responded by holding an all-hands meeting to support the BLM movement and condemn systematic racism, not just in society at large but also within our organization. My company was going woke; to me, there was no mistake about it.

After that day, the culture in my workplace started to change.

The informal D&I Council promptly updated its name to DEI (Diversity, Equity, and Inclusion) Council. It was granted more prominence to help amplify its voices. Many employees feared being seen as not being on board with what was happening. When I made national news with my June 2021 speech at the school board, quite a few coworkers, including some I didn't know personally or were in high positions in the organization, emailed me *privately* to give me support. Others who had learned the news about me pretended they did not know. And the majority were just going along to get along. The culture of conformity and fear has become the norm, not just for my company, but across the nation.

Meanwhile, pronouns began to be added to email signatures across the division. A DEI Committee was launched by the division head just for our division, who apologized in the division meeting for her white privilege and stated her commitment to DEI. Soon, a division online DEI page was created just for DEI posts. One of the posts was the "Antiracism Toolkit for Allies." The toolkit not only condemned white supremacy, but asserted that white people, including white liberals, perpetuate white supremacy simply by being white. Simply by *being*! Now, for the first time during my twenty-one years working there, staff began to see each other through the lens of race, exactly what CRT intends that people do.

When the first DEI Committee discussion session was scheduled, I was determined to speak up. And I did. At the session, I stated that I have been working in this company for more than twenty years. I have great working relationships with all my white colleagues. But now the toolkit made me realize that I have been surrounded by "white supremacists." Should *I* feel unsafe now?

That was brutal, but I had to say it because it was all true. And the division head was more than displeased.

In 2022, for the first time in my twenty-one years working there, I received a bad annual review. That wasn't all. Soon, I was asked to learn a programming language as part of my goals for the next six months. If I failed, I would be disqualified for the position that I was hired for and had held for twenty-one years. Mastering a programming language had never been part of my profession, my job description, nor my work responsibility. It was clear that I was not wanted there.

I could have fought back. But I decided to quit instead.

I have a much more important battle to fight and a much bigger arena in which to fight the fight; not for me, but for America. So, I went to work full-time for America.

I came full circle. By coming to America, the land of the free, I believed that I had escaped Communism. Now I found myself in the midst of the battlefield, fighting against Communism to keep this land free.

CHAPTER 4

Two Cultural Revolutions

Although I personally was a witness to China's Cultural Revolution as a schoolgirl, I didn't understand what was really going on, why it was happening, or what the real purpose was of the revolution. It wasn't until after I came to America and got my hands on reliable historical information and archival materials that I was able to better understand what had taken place around me in China decades earlier. I had to cross thousands of miles to America in order to learn what I had left behind in China. When you are in it, you are just trying to survive. You are not given the courtesy of an explanation. All you can do is what you are told.

Understanding the impetus of your situation is a luxury not afforded to you.

Nor did I know anything about America's Marxist movement that had started in the 1960s and planted the seeds of today's *woke* Marxist movement until long after I had come to this country. It took me a while to understand what I was starting to see in America. Once I was able to connect all the dots, clear lines started to emerge that help us see the larger picture.

I consider it unique, maybe even privileged, that in my lifetime I have experienced not just one but two of the most important cultural revolutions in human history, Mao's Great Proletarian Cultural Revolution (1966–1976) and the American cultural revolution of the 2020s (with roots dating back much earlier). Both are cultural Marxist revolutions and are synonymous with Communism.

In China and in every country that has ever been under a Communist regime, history has proven that these countries have been incubators for rebellion, chaos, and violence. The parallels between the America of today and the China of the mid-1960s haunt me. These parallels, which are the hallmarks of cultural Marxism, will destroy America as we know it, as they have every country across history. If we do not stop this now, you can bet your life that America will inevitably become a Communist-like state, top to bottom.

I've told you a lot about my story. Now, I want to go deeper into the two cultural revolutions. But before I do, I need to clarify my use of the terms *Marxism*, *socialism*, and *Communism*. I often use them interchangeably—as do some experts familiar with their respective meanings. My understanding of these terms is based on the Communist education I received in Mao's China.

In every school in Mao's China, we were taught that human/ social development encompassed six stages that were to occur in chronological order across a spectrum: 1) primitive society (hunter/gatherer society), 2) slavery, 3) feudalism, 4) capitalism, 5) socialism, 6) Communism.

We were taught that every country goes through the same stages of development while heading toward the same final destiny and ideal stage of human development: Communism. China, we were then told, was a socialist country, but we were well on the way to Communism. Yet we could not achieve Communism until all the countries in the world were liberated and had accepted socialism. We were taught that it was our duty to help other countries in their effort to become socialist. I did not think much about it then, but it's now obvious to me that Communism is *globalism*!

When I first heard people in the West referring to China as a Communist country, I would correct them by telling them China is a *socialist* country. No Communist country calls itself *Communist*, despite that the news media, textbooks, and various historical accounts say otherwise. Where Communism comes into play is that the ruling political party in these socialist countries is the Communist Party.

It didn't take me long to realize that the type of socialism most Americans refer to is different from the socialist system I lived under. These Americans have been duped into believing that this newly emerging version of socialism is a far better and fairer society than what we had in China—that this "idealized" version of socialism is one in which people willingly and peacefully share wealth and resources. Many Americans, especially young people who have been conned into wanting socialism, use Nordic countries as shining examples. The Nordic countries are not socialist, but capitalist countries built on a free-market economy. What the progressives are actually pushing is government control of all wealth and resource distribution—a kind of totalitarian socialism just like China, where only the dominant class benefits and the rest suffer. The corruption of the term *socialism* is intentional.

* * *

On June 15, 1976, shortly before his death, Mao was reported to have said that he had two accomplishments in his life. One was winning the Communist revolution by defeating the Kuomintang (Nationalist) government (1921–1949). The other was launching the Great Proletarian Cultural Revolution (1966–1976).[1]

The first revolution was a bloody revolution using military force to overthrow a sitting government in order to seize power. The Chinese Communist Party and the Nationalists had a torturous relationship. They collaborated to fight against their common enemies known as the northern warlords and later Japanese invaders, but the ideological divide made it impossible for them to coexist. The final showdown was the civil war of 1945–1949, ending with Mao claiming victory and forcing the Nationalist government led by Chiang Kai-shek to flee to Taiwan. The Nationalists lost because of their long record of mismanagement and corruption, while the Chinese Communist Party under Mao was able to gain both military strength and popular support with their alluring and attractive narratives and promises as well as the fact that Mao had Soviet Russia's full backing while the US abandoned its support to the Nationalists.[2]

Mao's second revolution was the Cultural Revolution. Ironically, the aim of this revolution was also to overthrow a sitting government—this time, his own. He wanted to destroy everything, burn it all down, and build a brand-new world over the "ashes." (Or fast-forward to today in President Joe Biden's words, "build back better.") This time he did not use military forces. He had a better weapon, the mobilization of the masses, including young students and those of the populace that felt disenfranchised. This would be a real revolution, a revolution to destroy traditional culture and the CCP's institutions. His goal was to remake China exactly in his image and to gain absolute power in the process.

Mao's quote about his two greatest accomplishments in his life makes it sound like that's all he did—fomenting and carrying out the two revolutions. It is important to mention that the time between 1949 (the founding of the CCP China) and 1966 (the launching of the Cultural Revolution) was not in any way an uneventful and peaceful time period. From the time that Mao took power, he launched endless political campaigns. Every one of those campaigns was a smaller-scale Cultural Revolution, leaving behind millions of victims who perished or were ruined for life.

It is important to know of one particular campaign, the Great Leap Forward (1958–1961), as it became the prelude for the Cultural Revolution. The Great Leap Forward was Mao's strategy to emulate what Joseph Stalin had done in Russia. Mao set a goal to surpass the steel production of Great Britain in ten years and the United States in fifteen years. Why steel production? Steel is necessary for weapon production. The Great Leap Forward had nothing to do with improving China's economy and people's lives. It had everything to do with building Mao's military might.

It was all just madness, based on the premise that peasants would stop working in the fields and start the steel making endeavor with homemade furnaces. As the steel making operations failed, so did the crops. The Great Famine (1959–1961) ensued, which claimed up to thirty million lives.[3] Some estimations go as high as fifty million. I was born during the famine. I heard a lot of stories from my mother about strict rations for food, which was barely enough, and everyone around her had swollen faces, hands, feet, and stomachs due to severe protein deficiency. And these were the lucky ones.

Through his Great Leap Forward catastrophe, Mao lost a lot of his prestige. Members of the Communist Party started to question his leadership. At the same time, his second-in-command, President Liu Shaoqi, and Liu's ally Deng Xiaoping, vice premier, stepped in to take care of the mess by focusing on rebuilding China's economy. That was a problem for Mao—somebody else was in charge, not him. He wanted to get his power back, and he knew it could be done by getting the masses involved; he knew he still had great influence among the Chinese people, especially the well-indoctrinated youths.

It was against this historic background that Mao launched his Great Proletarian Cultural Revolution in 1966. There was an actual official launch date of the Cultural Revolution: May 16, 1966. On that day, the CCP Central Committee released a document penned by Mao known as the May 16 Notification. It announced that the CCP had been infiltrated by enemies who sought to restore capitalism; and it declared: "The whole party must follow Comrade Mao Zedong's instructions, hold high the great banner of the proletarian Cultural Revolution, thoroughly expose the reactionary bourgeois stand of those so-called 'academic authorities' who oppose the party and socialism, thoroughly criticize and repudiate the reactionary bourgeois ideas in the sphere of academic work, education, journalism, literature and art, and publishing, and seize the leadership in these cultural spheres."[4] It was made very clear that the war Mao was about to launch aimed at the complete destruction of existing institutions and traditional culture.

Through this Great Cultural Revolution, Mao wanted to dispose of all the Party bureaucracies that he felt were not under his control—that would include pretty much the entire CCP leadership: local, provincial, and central—and replace them all with true revolutionaries who were loyal only to him.

Mao had another motivation for initiating the Cultural Revolution. He wanted to make sure that what happened to Joseph Stalin, Communist dictator of the Soviet Union (1922–1953), would not happen to him as well. Three years after Stalin's death, his successor, Nikita Khrushchev, denounced Stalin in his speech entitled "On the Cult of Personality and Its Consequences."[5]

Mao had been doing the same. He, too, had been creating his own cult of personality. By revising the Marxist-Leninist revolution, Mao believed that Khrushchev derailed the Communist cause and allowed capitalism back into the USSR. Mao was determined to ensure that the same would not happen in China. He identified Liu Shaoqi as "China's Khrushchev," a "revisionist," and China's number one "capitalist roader," a label given to those who followed the "capitalist road" of focusing on improving the economy rather than the class struggle.

Mao wanted to focus on class struggle. During the first seventeen years of Mao's reign (1949–1965), the CCP had eradicated all private ownership and established a state-owned and collectivist economy. Still, Mao believed that the ideological war against the old culture was not over. He was determined to fundamentally transform China into a Communist utopia once and for all by abolishing all the remnants of the old culture and by purging the right-leaning influence within the CCP. He wanted to remake China exactly in his own image: Maoism.

By the time Mao died in 1976 at the age of eighty-two, China was a wreck and on the brink of total collapse. It was a society deeply divided, with institutions abolished, almost all remnants of the Chinese civilization destroyed, the economy in total ruin, people living in extreme poverty, and millions of lives lost. The only winner was Mao. He not only obtained absolute power, but he also became like a god to the people.

The Cultural Revolution robbed me of my formative years that would have included a sense of well-being, safety, and a normal education. That span of ten years should have been my elementary and secondary education, preparing me for my next step in development—a college education. Apart from material deprivation, I was also one of the unwitting lab mice in Mao's social reengineering experiment. It took decades for me to detox myself from the Marxist and Communist junk they had put into my head.

As I continue my story, sifting through the rubble and ashes of what Mao brought to China, destroying my homeland with every campaign, you will begin to recognize the clear and unquestionable similarities between the Cultural Revolution in China and the current state of the cultural Marxist movement, woke-ism, taking place in the United States.

Before coming to America, I knew its basic history. Since arriving, I have spent the past three decades learning about the history and culture of my adopted country. I deeply care about and am fascinated by not only its history but also its exceptional place in the world. I am constantly reading and listening to books, preferably those about American history and the founding fathers. In addition to the countless books and documentaries I have consumed,

I take every opportunity to visit historical sites and the homes of those who made an irreplaceable impact on America's greatness. I am fortunate to live in Virginia where history remains still so tangible and accessible thanks to the thoughtful and attentive conservatorship of historical sites and artifacts by so many organizations. This is how I have become increasingly familiar with the captivating history of the United States. But in all that I read, in all that I had learned, somehow, I had missed the sinister infiltration of cultural Marxism into the social fabric of American society. Perhaps the same was true for you?

After the George Floyd–inspired riots of 2020, I knew it was time to really educate myself on how exactly Marxist ideology came to dominate our schools, our institutions, and even our families. How could a country, so beloved for its defense of individual rights, property rights, the Constitution, and the right to life, liberty, and the pursuit of happiness, allow such a deadly ideology to plant its seeds here? We are currently living, whether we know it or not, under the tyrannical thumb of American Marxism.

My research has taken me back more than eight decades, to the 1930s.

Although Marxist theories led to a successful Communist revolution in Russia in 1917, and later in countries like China, North Korea, and Cuba, this was not what Karl Marx had predicted. His prediction that capitalism would collapse in the most industrialized countries like Great Britain, Germany, France, and the United States has been proven wrong. Capitalism did just the opposite. It has allowed everyone, rich or poor—and, yes, even new immigrants, in America—to successfully create wealth. Benjamin Franklin's rags-to-riches tale became the American dream. The dream has been made reality time and again by people like Henry

Ford, Andrew Carnegie, Steve Jobs, and Oprah Winfrey. Count-less ordinary people like me, who came to this country with two hundred *borrowed* dollars, are also able to achieve their American dream. Why would anyone who enjoys the prosperity and com-fort of the American way of life want to give it up to join a bloody and violent revolution that gains nothing but chaos, suffering, and poverty?

Reality and facts do not dissuade Communists from their plan. Antonio Gramsci (1891–1937), a devout Italian Communist, developed a new idea for defeating capitalism. Instead of seiz-ing the means of production and abolishing private ownership through violent revolution, Gramsci figured that capitalism can be defeated by the destruction of its *hegemony*. Andrew Heywood, author of the book *Political Ideologies: An Introduction*, explains Gramsci's "hegemony" in an easy-to-understand way. Gramsci believed that:

> …the Capitalist class system is upheld not simply by unequal economic and political power, but by what he termed the "hegemony" of bourgeois ideas and theories. Hegemony means leadership or domination and, in the sense of ideological hege-mony, it refers to the capacity of bourgeois ideas to displace rival views and become, in effect, the common sense of the age. Gramsci highlighted the degree to which ideology is embedded at every level in society: in its art and literature; in its education system and mass media; in everyday language; and in popu-lar culture. This bourgeois hegemony, Gramsci insisted, could only be challenged at the political and intellectual level, which means through the establishment of a rival "proletarian hege-mony," based on socialist principles, values and theories.[6]

Welcome to cultural Marxism. Gramsci would be regarded as the father of cultural Marxism and grandfather of today's woke-ism. I believe that understanding Gramsci is the key to understanding woke-ism.

Gramsci was imprisoned by Mussolini from 1926 until his death in 1937. It was in prison that Gramsci wrote down his political theory in a collection of essays collectively called Prison Notebooks.

Interestingly, the man who helped bring Gramsci's philosophy to America by translating his works into English and promoting them was Joseph Buttigieg, father of Pete Buttigieg, the current US Secretary of Transportation in the Biden administration. After I learned this information, I went to Amazon and searched "Joseph Buttigieg." Sure enough, Gramsci's three-volume work, Prison Notebooks, came up.

Sharing Gramsci's ideology was a group of Jewish Marxist scholars belonging to a school of social theory called the "Frankfurt School" in Frankfurt, Germany. As Hitler rose to power, these scholars no longer felt safe. In 1935, they fled to the United States, where they became embedded in academia at Columbia University in New York City—the heart of modern Western culture at the time.[7]

These transplanted intellectuals were the forerunners of American Marxists. They grew in dominance and began to exert their influence on American educational institutions. They had a strategic plan to destroy Western culture, through the manipulation of America's students and academics, weaponizing their published materials and collecting "useful idiots" to read, teach, and popularize their ideology. The first of these publications was *Traditional and Critical Theory* by Max Horkheimer.[8]

The idea behind critical theory, simply put, is to "criticize" every aspect of Western culture—family, Christianity, law, freedom of expression, or the "bourgeois hegemony," in Gramsci's terms. "Criticize" was a word that was on the lips of every Chinese person, including me, during the Cultural Revolution. You will learn more about it as you continue to read.

Critical theory produced many wicked offspring like *critical race theory* (CRT), *critical feminist theory* (CFT), and *critical queer theory* (CQT). CRT was developed by Derrick Bell (1930–2011) as a framework for legal analysis. It was made even more potent by Kimberlé Crenshaw (1959–) with her formulation of the term *intersectionality*.

An article entitled "A Lesson on Critical Race Theory" on the American Bar Association website explains that CRT is "a practice of interrogating the role of race and racism in society that emerged in the legal academy and spread to other fields of scholarship."[9] CRT critiques how the social construction of race and institution-alized racism perpetuate a racial caste system that relegates people of color to the bottom tiers. CRT also recognizes that race *intersects* with other identities, including sexuality, gender identity, and others. I will talk more about CRT and intersectionality in the following chapter.

The works of the neo-Marxists that made up the Frankfurt School are so densely academic that they do not appeal to the average readers, only to the most serious of researchers. Fortunately, cultural Marxism critics, such as Dr. James Lindsay, a notable anti–cultural Marxism intellectual and author, has helped bridge the gap of understanding. Lindsay made it possible for average readers, such as me, to understand and digest the works of the Frankfurt School Marxists. He did this through his books *Cynical*

Theories: How Activist Scholarship Made Everything about Race, Gender, and Identity—and Why This Harms Everybody (2020), *Race Marxism: The Truth about Critical Race Theory and Praxis* (2022), and *The Marxification of Education: Paulo Freire's Critical Marxism and the Theft of Education* (2023). Lindsay's podcast, "New Discourses," has also helped in this regard. These scholars have helped laymen like me develop insight into the neo-Marxist theories and ideas that shaped the American cultural revolution, ergo woke-ism.

The works of the Frankfurt School are the theoretical foundations for what we now know as woke-ism. It is also an important characteristic of today's American cultural Marxism. It is a weapon used by progressive ideologues to justify and impose tyranny on traditional society.

Prominent billionaire Elon Musk refers to woke ideology as a "mind virus" and "arguably one of the biggest threats to modern civilization."[10]

Woke-ism, as I understand it, is an ideology believing that a more equitable society is necessary and can be created through the systematic deconstruction of capitalism. Those who are "woke" believe all existing institutions, traditions, and social norms—in other words, the entire Western civilization and free market system—need to be destroyed and burned to the ground, upon which a brand-new world over the ashes will be built, just like Mao did to China.

The Chinese word for woke is *juewu*, which means awareness or consciousness, a word that originated in Buddhism. During the Chinese Cultural Revolution, we were constantly urged to raise our political *juewu*, class *juewu*, or simply *juewu*. What it really meant was abandoning any independent thinking and letting ourselves be unconditionally guided by Mao Zedong Thought. It meant that every person had to loyally obey Mao's orders without question—ever. Mao's orders were similar to American woke-ism: to eliminate the Chinese traditional culture so that Marxist ideology would have complete dominance over China.

Note, though, that woke-ism is *not* the beginning of a *new* American cultural revolution. The revolution in America that led to woke-ism actually began during the 1960s.

It was in the 1960s that cultural Marxist ideology promoted by the Frankfurt Schoolers made its way out of the university libraries and classrooms and into the streets.

The 1960s and the 1970s were an extraordinary time on both sides of the Pacific Ocean. Two parallel cultural revolutions were launched; one in China and one in the United States (including the entire Western world), designed to either strengthen socialism or weaken capitalism by undermining and eliminating anything traditional.

The counterculture movement of the 1960s turned out to be the first phase of the American Marxist cultural revolution. Unlike the Chinese Cultural Revolution, there was no one leader or instigator—no Mao—in plain view making this happen.

One man who doesn't have blinders on is Roger Kimball, a noted art critic who also happens to be a notable conservative social commentator. Kimball is the editor and publisher of *The New Criterion*, and the author of numerous books. His first published work was *Tenured Radicals: How Politics Has Corrupted Our Higher Education*—a title that suggests a particularly timely study of the state of American college education deep into the twenty-first century, but which, in fact, was first published *more than thirty years ago*, in 1990! During my own research, I came across Kimball's remarkably insightful book, *The Long March: How the Cultural Revolution of the 1960s Changed America*, which details the first phase of the cultural revolution that took place here in America. It is worth noting that the term "long march" in Kimball's book title originated from Mao's Long March (1934–1935). It was a march of the Chinese Red Army led by Mao to escape the encirclement campaigns of the Nationalist troops. The march, from Jiangxi in southern China to Shaanxi of northwestern China, covered a total of 5,600 miles and saved the CCP from being wiped out by the Nationalists. The term was later used in a famous phrase, "long march through the institutions," which was adopted by German Communist Rudi Dutschke to describe a long-term strategy to infiltrate institutions in order to change the culture not only of the institutions but the whole of society itself.[11]

In *The Long March*, Kimball explains how radicals of the '60s applied the teachings of the Frankfurt School intellectuals such as Herbert Marcuse to their activism. Kimball also details how major personalities such as Susan Sontag, Allen Ginsberg, Jerry Rubin, and Timothy Leary launched a war against traditional American culture. It is not difficult to look back and see the similarities to "cultural hegemony" as envisioned by Antonio Gramsci. The entire landscape of Western values, morals, and traditions was turned upside down. Common sense, as theorized by Gramsci, was completely redefined. What played out in the streets and across campuses was a complete rejection of traditional values, morals, and sexual manners that had guided the American way of life for generations.

One of Kimball's most insightful arguments is that the 1960s cultural revolution was the offspring of the unlikely marriage of cultural Marxism and Freudian psychology. "Free love" became the slogan of the day. Sexual desire and sexual fantasies were to be acted upon, no longer repressed. "Make love, not war" was the mantra on the lips and T-shirts of '60s counterculturalists. The Woodstock festival in 1969, according to Kimball, "helped put into circulation a new demand for absolute freedom together with the promise of absolute ecstasy."[12]

An integral component of the countercultural movement was the women's rights movement in the 1960s, or second-wave feminism. I am a beneficiary of the work done by the first-wave feminists who fought for equal rights for women and made it possible for women to pursue their dreams beyond narrowly defined roles as wives and mothers. However, the second-wave feminist movement had a totally different agenda. They preached to women that being a housewife meant being complicit in a form of subjugation. Both Betty Friedan, a feminist writer and activist, and Gloria Steinem, a writer, political activist, and feminist organizer, remain two of the most recognizable figures of the decade. I will talk more about second-wave feminism in Chapter 7.

The '60s gave us the birth control pill, which made "free love" totally available without the burden of pregnancy. The birth control pill, coupled with rampant sexuality, eventually led to the 1973 Supreme Court decision *Roe v. Wade*, which recognized abortion as a constitutionally protected right.

Drug culture was another hallmark of the '60s cultural revolution. With the introduction of a new mind-altering substance called LSD, Timothy Leary encouraged an entire generation to "tune in, turn on, and drop out." This led to scores of young people descending on San Francisco and living on the streets, having "dropped out" of society.[13]

Although both of the cultural revolutions, in China and America, aimed at destroying traditional cultures, the similarities end there. The major difference was how sexuality and drugs were perceived. During the Cultural Revolution, sex and sexuality were not only repressed but also made into a total taboo. Western-style free sex and drug culture finally made its way into Chinese popular culture only after China opened its doors in the 1980s.

The two Cultural Revolutions originated from very different standpoints. The revolutionaries in China were seeking total elimination of free thought and demanding absolute obedience to Mao. In America, however, the revolutionaries were seeking total unrestricted freedom, devoid of responsibilities and moral compass. Yet both ended up at the same place: conformity and tyranny.

The American activists in the 1960s sought to liberate themselves from the social norms and constraints of the hegemony: free sex, free drugs, free abortion. By contrast, radical activists of today are the ones defining society's norm. They have the power not only to define, but also to keep redefining the norm, whenever necessary, and force the norms and their views on society at large.

The '60s counterculture movement, however, failed to cross the finish line in "fundamentally transforming" America. At best, they received an "incomplete" on their report card, but they weren't through. Although the movement seemed to have died down by decade's end, after the Vietnam War ended, it only changed strategy. These Marxist radicals persevered under cloak of darkness, toning down their public act while patiently working to achieve prominent positions at universities through their "long march" strategy. In past decades, they became the tenured professors taking control of much of academia. From their influential positions, they have succeeded in training new generations of anti-America and anti–free market revolutionaries. Their students are now in key positions in all our institutions: schools, court, media, corporations, the military, all levels of our government.

The woke revolution we are facing today is the result of that "long march." By the time conservatives became aware of what had happened and tried to object, it would take a herculean effort to right the ship.

It is important to know that in the 1960s, Marxism was also put into practice by the militant arm of the civil rights movement. The history of Black American Marxism is not new, either. The Black connection to Marxism goes back to—yes—Mao. In fact, BLM and its like-minded predecessors have been stealing from Mao's playbook for years. Don't forget, BLM is a self-identified Marxist organization. There is no disputing that. Its founders openly claim that they are "trained Marxists."[14]

They want us to believe that they are an offshoot of the US civil rights movement. They are not. They are the offspring of American Marxism.

Malcolm X, although sharing the goal of Dr. King, fighting for the freedoms of Black people in America, chose the route of violence "by any means necessary."[15] Then there's the Black Panther Party, a full-fledged Marxist organization. One of its founders, Huey Newton, took the trouble of going to China to meet with Premier Zhou Enlai in 1971 to seek support from the CCP for their fight for freedom.[16]

Another African American civil rights activist, Robert F. Williams, made his way to China as well, where he was able to meet

Mao. At Williams's request, Mao published his "Statement Supporting the American Negroes in Their Just Struggle Against Racial Discrimination by U.S. Imperialism" (August 8, 1963). In the statement, Mao compared the struggle for civil rights by Black Americans to a "class struggle," as this was Mao's motto.

W.E.B. Du Bois, a Black author, civil rights activist, and Communist, met Mao multiple times and attended the National Day celebration parade at Tiananmen Square with Mao and other top CCP officials in 1962.[17]

Newton, Williams, and Du Bois (and others like them) are followers of Marxism. They are the true ancestors of BLM, as they apparently rejected Dr. Martin Luther King Jr. and his "nonviolent protest" tact that was the hallmark of the civil rights movement. Dr. King used civil disobedience, rooted in the Constitution, the Declaration of Independence, and the Bible, to preach that "all men are created equal." His movement sought to give African Americans the same fair chance provided every citizen of this country by virtue of being created in the image and likeness of God. King never preached revenge or retaliation. He never taught his followers that they were victims, an oppressed people who would never achieve unless they themselves became the oppressors.[18]

Marxists, by contrast, put their faith in Communism; they put their faith in "the Party" as the way to "liberate" an otherwise subjugated people. When these Black American Marxists were in China receiving VIP treatment from Mao, they chose to ignore the obvious fact that the Chinese people were not free. They refused to see that Communism is color-blind totalitarianism. Those visits to China by Newton, Williams, and Du Bois were around the time Mao was at work, making sure there would be absolutely no free speech, no free expression for the Chinese people. It was the time when food, clothing, and dwellings were rationed by the government. It was also a time when one's life could be taken away by the CCP for any offense. These Black Marxists did not have to do any deep research. The Communist oppression of the Chinese people was there for everyone to see. The truth is that they refused to see it.

Another of these American Marxist forerunners, Angela Davis, is still alive and well at the time of this writing. She is a political activist, author, and self-avowed Communist. She studied under Herbert Marcuse, a prominent figure of the Frankfurt School. She earned her PhD at Humboldt University of East Berlin during the Cold War. Davis was an iconic figure in the Black Power movement.[19] "Yes, I am a Communist and consider it one of the greatest honors because we are struggling for the total liberation of the human race," Davis says in her autobiography.[20]

In a panel interview of Angela Davis and BLM cofounder Alicia Garza on *Democracy Now*, Garza called Davis one of her greatest teachers and that she has a bookshelf full of Davis's writings.[21] The influence of Davis on BLM is obvious.

Davis is now a professor emerita of feminist studies at University of California, Santa Cruz, continuing the work of the "long march through the institutions."[22]

The Vietnam War provided the backdrop to the '60s cultural revolution. Kimball quotes two counterculture icons in regard to Vietnam: Susan Sontag and Jerry Rubin. Sontag has said that "Vietnam offered the key to a systematic criticism of America," and Rubin went further: "If there had been no Vietnam War, we would have invented one. If the Vietnam War ends, we'll find another war."[23]

That's exactly what BLM did. It did not allow a good crisis to go to waste by fully taking advantage of the tragic deaths of Black Americans as a result of police shootings to further an agenda that had little to do with shootings of these individuals and more to do with furthering their goal of the undoing of America and capitalism, using the excuse that America is systemically unjust and racist. The death of Floyd was their Vietnam War. If there had been no George Floyd, they would have invented one. The progressives have never stopped searching for their "Vietnam War." At the writing of this book, they found a new Vietnam War: the overturning of *Roe v. Wade*.

American Marxism is a new development of Marxism based on America's unique social, historic, economic, and cultural conditions. It is "Marxism with American characteristics," just as the CCP's brand of socialism is "socialism with Chinese characteristics."

What is the "old-world hegemony" that American Marxists are trying to destroy and replace?

"Old" Concept:	Replacement:
Individualism	Collectivism
Constitutional protected rights	Government overreach
Equality of opportunities	Equity of outcome
Rule of law	Lawlessness and mob culture
Content of character	Identity (Skin color, gender, sexual orientation, etc.)

Free Market	Socialism
Christianity	Anti-Christianity (not atheism)
Nationalism	Globalism
Diversity of thought	Conformity
Justice for all	Customized justice, e.g., racial justice, social justice, environmental justice...
Freedom of expression	Censorship/political correctness
Parental rights	Children of the state
Common sense	Political ideology

Clearly, the progressives' patient and relentless decades-long march through the institutions has borne fruit. These staunchly woke-minded activists have been transforming our society steadily, little by little, and keeping much of their activity under the radar. But since 2016, the progressives started to turn up the heat too fast, too high. The complacent frogs in the pot suddenly realized they had been boiled alive. More and more people are seeing the sudden change in the political and social landscape that has swept through our country.

Marxism and Communism's infiltration in America is complete. The most compelling place to see this infiltration is in our military, which should have been the last place for this to occur. Some time ago, I had the honor to meet Space Force Lt. Col. Matthew Lohmeier. As a military leader, Lohmeier had firsthand experience with this infiltration. Unlike many who just keep their heads down and lips sealed, Lohmeier not only spoke up, but he also wrote a book to expose what is going on in our military: *Irresistible Revolution: Marxism's Goal of Conquest and the Unmaking of the American Military.* For that, he was relieved of his post.

Politics is downstream of culture. It doesn't work the other way around. The changing of political party control does not mean that culture will be changed as a result. It is important to understand that even if conservatives were to take over the White House and both houses of Congress, and maintain their majority in the Supreme Court, it does not mean that cultural Marxism would simply disappear. We can ban CRT in every school, but that won't stop Marxist teachers from injecting their beliefs into their instruction, mentorship, and coaching. Chances are, their efforts will become more strategic and focused and their voices will become even more insistent.

I want to alert people that we cannot depend on the few superheroes to fight against the Marxist machine for us. They, alone, cannot save us. This is a battle that cannot be won simply through legislation or policies, or Elon Musk buying Twitter, which are all crucial and necessary. It will be a long process to undo the indoctrination that happens in our schools, one that requires parents to talk to their children regularly about their own values, morals, and worldviews. To defeat cultural Marxism and restore America as we know it, we must take the long march *back* through our institutions. However, we do not have decades of time to leisurely take the long march back. We have to act now.

We are at a historic moment. The two cultural revolutions, launched about the same time in the 1960s, have converged again. America has entered into a woke cultural revolution, while Xi

Jinping has been reviving Maoism by pursuing a Chinese Cultural Revolution 2.0.

After more than half a century, the cultural Marxists are nearly succeeding in transforming American institutions. Yesterday's seemingly radical ideologies have become acceptable and even preferable to many. Gramsci's vision of a new hegemony will be fully achieved if we don't put a stop to it.

The good news is that the more extreme, radical, and woke the progressives get, the more Americans are becoming "awake," stepping off of the sidelines, out from behind their keyboards, and into the fight against the cultural Marxist revolution. A countercultural Marxist revolution is now underway; something I hope will become known as the Great Pushback! There is no better sign than that of the influential left-wing TV host Bill Maher when he did an episode in February 2023 comparing the similarities between today's woke revolution and Mao's Cultural Revolution. He followed that with a warning when he tweeted, "If you're part of today's woke revolution, you need to study the part of revolutions where they spin out of control."[24]

CHAPTER 5

Born Guilty: How an Ideology Divides

On October 26, 2021, at a Loudoun County School Board meeting in Ashburn, Virginia, a mother testified before the school board. Near tears, she shared, "My six-year-old (daughter) somberly came to me and asked me if she was born evil because she was a white person—something she learned in a history lesson at school."[1]

Watching and listening to this at home, I felt sick to my stomach, because this is absolutely a replay of something I experienced more than fifty years earlier in China when I was eight.

Millions of school students across America are being taught a new concept: they have been "born guilty." What do these young people, many of them easily influenced and indoctrinated into a "progressive" mindset, have in common? By virtue of simply being born with white skin, they are all guilty of the crimes that began here in America over four hundred years ago, when Black Africans were sold by Black slave traders to white European slave traders and taken to America. Further, it is taught that all whites, regardless of whether they or their ancestors fought against slavery or Jim Crow laws, or whether they came to America after the Civil War and the Jim Crow era, share in the responsibility of systemic oppression and innate racial bias toward people of color. CRT does nothing to lift up the lives of people of color. It teaches them that they are victims, and they are inherently and irrevocably oppressed by the system and their white fellow countrymen. The injection of CRT perspective and nuance into American school curriculums intends to achieve one thing: to divide.

China's Cultural Revolution was all about division. Mao split Chinese society into classes of oppressors and the oppressed, a Marxist concept based on the "sin" of our birth. Mao had his loyal and brutal young Red Guards in full swing, taking power from authorities at all levels. Schools were closed, and we spent our days watching the Red Guards' struggle sessions, one after another. We saw the Red Guards—and I'll cover them in more detail in a later chapter—as a symbol of power and an object of desire. Soon, children too young to be Red Guards organized themselves as Little Red Guards with their own badges. A call went out in my neighborhood for us to join the Little Red Guards. I eagerly answered the call and asked the leader to accept me. She was my neighbor and no more than twelve years old.

"I want to join," I told her.

She told me, "We must check your family background going back *three generations*. We must first make sure that your roots are *Red*."

Certain that I would meet that prerequisite, I led the young Little Red Guard leader to meet my mother and get the confirmation from her that I belonged to the *right* class. My mother hesitated at first when confronted by this girl's question before slowly telling the Little Red Guard leader that my paternal grandmother was a landlord, putting me and my family on the "wrong side" of the Revolution.

When my mother uttered these words, my heart sank. This was the same feeling I got sitting in the comfort of my American home more than fifty years later watching this young American mother speaking about her little girl's experience and her disturbing question. It was surreal. I couldn't believe that a little girl was being told she was "born guilty" because of her skin color—in an American school, of all places!

It was a traumatizing moment for me to discover my Black Class origin (those whom Mao deemed enemies of the state such as landowners, the wealthy, intellectuals). It felt like my world had collapsed. I immediately pleaded with the Little Red Guard leader not to tell other kids, but she callously shrugged off my request. As soon as we walked back outside together, she boldly yelled to a nearby group of Little Red Guards, "Xi's grandmother was a landlord!"

What this little Loudoun County schoolgirl felt that day was exactly what I had felt more than fifty years earlier as a schoolgirl myself—that I had been born evil, only not because of my race, but because of my grandmother's class.

Mao used his class conflict theory (CCT) to divide the Chinese people. Critical race theory (CRT) is nothing more than a modified version of Mao's class conflict theory to divide the American people. It is no coincidence or quirk of history that CCT and CRT are so similar in purpose. They come from the same source—Marxism.

* * *

If you want to divide a family, a community, an organization, or even a nation, you need to create a conflict. It is done by manipulation. Conflict through manipulation is what Marxism is all about. Classic Marxism manipulates the class conflict between the rich and poor by labeling them as exploiters and exploited, oppressors and oppressed, or villains and victims. Neo-Marxism, or cultural Marxism, needs more than just class conflict. It also needs identity conflict. With this division in place, Marxist elites can just sit back and watch the two sides fight.

Here's my take on the basic steps that Marxists typically follow in fostering division through manufactured conflict:

- Identify what can be used to divide people into opposing groups.
- Promote hate against, demonize, and dehumanize the group deemed as villains.
- Mobilize political campaigns against those deemed as villains.
- Use divisive narratives to keep the groups in perpetual conflict.

You can likely think about or look at the news regarding what is happening today in the United States and cite examples of each one of these steps. Like a broken record, these steps are replayed over and over again.

The Chinese Cultural Revolution of 1966 was not the first time Mao implemented Marxist division. Mao and the CCP were using division tactics ever since the birth of the Chinese Communist Party in 1921. Division is an essential part of Marxism. In fact, it is in the DNA of Marxism.

Guided by the Marxist class conflict theory, Mao conducted an in-depth analysis of the class structure of Chinese society as early as 1925 for the purpose of answering the most urgent question: "Who are our friends? Who are our enemies?" Mao reported his findings in a paper entitled "Analysis of the Classes in Chinese Society" (1926), in which he categorized the entire Chinese society into five main classifications, with many more subclassifications:

- landlord and comprador class,
- middle bourgeoisie,
- petty bourgeoisie,
- semi-proletariat, and
- proletariat.

Mao concluded that the landlord and the comprador class, including the right wing of the middle bourgeoisie, were the enemies of the revolution. The rest were supporters of the revolution. The line was drawn. Class and class struggle would become Mao's guiding principle for winning the revolution and for the future governance of the Chinese people.

Quantifying the designated classes, Mao estimated that five million of the Chinese people belonged to the enemy class, leaving 395 million allies on his side—an overwhelming majority, at least on paper. In Mao's typically coarse language, he said the mere spit from the 395 million would drown the five million enemies.

Mao's definition of classes and breakdown of percentages would provide the road map for Mao and the CCP to later gain and maintain power. By promising its 395 million "allies" free land and properties from the 1 percent, the CCP got their support and won the revolution in 1949.

Note how Mao's 1 percent (actually 1.27 percent, to be precise) versus 99 percent corresponds exactly with Bernie Sanders's 1 percent versus 99 percent. Is it just a coincidence?

After taking power in 1949, the Land Reform Movement (1950–1952) was one of the first mass campaigns that Mao and the CCP launched. To fulfill their promise to the 99 percent, they determined that all land owned by landlords would be confiscated and redistributed to poor peasants. Land Reform was about much more than just land. It would be a political campaign to create a systematic divide among the Chinese people by *class*.

One of Mao and the CCP's main tasks was to classify the entire peasantry. Mao had already done his homework in 1925 and tried out the tactics in CCP-occupied areas before 1949. They knew exactly how to carry out this campaign. It turns out, as expected, the tactics used in the Land Reform would be used repeatedly in subsequent political campaigns, including the Cultural Revolution.

The Chinese peasantry was categorized into five groups:

Landlords: Income came solely from collecting rent from tenant farmers.
Rich peasants: Worked on their own land and hired farm-hands to support the work.
Middle-class peasants: Owned land and were self-sufficient.
Lower-middle-class peasants: Owned land and supplemented their income by providing labor to other landlords.
Proletariats: Landless peasants.

These five categories grouped people into two camps: the landlords and rich peasants were condemned as the oppressors and labeled the *Black Class*. The poor and middle-class peasants were deemed as the oppressed and labeled the *Red Class*. The labels determined whether one was the enemy or friend of the newly established government of the CCP. These labels became one's assigned identity. They were hereditary and inherent upon birth.

The campaign was supposed to be peaceful. That was the written plan, but Mao had other ideas. He would strategically manipulate the populace to war against one another in order to achieve his own goals of division and control. Mao and the CCP could have used peaceful administrative measures to redistribute land. But their motivations had nothing to do with the benevolent redistribution of land for the good of China's development. Mao had two goals: first, to eliminate the landlord class, and second, to raise class consciousness/class *woke-ness* of the poor peasants and condition them to fight against the enemy class. The poor peasants would need to participate in the struggle against their class enemies in order to obtain the lands over which they were to gain ownership. In so many words, Mao was saying that the allies could have this land, but they were also going to have to fight, and possibly kill, for it.

The Land Reform was administrated by CCP work teams. One important part of their job was to coach villagers on how to participate in "class struggle," through which the CCP believed that peasants would become strong Communist followers. I can't help but compare them to today's DEI (Diversity, Equity, and Inclusion) officers now planted within our institutions.

Traditional Chinese villages were mainly communities formed by clans. The landlords and the poor peasants were often relatives. To break this predicament, the CCP work teams had to arouse the hatred of the poor against the rich.

These are some of the tactics the CCP used to arouse the hatred:

Guiding the peasant to find the origin of their poverty and suffering. "Speaking Bitterness" (*su ku*) was a successful approach to get the poor peasants to speak about their sufferings and grievances in struggle sessions and blaming them on the rich. Now the camps were formed: the poor versus rich, and us versus them.

Turning suffering first into anger and then into hatred. From "suffering" to "anger," the peasant masses naturally had completed the important transformation from mere complaining to revenge, and from speaking to action. This was the work teams' job, to coach the peasants to "discover" the roots of their suffering, make them angry, and turn their anger into hatred, then eventually into violence.

Weaponizing personal grudges and turning them into class hatred. To many peasants, the idea of "class hatred" was too abstract to grasp. The CCP work teams encouraged these peasants to turn their personal grudges against the landlords or rich peasants. Personal grudges often became the initial cause of violence in Land Reform.[2]

Without different skin colors to set people apart as in America, villagers wore a colored strip of cloth to identify the class they were assigned to. The color for landlords was white, rich peasants pink, and middle-class peasants yellow. The poor proudly displayed their color: red.[3]

The CCP also aggressively promoted hate by demonizing the landlords/rich peasants as monstrous villains. It was much easier to humiliate, mistreat, torture, and kill when the enemies were considered to be subhuman. Following the struggle sessions, the "people's court" would announce the sentence of death, imprisonment, forced labor, etc.[4]

It is impossible to accurately determine the number of landlords killed during the violent Land Reform, although various Chinese scholars have offered estimates of up to five million. Some scholars call the killing "classicide," which equates to a genocide of the rich.

My mother, who was a CCP cadre, told me about her experience of going to villages as a member of a CCP propaganda team that would support the Land Reform by using forms of entertainment to motivate the peasants to take part in the class struggle. After a struggle session, for example, members of the propaganda team often would get up on stage to put on a revolutionary performance. They did this while looking out over the bodies of enemies of the state who had just been executed and were now lined up in front of the stage.

Ironically, six years after the violent Land Reform, all redistributed land was taken back from the peasants by the state through yet another campaign, the people's commune campaign. By this time, many came to realize that they had been fooled by the CCP. That was not the first time, nor would it be the last.

To make the alien idea of *class* acceptable, Mao and the CCP also made ample use of media to propagate the idea of class and class struggle to the masses. Class struggle and hatred for the class enemy would be the main theme in all media, literature, art, and entertainment—all contributing to keeping the flame of hatred and division burning forever. All the CCP's "entertainment" propaganda portrayed landlords as the symbol of evil and source of suffering of the poor. The goal was to brainwash the population, especially the young, to hate and to keep fighting against the class enemies. As a young girl, I watched these shows endless times and knew the story lines by heart. So did millions of Chinese people.

One example was *The White-Haired Girl* (an opera, movie, and later a ballet). The story was about a father who had to sell his only daughter, Xier, to the landlord Huang Shiren to pay a debt. Xier's father committed suicide out of despair. Xier became a servant girl for the evil landlord, who abused her and attempted to rape her. Xier escaped Huang's manor and hid in mountains and lived like a wild animal. Her hair eventually turned white. The villagers who caught glimpses of her called her the "white-haired fairy." Eventually, the CCP liberated the village. Xier was rescued and returned to the village, while Huang was struggled against and executed. The moral of the story was that the evil of the landowning class was the source of the suffering of the proletariats and the CCP was the savior of the Chinese people.

All the propaganda was aimed at raising the Chinese people's class consciousness and their hatred toward the *Black Class*. In my young mind, there was not the slightest doubt that the *Black Class* was made up of bad people and that they were to be deservedly seen as public enemies.

The reality is that most of the CCP founders, including Mao Zedong, Zhou Enlai, and Deng Xiaoping, were from landowning and wealthy families. That is why they could afford to have education as well as the time and perspective to entertain the idea of starting a revolution in China. They had personal knowledge of how their parents and ancestors had managed to accumulate wealth and obtain land, putting them in position to know how a Land Reform could work and divide people in the process.

In 1937, the progressive American journalist Edgar Snow published a highly influential book entitled *Red Star over China: The Classic Account of the Birth of Chinese Communism*. It included an interview with Mao in which the Chinese leader discussed his father and family background.

When he was in his early teens, Mao's family of five owned about four acres of farmland, which was sufficient to provide them with enough rice and even some surplus. Later, his father started a grain trading business that brought in additional income. After reaching the status of a "rich" peasant, his father devoted most of his time to the business and hired farmhands to take care of the farm work. "My family ate frugally but had enough always," Mao recalled.[5]

The story of Mao's father was a typical one of how ordinary peasants managed to accumulate wealth through hard work, a frugal lifestyle, and good business sense. Mao didn't accuse his father of exploitation and oppression of the less fortunate while steadily accumulating wealth. Because there was no exploitation and oppression. Yet, he forced the Chinese people to believe that the only way to get wealth was by exploiting and oppressing the poor. In Communist theology, the original sin is wealth.

My paternal grandmother was from a well-to-do family. Part of her dowry was about seventeen acres of land. Her marriage to my grandfather was not a happy one. After four children, he left her and went on to marry three more wives. She had to rent out her land in order to generate sufficient income to raise her four children. As a result, she was classified a landlord, and her land and house were confiscated. She was at least lucky to have escaped struggle sessions or violence. She had moved to the city of Xi'an a few years before the Land Reform. But her children and grand-children, including me, did not escape the fate of being labeled as "Black Class."

Land Reform was followed by the so-called joint state-private ownership campaign, which nationalized all private businesses and industries. Class classification was expanded to accommodate the urban population. "Class origin" going back three generations was codified. Essentially, every Chinese person was assigned a label, a political identity, based on their family lineage. The label was part of the required information on all government papers, similar to one's ethnicity here in America. I filled out many gov-ernment forms during my first twenty-six years in China. Some required information of class origin going back two generations, some three. For the former, my class origin is "revolutionary cadre," for the latter "landlord."

Promising equity, Mao made China a society with two per-manent classes: Red Class and Black Class. In his paper "On the People's Democratic Dictatorship," Mao declared that the Red Class would enforce the people's democratic dictatorship, that is, to deprive the Black Class not only of all its rights, but also all of its humanity. The word *renmin*, meaning "people," now was reserved for the Red Class. "Class enemy" or simply "enemy" was to be used exclusively to refer to the Black Class; therefore, any atrocity committed against the Black Class was justified. While the Red Class rose to dominance, more and more people found themselves falling into the Black Class. It happened to them not because of their class origins. It happened to them because they had failed to be in lockstep with the Party's direction. If one was found to take the wrong standpoint, or worldview, the bourgeois instead of proletariat standpoint, one could be stripped of their Red Class status and be condemned to the Black Class and, thereby, become an enemy of the state. After all, class was but a tool for the CCP. It was really about ideology.

Through endless political campaigns, more categories were added to the Black Class: rightists, counterrevolutionaries, and bad influencers. During the Cultural Revolution, additional Black Class categories were further identified: traitors, spies, "capitalist roaders," and lastly, the ninth, intellectuals. Intellectuals were also called *lao jiu*, or the number nine. The more popular name was "stinky number nine."

Knowing what Mao did to China, it is much easier to see how the progressives have been doing exactly the same thing in America. It is no coincidence. Both Mao and the progressives are followers of Marxism. Mao has surely been an inspiration for present-day American Marxists. Not a comforting thought.

We have long known that simply trying to divide Americans by class to bring down America doesn't work. The progressives have a better tool: identity Marxism. No identity is more potent than the immutable characteristic of race. Marxists have been running with that tactic for a long time because of slavery and America's troubled history with race relations.

CRT is tailor-made for America. It divides Americans crudely into two opposing groups: white and non-white. The historical racial category of "Black" has been expanded to include all non-whites as shown in the new term BIPOC (Black, indigenous, and people of color). The categorization, unique to America, accomplishes two goals: to divide and to unite. It intends to separate out white Americans as one single entity, and to "unite" all ethnic minorities and people of color to create solidarity against those who are white.

Many articles, commentaries, and books have been written about CRT concerning its origins and complex development. My understanding of it derives from my understanding of Mao's class conflict theory (CCT). It is a worldview: a lens with which to view the world. When we apply the CCT lens, we see *everything* in terms of class. When we apply the CRT lens, we see *everything* in terms of race. Renowned author Dr. Carol Swain refers to it as "fundamentally a racist worldview."[6]

James Lindsay, one of the most influential contemporary critics of cultural Marxism, calls CRT "race Marxism" in his recent book, *Race Marxism: The Truth about Critical Race Theory and Praxis* (2022). It makes perfect sense. It is truly a variation of the Marxist theme. This is no accident, but a carefully thought-out strategy.

One of the most prominent CRT evangelists in America is Robin DiAngelo, author of *White Fragility: Why It's So Hard for White People to Talk about Racism*. She argues that one's race determines one's worldview. According to her, *whiteness* is a standpoint that "views white people and their interests as central to, and representative of, humanity."[7] DiAngelo tries to convey the idea that white people are natural-born racists because of their whiteness standpoint. In addition, anyone, including non-white people, who takes the "whiteness standpoint" or "thinks like" a white person is also a racist.

It's typical for outspoken Black conservatives to be smeared as "Uncle Toms" or accused of being the "blackface of white supremacy." Appearing on Joy Reid's MSNBC show *The ReidOut* in November 2021, Georgetown University professor Michael Eric Dyson verbally smeared his fellow African American Winsome Sears after she won the historic race for lieutenant governor of Virginia. He said of Sears: "There is a black mouth moving but a white idea running on the runway of the tongue of a figure who justifies and legitimates the white supremacist practices."[8] It is clear that Dyson attacked Sears for her conservative beliefs; in other words, her "whiteness standpoint." It is evident that the applied prism of CRT is more than a critical analysis of race. It is really, and more profoundly, about political ideologies, exactly like the way Mao applied his CCT to people who dared to think differently.

The progressives do offer the path to salvation for "racists": by giving up the "whiteness standpoint" and embracing the Marxist race standpoint now known as CRT. Progressives believe that it is not enough to simply not be a racist. One must be an anti-racist. To achieve the anti-racist status, one must follow Ibram X. Kendi's prescription laid out in his book *How to Be an Antiracist* and fight racism through measurable actions daily. The same was true for

Mao, who preached that if you were born of the Black Class, you still had the potential to be saved, but only if you cut your family ties, confessed your sins, and devoted yourself to studying Marxism and Maoism and thoroughly reforming your thoughts.

That is exactly what the white liberals (or *bai zue*, a derogatory label given to them by Chinese netizens) are doing. As reported by the *Los Angeles Times*, many white celebrities, who partner with the NAACP to "take responsibility" for racism, identify themselves as *anti-racists*. In the wake of George Floyd's death, entertainers such as Sarah Paulson, Aaron Paul, Kristen Bell, Kesha, Justin Theroux, Debra Messing, and Julianne Moore reportedly partnered with the NAACP to produce a publicly released video "denouncing police brutality and checking their privilege for the #ITakeResponsibility campaign."[9] The video's message came through loud and clear: If you are white, you are guilty of white privilege, and responsible for police brutality and the sins committed by people who look like you.

I found out rather quickly after arriving in America that I had been magically transformed from a descendant of the oppressor Black Class to a member of the oppressed group of a marginalized minority, the American version of the proletarians. To my dismay, I—still exactly the same person—found out recently that my oppressed status has been downgraded to "white adjacent" by the same progressives that previously assigned me a victim status. What is the reason? Asians are too successful!

In spite of the success of CRT tactics, the progressives know that their reliance on race-based Marxism will still not be enough to ultimately divide the American people. After all, we are a nation of free people and the world's greatest constitutional republic. The Marxists in America will have a much harder time forcefully dividing people than Mao and the CCP ever did in China. Mao dealt with a people who never had any rights and who knew nothing but brutal tyranny. Getting the masses in line and keeping them controlled wasn't as complicated as it is in America.

The progressives depend on identity Marxism by constantly expanding the manufactured list of "identities." They will never stop adding to it. Without identities to divide Americans into tribes, they would, in fact, be neutered.

Here are some of the "identities" embraced by the left to divide Americans today:

- **Class:** Poor vs. rich. Bernie Sanders is the epitome of class rivalry, in the same way that Mao was famous for. In Sanders's own words on Twitter, "At the end of the day, the 1 percent may have enormous wealth and power. But they are just the 1 percent. When the 99 percent stand together, we can transform society."[10]
- **Sex:** Women vs. men. In her 2018 Golden Globes speech, Oprah Winfrey summed up that "'brutally powerful men' had 'broken' something in the culture. These men had caused women to suffer: not only actors, but domestic workers, factory workers, agricultural workers, athletes, soldiers and academics."[11] Men have become the enemy; especially white men, I may add.
- **Sexuality:** LGBTQQIP2SAA (ad infinitum) vs. heterosexuals. They lump all who are not traditional heterosexuals together under one ever expanding label, regardless of whether the individuals within each group agree or not. Their common foe is supposedly the "oppressive" heterosexuals.

- **Gender:** Transgender vs. cisgender vs. gender nonbinary. The gender divide is the most bewildering division so far, a new addition to cultural Marxism. It started with the divide between *cisgender* (those whose personal gender identity corresponds with their birth sex, including both homosexuals and heterosexuals) and transgender (those whose personal gender identity does not correspond with their birth sex and who wish to transition to the opposite sex, i.e., from male to female and vice versa). The divide now has evolved beyond trans and gone beyond the confine of male and female. Now we are told by the "experts" that "there is no fixed number of gender identities. They occur on a spectrum, which really means that the possibilities are infinite. Each person might find that a certain point on the spectrum feels most comfortable and accurate, and this may change over time," according to *Medical News Today*.[12]

- **Religion:** Non-Christians vs. Christians. Christianity has been deemed oppressive. The latest label for a bigot from the progressives is "Christian nationalist." I will discuss this topic in much more detail in Chapter 8.

- **Ableism:** Disabled vs. able-bodied. In 1990, Congress passed the Americans with Disabilities Act, which protects individuals with disabilities from discrimination. Somehow, disability has become a political identity. In October 2022, NBC News interviewed John Fetterman, the then Democratic nominee for US Senate in Pennsylvania, who suffered a stroke that May.

NBC News was accused of "ableism" for daring to report Fetterman's difficulty in engaging in conversation and the need for closed captioning for the interview. Only in the age of woke-ism is the question of a political candidate's health and ability to serve off-limits.[13]

- **Ageism:** Old vs. young. Like Americans with disabilities, we also have laws protecting older people with the Age Discrimination in Employment Act of 1967. But that should not mean we don't have the right to question the mental capacity of the person who holds the most important job in the world, the office of the president of the United States. When journalists report that Biden's repeated incidents of gaffes are associated with senility, they are called "agists."[14]

- **Body weight:** Fat vs. thin. Being overweight now earns one a victim status. Being fit, on the other hand, has become a symbol of oppression.

- **Citizenship:** Immigrants vs. native-born. Being an immigrant somehow has become an advantage. The "inherent victimhood" of simply being a recent immigrant has ended up in the oppressed category by progressives' divisive narrative.

- **Political affiliation:** Progressive vs. conservative. It is no longer a matter of differences in political viewpoints. CNN anchor Don Lemon openly condemned the entire Republican Party by declaring that Republicans must be treated as a danger to society by media and cannot be "coddled."[15] Conservatives now find themselves in the category of the oppressors.

- **Profession:** This is relatively a new development in the dividing of Americans. Now certain professions have been deemed evil. The progressives try to convince us that anyone in a law enforcement position (police, border patrol, US Immigration and Customs Enforcement [ICE], etc.) is inherently a racist, white supremacist, or oppressor. Current US Vice President Kamala Harris once compared public perceptions of ICE to that of the KKK in a Senate hearing.[16]

- **Vaccination status:** Vaxxed vs. un-vaxxed. The latest, but definitely not the last, divisive tactic to set citizens against one another. People who question the mRNA COVID vaccines and reject to be vaccinated have been treated as threats to humanity. Biden threatened with the following words: "We've been patient, but our patience is wearing thin. And your refusal has cost all of us."[17]

The above is by no means a complete list. Be assured. More is coming and will be used to further divide our society now that the progressives have uncovered a gold mine as an unlimited source for identity creation: trans____ (fill in the blank). All one needs to do is to identify themselves as anything they desire and therefore qualify as a victim.

The list of identities will continue to grow thanks to the concept of intersectionality. The term was coined by Kimberlé Crenshaw, professor of law at Columbia University and UCLA. The intention of intersectionality was to illustrate how one's victim status depends on how many ways their identities intersect. In addition, intersectionality can be seen to serve as a metric to determine how oppressed an individual is. For example, a woman is a victim due to her gender. A Black woman, however, is twice a victim because of her gender and race.

Crenshaw explains in an interview that "intersectionality is a lens through which you can see where power comes and collides, where it interlocks and intersects. It's not simply that there's a race problem here, a gender problem here, and a class or LBGTQ problem there. Many times that framework erases what happens to people who are subject to all of these things."[18] Do you notice the choice of the word *lens*? She is correct. All identity ideologies are simply lenses through which one *chooses* or is conditioned to see the world.

The creation and advancement of the idea of intersectionality helps to endlessly divide people and weaken our communities. For example, among feminists, there is now a division between white feminists and Black feminists, as well as lesbian/trans feminists versus hetero/cis feminists.

In addition, intersectionality has created an American version of a political caste system. Based on the intersectionality doctrine, a white person who is male, cisgender, able-bodied, conservative, middle class, Christian, working in law enforcement, and un-vaxxed has no intersectionality. Zero! That means that he belongs to the lowest political caste because he is viewed as the ultimate oppressor and will be the most targeted by the progressive Marxists. Conversely, the highest-ranking member of this new political caste would be someone who is trans, Black, disabled, poor...or a BLM activist, which by itself carries tremendous clout and inculpability. Just like in Mao's China, the most "oppressed" now possesses the highest social superiority.

Using the intersectionality principle, I figure this is where I stand:

I am female: +1.0

I am an immigrant: +1.0

I am Asian: +1.0

Asians are white adjacent: -0.5

I am a senior: +1.0

I am cisgender: -1.0

I am heterosexual: -1.0

I am able bodied: -1.0

I am not vaccinated: -1.0

I am a member of the middle class: -1.0

I am conservative: -1.0

That awards me with an intersectionality score of -3.5! I'm sure I could further score myself, but I think you get the picture. Isn't it interesting that I do not fare well with either CCT or CRT?

Consider a problem with intersectionality: What are we to make of a poor, white person? The almost always politically controversial and far-left actress Jane Fonda once asserted that even the poorest whites had privilege, during an interview on CNN with Don Lemon,[19] a Black millionaire with a net worth of twelve million, according to celebritynetworth.com. Let there be no confusion, however; Mr. Lemon is still considered *oppressed* by the progressive Marxists. Crenshaw's intersectionality spectrum certainly removes all doubt of this.

Intersectionality is the gift to Marxists that keeps on giving!

I once tweeted this: "Nazism divides people along ethnic, racial, and religious lines. Communism divides people by class.

Woke-ism divides people by both and more!" This is the sad reality we are facing.

There is, however, a difference between the CCP and woke ideologues. Mao always set the majority against the minority, although the minority kept changing. One of his favorite words was "masses," or *qun zhong*. He wrote extensively on the masses, such as how to organize, mobilize, and motivate them. He believed in controlling the masses to achieve his political goals. The "woke" progressives are doing the exact opposite. They are setting minority groups against the majority. It is for this reason the progressives must aggressively keep creating new victim identities and use intersectionality to ever expand their victim base.

In order to motivate these "victims" to fight, the progressives depend on arousing hatred toward the "oppressors" by demonizing and dehumanizing them. This is how they pave the way to eventual violence. Mao was a master of this tactic, as I demonstrated with the example of China's Land Reform campaign. The American Marxists have proven themselves to be excellent students.

As was done for Mao and the CCP, the mainstream media and entertainment industry in America have long fallen into the hands of the progressives through the long march. They have become CCP-like propaganda machines promoting the progressives' political ideologies and molding the viewpoints of many viewers on a mass scale through manipulation. The news media has been very successful in creating a narrative that white supremacy is the cause of all our problems, that our nation's law enforcement community is inherently, systematically racist, and that police officers are hunting down and shooting dead innocent, unarmed Black men with impunity. They perpetuate the belief that members of the LGBTQ+ community are living in a world of constant persecution and marginalization. They paint conservatives as extremists, domestic terrorists, and as a danger to democracy. The goal, as I am sure you have figured out by now, is to foster hate.

What the left hates most is, no doubt, Trump. Seared into the minds of many of us is the image of comedian Kathy Griffin parading a replica of the decapitated bloody head of then sitting President Donald Trump.[20] Why such hatred? Because Trump was deemed an archetype of white supremacy, a fascist, Hitler; therefore, public enemy number one! But the real reason is that Trump is regarded by the left as the biggest obstacle to their Marxist agenda.

Fostering hate is something Joe Biden has been doing ever since he entered the White House. One example is his speech at Philadelphia's Independence Hall on September 1, 2022. In the speech, he declared and attacked his enemy, the MAGA Republicans, calling them a threat to this country and a "clear and present danger" to our democracy.[21] Once the enemy is identified, the next obvious step would be the enforcement of the "proletarian dictatorship." The two Marine honor guards standing at attention behind Biden, their commander in chief, together with the blood-red backdrop appeared to make that point.

The hatred against fellow Americans with a different political view demonstrated here is the same hatred that eventually drove the Chinese peasants to kill those landlords during the Land Reform, and later the Red Guards to kill their teachers and other "counterrevolutionaries." This is a very dangerous path that we are on!

Those in charge of the Chinese Communist Party and the

progressives are the elites of their respective eras. They attempted/attempt to divide people to fight against the groups that they, the elites themselves, are a part of. The CCP elites demonized the landlord and property class, but the majority of them were members of that class themselves. Almost all of the progressive elites in America are white themselves. It's not an attempt on the part of white leftists to be simply traitorous or remorseful of their class or race. They are simply using divisive Marxist tactics to gain power for themselves.

In Mao's China, everyone tried to claim the lowest social status. Being anything else would place them squarely in the Black Class, the enemy of Mao and the state. Wealth became the cause of one's misfortune and suffering.

We have seen a similar phenomenon in America. "Whiteness" is the new "original sin," something to be ashamed of and something to disavow. There have been incidents where white people have falsely claimed to be a member of historically marginalized communities.

Rachel Dolezal stepped down as the leader of the Spokane chapter of the NACCP in 2015, proclaiming, "I identify as Black." She wasn't.[22] Progressive Massachusetts Senator Elizabeth Warren is another example of someone who identified herself as Native American.[23] Such pretenders feel the need to identify as victims, because they understand the benefit and privilege in doing so, which I called "victim privilege."

Divide and conquer is an old tactic. Older than Marxism. But it is cultural Marxism that perfected it and weaponized it to achieve their goal of destroying America. America has only once before been so divided. And the divide runs so deep. It has broken up our society, our communities, and even our families. People seem to be at each other's throats and treat their fellow Americans as enemies. This is exactly what the American Marxists have desired. Yet, division is only part of the grand scheme for bringing down America. In the remaining chapters, I will attempt to unveil their entire scheme.

CHAPTER 6

Red Guards: Stormtroopers of the Revolution

I remember the massive Red Guard rallies. It was 1966, shortly after the launch of the Cultural Revolution. I watched them in my hometown of Chengdu on the news digest, which was shown on a large movie screen outdoors, as television did not exist here yet. How exciting this was for me.

Imagine being a little girl and watching kids only a bit older than myself ecstatic as they screamed, "Long Live Chairman

Mao!" over and over again. These young Red Guards were waving Mao's *Little Red Book* with tears streaming down their faces. As my young and pliable mind got caught up in the rally, I wanted so much to be a part of this historic movement and to be one of them, the Red Guards. If I had only known then what I was about to so painfully learn. To this day, I am haunted by the images of Mao waving to the Red Guards from Tiananmen Square—an iconic moment that has become a symbol of that era.

To launch a revolution, one needs revolutionaries. Both Lenin and Mao won their violent revolutions by mobilizing the proletariat. These revolutionaries were soldiers armed with weapons. But for a cultural revolution, a different kind of revolutionaries is called for. Instead of being armed with real weapons, they are armed with ideologies—Marxist ideologies. Mao had his revolutionaries, known as the Red Guards, tailor-made for him from his government schools. The American progressives have theirs from the same place: government schools. They are the social justice warriors, the American Red Guards.

Mao was the architect and driving force behind the Chinese Cultural Revolution, but it wouldn't have been what it was without the Red Guards. The Cultural Revolution would not have been as violent and cruelly effective had it not been for these youths who took over schools, rampaged through large sections of society with their fear-producing intimidation tactics, and eventually brought down the entire CCP bureaucracy. The Red Guards became synonymous with the Cultural Revolution.

Who were the Red Guards? They were mostly teenagers who transformed themselves from students into unruly yet deadly political activists. They were an enforcement wing of Mao, in their minds answering to no one but Mao—and no one was empowered to stop them. They were without training, organization, or scruples—brainwashed. In other words, perfectly useful idiots.

The Cultural Revolution as a political campaign was kickstarted through the release of the May 16 Notification by the CCP Central Committee. It laid out the goal for launching the revolution "to rectify those in power within the Party who are taking the capitalist road."

Days later, on May 25, a big-character poster appeared on the campus of Beijing University directly attacking the University's Party Committee and the Beijing Municipal Party Committee, accusing them of suppressing staff and students' strong urge to participate in the Cultural Revolution. Mao called the poster "the nation's first Marxist and Leninist big-character poster." A few days later, the Central People's Radio Station, mouthpiece of the CCP, broadcasted the full text of this poster, prompting a nationwide rebellion.[1] In response, big-character posters popped up everywhere on Beijing campuses.

On May 29, the word *Red Guards* appeared in a big-character poster on the campus of the prestigious Tsinghua University Middle School in Beijing. The name immediately caught on and became the official name for the rebelling youths all over China. May 29, 1966, became the birthdate of the Red Guards. They would eventually grow to over eleven million strong.[2]

On July 28, 1966, members of the Tsinghua University Middle School Red Guards sent a letter to Mao asking him for his support of their rebellious activism. In the letter, they used Mao's quote "Rebellion is justified." Mao replied to the letter on August 1, 1966, proclaiming his full support for the Red Guards in their rebellion against the bourgeois and reactionary school authorities, which included teachers."[3]

Four days later, on August 5, Mao published "Bombard the Headquarters—My Big-Character Poster" in the official CCP newspaper, *People's Daily*, to declare his "enthusiastic support" of the Red Guards. The news spread like wildfire. The Red Guard movement was formally launched with Mao's approval.

Knowing their value to his cause, Mao was very hands-on with the Red Guards. On August 18, 1966, he showed his support for the Red Guard movement by attending their mass rally in Tiananmen Square. The crowd was estimated to be one million, making it the biggest rally ever in China's history. For good measure, Mao wore an army uniform to match the Red Guards' mock army uniform.[4] He took great pains in showing that he not only commanded great influence over them as their inspirational shepherd, but that, in essence, he was one of them.

The mass rally was widely hailed as a great success. It inspired Red Guards from around the country to come to Beijing to meet with Mao. This Red Guard pilgrimage was called *da chuan lian*, which translates to "big linkups." Mao encouraged the big link-ups with the order that free transportation, food, and lodging be provided for the Red Guards.[5] By this time, he had already won both the hearts and minds of the Red Guards. As people would soon find out, anyone on the wrong side of Mao could expect years of misery at the hands of the young, rowdy, Mao-led Red Guards.

As millions of youths from all over China journeyed to Beijing to join the Red Guard movement, some referred to the big linkups as "free Red Tourism." The soon-to-be militants moved from city to city with great enthusiasm and zest. In a time when travel was a luxury, these Red Guards were able to journey around the country for free. They were supposed to link with other Red Guards to exchange ideas and provide support for one other. Wherever they went, they caused chaotic scenes in major cities.

While Mao had total control over the dissemination of information via radio and print (television was still unavailable), the big linkups were his key to a mass movement by mass mobilization. The big linkups served to keep him connected and spread the message to hundreds of millions of Chinese people by word of mouth as effectively as Twitter or Facebook today.

Mao would meet with the Red Guards seven more times over the next four months, with the last of the eight rallies taking place November 25, 1966. By then, the number of mass rally participants had reached eleven million in total.[6]

This was a first for China and her people. Never in Chinese history had such rallies taken place. They were big, dynamic, and drew millions of Chinese people from all over. The Red Guards were fully mobilized, under Mao's spell, and excited to execute his orders. He was their Red Commander in Chief and they were his loyal Red Guards.

I remember watching all eight of those rallies. When my sixteen-year-old cousin showed up from Xi'an, a city about five hundred miles from Chengdu, I nearly died with excitement. We had never met before, but I knew all about her. To me, she was everything that was great in the world! She was one of the big linkup Red Guards, a member of Chairman Mao's propaganda team of twenty other young Red Guards, and I looked up to her as if she were a movie star! I begged my parents to let me take the twelve-hour train ride back to Xi'an with her. Astonishingly, my parents said yes.

The journey together was one I will never forget. The excitement of traveling with my cousin, who was practically an adult at sixteen years old and a member of the Red Guard, was almost too much for me to handle. I committed to doing everything she said and never complaining, which included being placed on the luggage rack in the train car because all the seats and floors were taken by the real Red Guards. It was a very long train ride, but we stopped several times at small stations, where my cousin and her team deboarded to go to factories or work units to give Red Guard performances, which included reciting Mao's quotations, singing revolutionary songs, and dancing revolutionary dances.

I was so proud to be with my cousin and, boy, did I get so much attention. Although just a tagalong, I was given the important job of leading the team by carrying Mao's portrait onto the stage at each show. I received extra applause you can imagine a little girl would get when joining a grown-up performance. It was exhilarating. I was full of pride at the cheers from the packed halls. I felt like a celebrity myself!

I got to eat meals with my cousin and the team of Red Guards, and we all slept on the floor together. Without understanding the real purpose of the Red Guards, I was in heaven at being a part of this group. Cold and wet from snow, we finally reached Xi'an, where I was placed into the care of my grandmother, who I was meeting for the first time. I begrudgingly had to say goodbye to my cousin and my exciting revolutionary journey. I stared at my grandmother, conflicted. My grandmother was a landlord. This status made her a class enemy of the Red Guards. I got to know her over the months I spent in Xi'an. I am happy we had that time together, as I would not see her again until I was in high school. Sadly, that would be the last time I would ever see her.

Along with big linkups, there were "four bigs": big free speech, big openness (no more rules or regulations), big-character posters, and big debate. The Red Guards took full advantage of their right to "free speech" by gathering in the streets and in public spaces to engage in debates. I remember watching Red Guards "debate" with each other with handheld megaphone speakers where each side tried to draw out the voice of the other side. It was essentially a shouting match between opposing sides, each declaring that they possessed the correct understanding of the true meaning of Mao's principles.

There was one Red Guard who stood out from all the rest. His name was Sidney Rittenberg. He was a middle-aged American. Rittenberg stayed in China after his US military assignment there ended in 1944. He was an enthusiastic supporter of Mao and Mao- ism despite his being jailed twice by the CCP. During the Cultural Revolution, Rittenberg became a rebel and managed to make his way into Mao's inner circle, which for anyone would have been quite a feat.

In his memoir *The Man Who Stayed Behind*, Rittenberg gives his account of the Cultural Revolution. Included is a segment in which Rittenberg recounts Chinese Premier Zhou Enlai enthusi- astically talking about the four bigs:

Look at these big-character posters. People can put them any- where they like, and write anything they like on them. This is a scene of popular liberties such as no other country has ever had. Does Lyndon Johnson allow students to paste up sharp criticisms of him in the White House? No other country can do that. But we can do it here, and we are doing it. People can criticize anyone at all, except for our Great Leader Chairman Mao, and his deputy commander-in-chief, Vice Chairman Lin Biao, and the Central Cultural Revolution Group.[7]

In other words, the "free speech," according to Zhou, allowed people to criticize anyone except those who were in charge and directing the Cultural Revolution! Does it ring a bell? In today's woke world, free speech is allowed as long you are aligned with the woke-sters. Otherwise, it is hate speech and needs to be banned.

Zhou encouraged Rittenberg, who was working in the CCP's broadcast administration, to spread the news to the world: "We should broadcast this great democracy so that listeners all over the world know about it."[8]

With Mao as their guardian angel, the Red Guards had free rein, freed from any "restrictions." The Red Guards could debate, criticize, and denounce anyone and anything, as long as it was not Mao, his handpicked successor Lin Biao, or the Central Cultural Revolution Group.

The Red Guards not only used their words, they also employed effective guerrilla marketing tactics to reinforce their messaging in memorable ways. They used trucks, known as "propaganda vehicles," to broadcast their messages or play revolutionary songs at near-deafening volumes over their loudspeakers. These propaganda trucks grabbed additional attention via adorned signs and Red Guards who threw pamphlets at passersby.

I witnessed so many events as part of the early stages of the Cultural Revolution that were both exciting and volatile at that same time. What started out this way, would soon become anything but exciting. The Cultural Revolution would soon become violent and deadly. The enchantment I felt as a young child witnessing the Red Guards in action would soon become the distant past.

* * *

While common debates were centered around how extreme one group would be on a political spectrum, there soon emerged a significant debate related to class origin.

The original Red Guards were those who were considered "naturally red," meaning they were the descendants of the Revolutionary old guards. One of their leaders published a big-character poster with the slogan, "If father is a revolutionary, the son is a hero. If father is a reactionary, the son is a bastard." This propaganda fueled the "bloodline theory." The "old" Red Guards used this theory to legitimize themselves and their parents as "grandfathered in" to the preferred class of people. Just as they used this theory to legitimize their own status, they used it to delegitimize the people of the Black Class, using intimidation and violence to dehumanize them, and preventing their children from joining the Red Guards and wearing Mao's badges.

To the surprise of these Red Guards, the Central Cultural Revolution Committee stood against the "born red" slogan, suggesting it be changed to, "If father is hero, son will carry it on. If father is reactionary, son will rebel." The reason given was that this was good for uniting the majority.[9] These born-red Red Guards would soon find out the real reason.

This positioning allowed for youths from the Black Class to participate in the Cultural Revolution. One of these young men was Yu Luoke. Yu published his article "On Class Origins" in a Red Guard newspaper. He was a member of the Black Class. Because his father was labeled a "rightist" during the Anti-Rightist Campaign in 1957, Yu could not go to college even though he had excellent grades. Instead, he was given a menial job in a factory.[10]

Using Marxism as his basis, Yu argued in his manifesto that children of the Black Class should be allowed to participate in the Cultural Revolution. What should matter most, he said, was how individuals created their own *political identity*, and one should not be bound by one's family pedigree. Yu's daring statement in this regard was a dazzling one. He argued that "the fact that Marx, Lenin, and Chairman Mao, the great leaders of proletariat revolutions, were not from good family background is by no means accidental. The crux of the problem lies not in one's birth, but in thought reforming."[11]

Yu's article had a far-reaching impact, resulting in large numbers of people of the Black Class joining the Red Guards. The target of their rebellion is what Mao really wanted: rebelling against the CCP ruling class and establishment. Although Yu's manifesto helped Mao's cause, his argument fundamentally challenged Mao and the CCP's class-division principle. He was arrested and later executed at the age of twenty-eight in 1970. Making this story more horrific, the CCP exercised their very long history of forced live organ harvesting from prisoners. Before his execution, Yu's cornea was harvested for a model revolutionary laborer.[12]

A new breed of Red Guards emerged. They would identify themselves as "rebels." The original Red Guards were mainly children of the CCP cadres. They were now called "loyalists." The "rebel" Red Guards incorporated people from all walks of life, including those from the Black Class. The Rebels had their eyes on the members of the ruling class. They were the parents of the "loyalist" Red Guards, Mao's real target.

On August 22, 1966, Mao and the CCP Central Committee issued "Regulations of the Ministry of Public Security on Strictly Prohibiting the Dispatching of Police to Suppress Student Movements."[13] In today's world, that would be known simply as "defunding the police."

Part of the regulations stated that the people's police should enthusiastically support the revolutionary student movement; police would not be allowed to enter campuses (where much of the violence was taking place). It also stated that, should a revolutionary student hit the police, the police would not be allowed to fight back. Are police in America being intimidated into not fighting back if attacked?

Mao not only wanted to paralyze law enforcement, but also totally abolish the entire criminal justice system. In 1967, the CCP Central Committee issued a document requiring all public security administrations across the country be placed under military control. "Destroy the criminal justice system" became their slogan. Ninety-five percent of justice personnel were expelled to rural areas for reeducation. The unfortunate ones lost their lives to the violence and persecution.[14]

By then, the obstacles were all cleared. Nothing would stop or slow down the Red Guards from their rebellious acts and pronouncements on behalf of Mao and the Cultural Revolution. Rittenberg, the American Red Guard, described in his book the scene of the Red Guards raiding stores in Wangfujing, the busiest shopping district in Beijing:

> All of us watching this scene felt the same way about it. These were children, really, high school age or under. They had no guns, no weapons, no real strength. If any of the people they were harassing had decided to fight back, these kids couldn't have defended themselves. But none of us saw anyone fight back or even try to defy the Red Guards. Everyone did exactly what he or she was told. All these grown men and women stood by while children smashed their signs, clipped their pants, cut their hair. With the backing of Mao, these kids were emboldened, and the people simply acquiesced.[15]

After law enforcement was neutralized and the Red Guards fully mobilized, chaos descended, just as Mao had designed: "Let there be chaos, from which a new order will emerge. This should be repeated every seven or eight years."[16] As a dictator, Mao could openly state his plan. Although without an open statement, the American progressives instigate chaos every four years, instead of Mao's prescribed seven or eight years. And interestingly, it always falls on the presidential election year. Coincidence?

August 1966 in Beijing would be forever remembered as Red August. Red because it was bloody. It was a month of Red terror and the beginning of the widespread violence that became the hallmark of the Cultural Revolution.

In August, Red Guards conducted a series of massacres in

Beijing. Wang Youqin, a Cultural Revolution scholar, provides the statistics: "According to internal reports at the time, from August 20 to the end of September, 1,772 people were killed in Beijing. Some people believe that the actual number may be larger than this. The peak period of killing people was between the first and second time Mao Zedong met the Red Guards in Tiananmen Square, that is, between August 18 and August 31."[17]

The first killing took place in the Girls' Middle School Affiliated with Beijing Normal University, where teachers and administrators were the first group of victims. They had been labeled as class enemies because their positions in society had identified them as bourgeois intellectuals. Bian Zhongyun, the female deputy principal, is believed to have been the first person killed in the massacre. She was attacked and beaten to death by a group of young students wielding nail-studded wooden sticks and boiling water. After they came down from the excitement of their brutal murder of Bian, these students worried about suffering unintended consequences due to their rebellious actions. They reported the incident to the Beijing Municipal Party Committee and the office of Premier Zhou Enlai. There was no response.[18] The day was August 5, 1966. It is the day that Mao had given the Red Guards a license not just to rebel, but also to kill.

Song Binbin was one of the Red Guards alleged to have been involved in killing Bian Zhongyun. Song was chosen to represent the Beijing Red Guards at the Mao-led mass rally on August 18 that year. She was given the coveted position of placing the honorary Red Guard armband on Mao during the rally. Song quickly rose to fame after a conversation she had with Mao about the meaning of her name. Her subsequent actions made their way to the masses via all of the major CPP news outlets; Binbin (meaning *gentleness*) changed her name to Yaowu (meaning *war-like, martial,* and *violent*) at Mao's suggestion. Song Yaowu instantly became a national celebrity, the face of the Red Guards, and a national symbol of Mao-backed violence.[19]

In my mind as a child, Song Yaowu was a hero. I was not aware of her alleged participation in the killing of the deputy principal of her school. Even if I had been, I would have accepted the Red Guards' justification that the principal was an enemy of the state and deserved to be killed. I would have accepted this because of the indoctrination I and millions of others went through.

The Red Guards also humiliated and tortured their victims. Those who could not tolerate the brutality they were forced to endure by the inhumane Red Guards chose suicide. Sadly, suicide became commonplace during the Cultural Revolution. One such instance has stained my memory: After a long struggle session wrought with beatings and humiliations, someone our family knew returned home to his wife. There, he was met by ridicule and shaming by her; she was only concerned with how he would negatively affect her politically. She was so disgusted by him that she said he would be better off killing himself. He did. Adding to the long list of those who committed suicide was the half-sister of Xi Jinping, China's current dictator. After their father was purged by Mao in 1963, the entire family fell into the Black Class, and became a target of persecution by the Red Guards.[20]

As you know by now, when the rebel Red Guards joined the ranks, they were ready to take down the CCP leaders and bureaucrats. It was not difficult to identify those leaders and bureaucrats. They were those in charge, up and down the chain of the CCP ruling machine. The average Chinese person had long regarded these CCP bureaucrats as the new oppressors with unwarranted privilege. Those of the Black Class never forgot what these CCP bureaucrats had done to their parents—none of it good. Now it was their chance to get revenge.

I did not just hear of stories of struggle sessions. I witnessed them. One struggle session I witnessed was that of Li Jingquan, the governor of Sichuan (1949–1966). Although he supported all of the campaigns put forth by Mao and implemented radical policies during the Land Reform and Great Leap Forward, resulting in the deaths of more than eight million people in Sichuan Province, he became an enemy of Mao and was given labels such as "counterrevolutionary revisionist" and "capitalist roader." He was accused of making Sichuan Province an independent kingdom of his own.

Li Jingquan and his wife were beaten over and over again in struggle sessions that were never-ending. She finally committed suicide by hanging. For the sin of defending his father, Li Jingquan's second son, Li Mingqing, was beaten to the point of near death by the Red Guards, only to be delivered to the crematorium where he was cremated alive.[21] Li and his wife were not innocent. They had overseen many bloody struggle sessions against the landlords during the Land Reform campaign, and now they were at the receiving end of the same struggle! No position or degree of loyalty to Mao was enough to keep CCP officials safe from succumbing to the same fates they handed out. As the saying goes, what goes around, comes around. And it did. It became a common occurrence for these high-ranking CCP officials to be murdered at the hands of the Red Guards.

With the great power bestowed upon them by Mao, the Red Guards became more and more brazen, attacking anyone and anything they deemed counterrevolutionary. On July 7, 1967, more than three thousand Red Guards attempted to raid Zhongnanhai, the central headquarters and residence of the Chinese Communist Party leaders. Zhongnanhai is like America's White House. The aim of the guards was to "arrest" Liu Shaoqi, the president of China; Deng Xiaoping, the vice premier of China; and Peng Zhen, mayor of Beijing. The three were all deemed counterrevolutionaries, making them presumed enemies of Mao. The Red Guards might have been successful had it not been for Premier Zhou Enlai.[22] During the Cultural Revolution, Zhou was one of the few old guards Mao did not purge and still had the authority to intervene on Mao's behalf.

It may not be a leap to say that the riots by the violent mobs close to the White House after the death of Floyd in 2020 were not too far off from the actions of the Red Guards. The riots around the White House became such a concern to the Secret Service that agents rushed then president Donald Trump to a White House bunker.[23]

The Red Guards did a hell of a job pulling down the CCP leaders from their position of power. It was over attempted power grabs and fractional contention that infighting broke out. The factions kept growing and went beyond just "loyalists" and "rebels." They were now fighting for their own interests. No faction wanted to share power. For this reason, large-scale violence between factions broke out all over the country, with average people too close to the fray becoming collateral damage as a consequence. The Red Guards raided many military arsenal facilities, while no one dared to intervene because they lacked Mao's orders to do so. Now the Red Guards were armed with deadly weapons instead of just sticks and rocks.[24]

The fighting between Red Guard factions eventually rose to the level of an actual civil war. John Gittings, writing for *China Beat*, described the mode of warfare used by one Red Guard faction against another: "In 1968, Red Guard factions battled one another at Beijing's Qinghua [Tsinghua] University. Red Guards told the writer and historian William Hinton about how the struggle on the campus in April of that year escalated from stone slingshots and wooden spears to revolvers and hand grenades. One group welded steel plates onto the body of a tractor to convert it into a tank. Ten students were killed and many more badly injured in the next three months till July 1968 when Mao Zedong finally sent in groups of local workers, backed by the army, to restore order."[25]

Killings by the Red Guards had started under the same banner of "fight to death to defend Chairman Mao." Chongqing, where many defense factories stood, was a city neighboring my hometown of Chengdu. It was also the location of one of the very worst battles where the Red Guard's bloodthirst was on full display. Tanks and artillery were deployed. Countless young lives were lost. I remember eagerly listening to my well-informed neighbor sharing her latest news about Chongqing in our communal kitchen in the evening during the time when the worst fighting was taking place. As you might imagine, one would never be able to find news like this in official papers. The papers only published good news approved by Mao and his inner circle. Today, there is a cemetery, aptly named Red Guard Cemetery, in Chongqing. The personal stories of the more than four hundred souls buried there died with them.

Yang Guobin, author of *The Red Guard Generation and Political Activism in China*, reached this conclusion:

> The study of factionalism in Chongqing shows the centrality of ideas and ideals to collective violence. The most important factor in influencing participation in the Red Guard movement was not class interests, nor manipulation of the masses by the party leaders, but the sacred culture of revolution that had formed prior to the Cultural Revolution, which had come into full play during it. The case demonstrates that human beings are capable of, and, indeed, may be attracted to, death to prove their devotion to an idea. And the more sacred the idea is made to be, the more deadly it may become.[26]

While there was a tremendous amount of violence happening across the country, whether to benefit Mao's vision or for the Red Guards' own personal reasons, not all were on board with the mission. Wang Rongfen, a student at the Beijing Foreign Language Institute studying German at the time of the Cultural Revolution, would prove to be an insightful and courageous young woman. Her study of the Nazi regime in Germany served her well as a participant of the 1966 August 18 rally in Tiananmen Square. She quickly identified the frightening similarities between the student soldiers wearing the green shirts in China and Hitler's youths who wore the brown shirts in Nazi Germany.

Personally compelled to do so, Wang wrote Mao a letter—using her real name and address—accusing him of leading China on a ruinous path. Wang was subsequently arrested and sentenced to life in prison. After the Cultural Revolution, she was released and immigrated to Germany.[27] This is a powerful story that demonstrates the importance of learning and understanding history so that the atrocities of our past are not repeated. It is imperative that Americans today understand history, as we are currently making the same mistakes of those before us. Instead of falling prey to indoctrination, Wang had the ability to think for herself, the confidence and the bravery to stand up for her convictions of doing what was right. Because of her studies, she was able to question what she was being told to do and decide that she was not going to repeat the mistakes made in Nazi Germany three decades earlier.

In 1968, as the Red Guards were waging a civil war among themselves, Mao's proverbial pendulum was swinging in a new direction. He ordered the People's Liberation Army (PLA) to suppress the most radical faction of the Red Guards. By "suppress," Mao meant kill.

By late 1968, the purpose of the Red Guards had run its course. They had successfully seized all power from Mao's enemies and had neutralized the old CCP bureaucrats. On July 28, 1968, Mao summoned the Red Guard leaders and told them that they had "disappointed" him with their infighting, and therefore the power seized by Red Guards was now going to the "workers, peasants, and soldiers," who, in Mao's mind, were the true leaders of the Cultural Revolution. So, just like that, the Red Guards were hastily disarmed, and the group was dissolved.[28]

In December 1968, Mao issued this order: "It is very necessary for educated youths to go to the countryside and receive reeducation from the poor and lower-middle peasants." The tables turned on the youth, the generation that rained terror on the people of China under Mao's watchful and approving eye. Mao's focus swung from his enemies to his Red Guards. Mao was convinced that probourgeois thinking remained in the minds of the spoiled and entitled youths. Mao directed all urban youths to be reeducated by the peasants, getting their hands dirty by doing manual labor with peasants. As a result of the movement, nearly seventeen million youths were exiled to rural areas across China. I was among one of the last groups of youths sent to the countryside before Mao died in 1976. Many of these young people would lose the opportunity to go to college. They would later be called the "lost generation."

As part of the Down to the Countryside Movement, the Red Guards were kicked out from urban areas where they had become increasingly regarded as a nuisance to everyone and a potential threat to the emerging order. The other reason was that the economy in ruins had nothing to offer to these youths.

After Mao's death in 1976, Deng Xiaoping seized power. He restored most of the bureaucrats to power as well. These CCP officials did not forget what the rebel Red Guards had done to them and others. Many of the rebel leaders were subsequently prosecuted and punished. There goes again the vicious cycle of hatred and revenge of the Communist machine.

One of the most important things to understand is that, while Mao's intention was to create chaos among the people, which would provide him with a ripe environment in which to build a new world order exactly according to his own design, that very same chaos became a monster that eventually destroyed everything on its path, including the CCP itself.

* * *

In twenty-first–century America, the "Red Guards" of our place and time are alive and they are multiplying. America's version of China's Red Guards is a combination of radical activists, BLM, and Antifa. They are on college campuses (and increasingly in high schools), city streets, workplaces, and every corner of the American landscape. These groups are nothing new in America. They have been around for decades, under different colors and banners, creating chaos and causing destruction in the name of one cause or another. The more passionate they are, the more they bend or totally break the rules—all in the name of social progress and justice.

Just like the Red Guards, whose ranks came out of schools, so did radicalized activists, starting in the 1960s, emerge on American campuses, influenced in large part by the Frankfurt School Marxists. As Jerry Rubin, leader of the Yippies, put it, "We're using the campus as a launching pad to foment revolution everywhere."[29]

This was when college student activism became political, radical, and militant. College campuses were epicenters for the counterculture movement and Marxist cultural revolution. Communist-thinking influencers such as the charismatic Jerry Rubin (1938–1994) became leaders of these radicalized student groups. Millions of American college students, and some in high school, thought they were taking part in a worthy cause.

The real political campus protests started in the 1960s. In 1964, students at the University of California, Berkeley launched the Free Speech Movement to protest the university's restrictions on students' political activities. The restriction had its origins in the McCarthyism of the 1950s, referring to US Senator Joseph McCarthy's campaign to root out American Communists. His pursuit was regarded as overzealous and made him a rallying icon for student activists who came on the scene a decade later. The student movement succeeded in forcing college administrations to back down and grant the students their goal of free speech and rights to political activism on campus.[30]

More than fifty years later, UC Berkeley students are again protesting, and again it's about free speech, although now the targeted issue has been reversed. In 2017, they wanted to stop (without success) the conservative talk radio host Ben Shapiro from speaking on campus. No free speech for him![31]

Looking back at the 1960s, we can see how 1968 was a banner year for college student protests across America, including East Coast Ivy League schools who weren't to be outdone by their West Coast counterparts. Columbia University in New York City was a site for a series of protests in 1968. The goals were to 1) stop the building of a gym on public land in Morningside Park, 2) sever ties with a Pentagon institute doing research for the Vietnam War, 3) gain amnesty for demonstrators, and 4) induce the early resignation of Columbia's current president. The New York City police ended the campus siege by coming in and forcibly removing the student protestors in a scene marked with violence.[32]

A year later, in 1969, one student movement turned into armed insurrections. It started with an incident involving Father Michael McPhelin, a visiting professor from the Philippines. Here is an account of what took place:

> ...black students...charged a visiting professor of economics with racism because he had dared to judge African nations by a "Western" standard of development. The administration required an apology from the professor; he complied, but the students were not satisfied and took possession of the

economics department, holding the chairman and his secretary prisoner for eighteen hours...[33]

I read this excerpt from Roger Kimball's *The Long March* to a friend over the phone and asked him to guess when the incident took place. He answered without hesitation, "This week?" No, it took place more than fifty years ago, at yet another Ivy school— Cornell University. This 1969 incident—the violence, threats, and cancel culture, in combination with a passionate social justice protest—is very similar to the tactics of BLM in the new millennium.

A Cornell Black militant student group called Afro-American Society (AAS) armed themselves and occupied Willard Straight Hall, the school's student union building, until their demands were met. What was the basis for AAS's grievances? Racial injustice. The irony is that many of these rebel students were admitted to Cornell because of affirmative action. While the university was doing its part to make up for injustices of the past, these students felt they were owed more. "They then began issuing various demands: for separate, black-only living quarters; for an Afro-American Studies Program, again, for blacks only; finally, they demanded that the university create an autonomous degree-granting college-within-a-college for the exclusive use of black students, the aim of which was to 'create the tools necessary for the formation of a black nation.'" One statement informed the world that "whites can make no contributions to Black Studies except in an advisory, non-decision making or financial capacity."[34]

Dr. Thomas Sowell, senior fellow of the Hoover Institution (and himself an African American), called the day of the armed occupation "the day Cornell died."[35] In many ways, that was also the day that American higher education died. Since that day, academia has yielded itself to the progressives' political correctness, social justice, and lawlessness. Violence defeated reason...the American Red Guards were born.

In 2019, Cornell University placed a permanent plaque on Willard Straight Hall to commemorate the fiftieth anniversary of the occupation. Whether the plaque is meant to honor the students who were involved, pay respect to Father McPhelin, or was displayed as a cautionary tale for where woke America is headed is perhaps open to interpretation by the reader. It reads:

> Cornell was one of the centers of student protest and activism in the 1960s against the Vietnam War and the denial of civil rights in the United States. In April 1969, over a hundred Black students occupied this building for thirty-three hours, bringing to Cornell the national Civil Rights Movement's struggle for racial and social justice. After a peaceful, negotiated ending to the building occupation, Cornell set out to become a leader in its commitment to the ideals of a diverse and inclusive university.[36]

I'll give my own interpretation of the fiftieth anniversary plaque: It is there to commemorate the American Red Guards' mob culture, which is not only celebrated but also institutionalized.

Fifty years later, the second phase of the American cultural revolution arrived. Campus protests again became commonplace. The theme stays the same: to protest against conservative speakers or conservative faculty members. In other words, abolishment of free speech and the dismantling of our systems in the name of stopping "hate."

I could go on for another fifty pages just summarizing these Marxist, Red Guard–like activities swarming college campuses, such as the University of Missouri protests that took place in 2015, or the 2017 protest against author Charles Murray at Middlebury College in Vermont, or the time in 2017 when controversial biology professor Bret Weinstein was targeted by students at the exuberantly liberal Evergreen State College in the state of Washington, where he worked, for various politically incorrect opinions he had stated.[37] The manner in which Evergreen students surrounded Weinstein and tried to silence him was uncannily similar to a Chinese Cultural Revolution struggle session by Red Guards in the 1960s. Yes, it looked like a struggle session; except if this had been the Chinese Cultural Revolution, Weinstein likely would not have made it out of there alive had he dared to engage in argument back like he did at Evergreen.

Never did I imagine that one day I would also join the ranks of speakers banned on campus. In April 2023, the students of the Turning Point USA chapter at Whitworth University, a Catholic school in Spokane, Washington, invited me to speak. The student government, however, voted nine to four rejecting me to speak on campus. What were their reasons? My views were harmful! Based on the released meeting minutes, the members of the student government reached their conclusion by going over my tweets, especially one in which I listed terms I identified as "woke," which included the terms *BLM, environmental justice, LGBTQQIP2SA*. The most astonishing reason was that I compared the Chinese Cultural Revolution to today's Woke movement. Instead of letting me speak and challenging me face-to-face where they disagree, they chose to simply cancel me. Ultimately, I wound up speaking off-campus to a good turnout, which included students, faculty, and local residents, and it went really well.

What is the difference between the 1960s campus student protests and those of today's campuses? Students in the sixties demanded free political speech for themselves on campus. Today, students demand that free speech be limited to only that speech which is approved by them to be allowed on campus. This invariably prohibits the voices of conservative speakers. We should ask ourselves how China's Red Guards of the past are similar to America's Red Guards of today. For one thing, the Chinese Red Guards were targeting the Black Class and the CCP bureaucrats. The American Red Guards were (and are) targeting the new American Black Class, the conservatives. The Chinese Red Guards started with verbal attacks, using big-character posters, but ended up physically beating and eventually killing their targets. American Red Guards started with verbal attacks and are now advocating for physical coercion and violence. A 2021 survey of the top 150 colleges in the US found that nearly 25 percent of students said it is acceptable to use violence to shut down a controversial speaker. The number jumps to nearly 50 percent at several elite women's colleges.[38]

Both Chinese and American Red Guards have one thing in common: intolerance—they demand tolerance of others, but not of themselves. The Chinese Red Guards went after those Mao could not tolerate. The American Red Guards have gone after those the progressives can't tolerate. To many of today's college students, "speech is violence." Not *their* speech; only the speech of those with different viewpoints. Lisa Feldman Barrett, a professor of psychology at Northeastern University, in her *New York Times* opinion piece "When Is Speech Violence?" argues that "if words can cause stress, and if prolonged stress can cause physical harm, then it seems that speech—at least certain types of speech—can be a form of violence."[39]

The Chinese Red Guard movement eventually took their mayhem and violence from the campuses into the streets, turning what had been a student movement into a movement embraced by the general public. Similarly, when radical American students graduated from schools, taking their passion for rioting and violence in the name of social justice to the streets in cities and communities nationwide, the plight of the social justice warriors grew, as did their numbers. These American radicals are looking and behaving like the Red Guards of China's Cultural Revolution. And, just like Mao giving the nod to the havoc wrought by the Red Guard, so do the progressive elites and their controlled justice system nod to the mobs. We see this pervasively in mainstream news outlets, in social media, and in our government.

BLM, as I explained in Chapter 3, is the direct descendant of the militant branch of the Civil Rights movement. In his book *BLM: The Making of a New Marxist Revolution*, author Mike Gonzalez, a senior fellow at the Heritage Foundation, details BLM's origin and development. He traces BLM back to the Black Panthers and Black Liberation Army, both of which turned their backs on the nonviolent teachings of Dr. King. They embraced not only Communism but also Maoism. Gonzalez also establishes a connection between Bill Ayers, cofounder of the extreme radical terrorist organization Weather Underground, with BLM.

Black Lives Matter did have a beginning. It was founded in 2013 by three African American women: Alicia Garza, Patrisse Cullors, and Opal Tometi. This was in response to the acquittal of George Zimmerman, who in 2012 fatally shot Trayvon Martin, a seventeen-year-old African American male who was walking to his father's fiancée's townhome in Sanford, Florida.[40] Zimmerman said he shot Martin in self-defense. With national media focusing on Zimmerman and the case, he was eventually tried for murder before a jury acquitted him, and that didn't sit well with BLM's founders. Guilt or innocence obviously is not a factor here.

BLM is a Marxist organization. We know this to be true because you can hear it directly from cofounder Patrisse Cullors when she called herself and other BLM founders "trained Marxists" in a surfaced clip from a Real News Network interview.[41] Cullors addresses the question of whether she is a Marxist on her own YouTube channel.[42] In that video, she manages to avoid repeating her claim that she is a trained Marxist. Instead, she said she believes in Marxism because it is an ideology that criticizes capitalism. She made it clear that BLM's target is capitalism. "I'm working on making sure people don't suffer," she said. She tried to dissuade people from seeing her as a Marxist/Communist by asserting that many people called Dr. King a Communist before his assassination, but now everyone loves him.

Dr. King is on record rejecting Communism as he stated, "Communism is based on an ethical relativism, a metaphysical materialism, a crippling totalitarianism, and a withdrawal of basic freedom that no Christian can accept."[43] He embraced the Constitution and the American dream: "And I knew that as they were sitting in, they were really standing up for the best in the American dream, and taking the whole nation back to those great wells of democracy which were dug deep by the Founding Fathers in the Declaration of Independence and the Constitution."[44]

Even if they try to say otherwise, BLM leaders are not followers of Dr. King. They are not followers of Malcolm X, either. Although Dr. King and Malcolm X took drastically different approaches—the former one of nonviolence and civil disobedience, the other a militant who believed in "by any means necessary"—their goal was the same. They both were fighting for the freedom and equality of Black people.

That's not the case with BLM. BLM members are true Communists. Like their forerunners, BLM also received support from the CCP just as the Black militants did from Mao in the 1960s. Both the *People's Daily Online* and the English-language newspaper *Global Times*, under the CCP's flagship publication *People's Daily*, ran articles supporting the BLM movement. An article entitled "Hypocrisy of American Civil Rights" by *People's Daily Online* even echoes Mao's 1963 statement in which he compared the Civil Rights Movement to *class struggle*: "We have really seen a 'Black Lives Matter' movement that has caused a global sensation, but we should also see the profound class nature beneath it."[45]

According to Mike Gonzalez, author of the book entitled *BLM: The Making of a New Marxist Revolution*, the Chinese Progressive Association (San Francisco) (CPA San Francisco) is the financial sponsor of the Black Futures Lab and the Black to the Future Action Fund, both associated with BLM founder Alicia Garza. CPA (San Francisco) was founded as a Maoist organization in 1972. It has since been doing pro-CCP work in America.[46]

Since the organization came into being in 2013, BLM has done nothing in terms of making the lives of Black Americans better. More than 90 percent of Black homicide deaths are at the hands of Black offenders.[47] Have you ever heard anything whereby BLM addressed all the Black people killed in 2020, even a simple statement of sincere grief? You didn't, because those Black lives did not matter to BLM.

The death of Floyd amid the COVID pandemic lockdown created the perfect storm. It was in the year 2020 that BLM activism turned the protests against police brutality into a full-blown Marxist upheaval aimed at destroying our society. Never letting a good crisis go to waste, the death of Floyd was their Vietnam War moment, not only for BLM to heighten awareness for their cause, but also to expand and grow their organization and their personal wallets.

Did you know that BLM started most of the riots in 2020? As reported by the *Federalist*, a study has shown that up to 95 percent of the 2020 US riots were linked to BLM.[48] Like you, I am not surprised by that, either. Yes, the summer of 2020 will forever be remembered as the summer of unrest and violence. It runs parallel to the Red Guards' Red Terror in August and September of 1966. The Chinese Red Guards managed to kill thousands of people and terrorize the capital city of Beijing much of those two months, not to mention the violence and death that ensued during the following two years. While in a five-month span in 2020, we watched BLM-influenced rioters burn and vandalize our cities; people died. Many of the victims are the very people the BLM movement claims to be fighting for. In addition to the loss of lives, BLM may have caused up to $2 billion worth of damage.[49]

While America was suffering, the progressive media cheered the rioters and looters on. I am interested to know whether Vicky Osterweil, author of *In Defense of Looting: A Riotous History of*

Uncivil Action, knew about the Red Guards' slogan: "Stealing is justified. Robbery is no crime. Long, long live the revolutionary bandit spirit."[50] In an interview with National Public Radio (NPR), Osterweil said that looting is a powerful tool to bring about real, lasting change in society.[51] The Chinese Red Guards would agree with her!

Antifa also plays a significant role in the American Red Guards movement, even though Democratic leaders—to include Joe Biden—go out of their way to trivialize Antifa as merely a fringe annoyance, or, as Biden put it, nothing more than an "idea."[52] Former House Judiciary Committee Chairman Jerrold Nadler called Antifa "imaginary."[53] Scary stuff considering that as of this writing, Biden and Nadler have significant roles in running this country as members of the majority party.

Antifa is an abbreviated term for *anti-fascism*. Beyond that, there seems to be little agreement on its definition. Searching the internet, you will find a variety of descriptions, although zeroing in on one all-encompassing term or phrase remains elusive:

An amorphous movement
A leaderless, nonhierarchical organization
A left-wing anti-fascist and anti-racist political movement[54]

Most Americans, including me, first learned about Antifa from the Unite the Right rally and counterprotests held in Charlottesville, Virginia, in the summer of 2017. The beating of journalist Andy Ngo in Portland in 2019 brought further national attention to Antifa, certainly showing it to be more than just an "idea." Ngo's status as an Antifa target was born of the fact that he is a conservative journalist who has been covering Antifa since early 2017, which by itself makes him more knowledgeable about Antifa than most journalists. In his book, *Unmasked: Inside Antifa's Radical Plan to Destroy Democracy*, Ngo documents the history and development of Antifa as a violent, left-wing extremist movement. While conceding that Antifa apparently lacks a single leader, Ngo says, "There are indeed localized cells and groups with formalized structures and memberships."[55] In 2020, the Trump administration announced their desire to label Antifa a domestic terrorist organization.[56]

Ngo traced Antifa back to Antifaschistische Aktion, a group founded by the German Communist Party in 1932. The American Antifa not only took its name, but also its logo, with two flags that represent anarchism and Communism. BLM also used symbolism with Communist roots, such as their raised fist. Ngo describes American Antifa as a "unique crosspollination of several radical ideologies: Marxism, anarchism, and critical theory."[57]

Antifa and BLM share the same goal of ending capitalism and America. They share the same belief in violence and lawlessness, and by any means necessary. They also use the deceptive branding of anti-fascism to mask their true intention and to suppress free speech and create confusion. Both Antifa and BLM are Marxists, through and through.

The Red Guards became an unstoppable force for the simple reason that they had Mao's full support. In 2020, so many Americans helplessly watched American cities set on fire and wondered why the mayhem and violence could not be stopped. It was because the radical activists had the entire progressive machine backing them.

Ngo explained in his book, *Unmasked*: "Indeed, if the riots of 2020 prove anything, it's that a sizable portion of Democratic politicians, intellectuals, academics, and journalists find riots and looting justifiable if committed in the name of 'racial justice.'"[58]

Mao dismantled the CCP's criminal justice system to pave the way for his Red Guards so that they could act with impunity. The progressives have been doing the same in America for *their* Red Guards by not only defunding the police but also by demonizing law enforcement as a profession. They have been successful in undermining police forces, as police officers have been quitting in droves since 2020.[59]

As for those lawbreakers who were arrested, they were provided a grassroots bail fund to free them, which was backed by then senator Kamala Harris.[60] Harris also was on the side of an accused criminal rather than on the side of law enforcement by personally meeting with and voicing support for Jacob Blake in Wisconsin. Blake was shot by police for resisting arrest during a domestic dispute in Kenosha, Wisconsin, in August 2020.[61] New York City dropped charges against hundreds of BLM/Antifa rioters and looters, despite many of those being caught and identified on video, many of whom were seen smashing windows, stealing goods, and setting businesses on fire.[62]

Ngo singled out Congresswoman Alexandria Ocasio-Cortez as being responsible for legitimizing Antifa by relentlessly calling the Trump Administration "racist" and saying he should be defeated by any means necessary. "No other politician as high profile as (her)," Ngo writes, "has managed to mainstream the Antifa agenda, making it politically palatable and even advantageous to espouse radical, extremist views."[63] Renowned former Fox News host and commentator Tucker Carlson perhaps summed it up best in his nightly broadcast *Tucker Carlson Tonight* on January 23, 2023 when he stated: "Antifa is the armed instrument of the permanent Democratic establishment in Washington."[64]

As for financial support, independent investigative journalist Ashley Rae Goldenberg, in a June 2020 report in *Conservative Firing Line*, compiled a list of 269 companies that she alleged were supporting Antifa and/or BLM, including the likes of Adidas, Amazon, American Airlines, Apple Music, Armani, AT&T, and Atlantic Records—and that's even before we get to the *b*'s in Goldenberg's long alphabetized list.[65]

Ngo points to the National Lawyers Guild, a far-left legal organization, as the one entity providing legal aid to Antifa.

BLM/Antifa and the SJWs (social justice warriors) made sure that everyone knew their demand: defund the police; no justice, no peace...In the city of Seattle, Washington, in 2020, the protestors got the chance to put their demands into practice, with the blessing of Democrat mayor Jenny Durkan. They built a police-free, socially and racially just, and self-governing commune where people of color were not only protected as equal but also were put on the top of the so-called "reverse hierarchy of oppression."[66] Welcome to the Capitol Hill Autonomous Zone (CHAZ), also known as the Capitol Hill Occupied Protest (CHOP). Capitol Hill consists of an area of about six blocks near downtown Seattle.

The saga lasted for twenty-four glorious days, during which CHAZ managed to see rampant crime that included four shootings, two homicides, arson, and numerous counts of alleged sexual assault.[67] Sadly "all the identified victims were black men—precisely the demographic for whom the CHAZ had claimed to offer protection. In the absence of a legitimate police force, armed criminal gangs and untrained anarchist paramilitaries filled the void. Almost every night, gunshots rang through the streets. The first homicide victim was killed in an outburst of gang violence; the second, reportedly unarmed and joyriding in a stolen car, was gunned down by the 'CHAZ security force,'" reported Christopher Rufo for the *City Journal*.[68]

There is no need for us to imagine the "better" society BLM/Antifa/SJW could create for us. We have CHAZ to look at. It was a glaring case of inmates running the asylum, much like the Red Guards controlling Beijing and other cities across China during the Cultural Revolution.

In 2020, the whole world appeared to be on board with BLM's cause. The *New York Times* claimed that "Black Lives Matter may be the largest movement in U.S. history."[69] Only two years since 2020, BLM's heyday seems to be behind it. Scandals keep bubbling up.

Among them is the report by Sean Campbell of Columbia's Journalism School on April 7, 2022, that Black Lives Matter Global Network Foundation bought a $6 million home with donation funds. What is its justification? It claimed that the luxurious home is to be used for "Black creatives to create their art and influence things for the movement" and "as a safe house when people were feeling threatened or receiving death threats, other things."[70] I wonder how many Americans will believe it. Campbell, writing for liberal outlets, seemed skeptical.

In May 2022, it was reported that Cullors, the organization's onetime executive director, paid $840,000 to her brother for "security services."[71]

This just goes to show that not only are BLM/Antifa not in the fight for Black lives, but they are also in it to enrich themselves.

Any doubt about the legitimacy of the above-mentioned story will be relieved by knowing that the allegations against the BLM founders also came from BLM chapters. Twenty-six of them are suing the organization's leadership over an alleged ten-million–dollar theft from the charitable contributions for personal expenditures.[72]

Although BLM leaders have been dismissing these allegations, more and more people have begun to see their hypocrisy, including their closest allies. In late September 2022, a month before the midterm election, then-candidate for the Senate, Democrat John Fetterman of Pennsylvania, an ardent supporter of BLM, removed the BLM section from his campaign website.[73] Is it because Fetterman has realized that people are fed up with BLM-created chaos? Obviously, he noticed that affiliation with BLM has become a liability rather than an asset. It is inevitable that more and more Americans will awaken to the fact that BLM is toxic.

＊ ＊ ＊

Since 2020, American Red Guard–led "protests" have become increasingly common in the American political landscape. We see them in state capitols and legislative sessions. We see them outside and inside Catholic churches. And we see them in public spaces on highways and in subways. While shouting slogans such as "stop gun violence," "protect trans kids," "defend women's reproductive rights," "save our environment," or "social or racial justice," the intent of these "protestors" is clear: to *intimidate* and *disrupt*. The way in which they are mobilized and activated is unmistakably a reminder of the Chinese Red Guards during the Chinese Cultural Revolution.

Both Chinese and American Red Guards are the stormtroopers of the Revolution. BLM and Antifa may think they will always possess power and influence. So did the Red Guards. Let's not forget what eventually happened to Mao's Red Guards. Mao discarded them like garbage after their usefulness was over.

CHAPTER 7

Cancel Culture: War on the Old World

One day in 1966, my mom took me to a dumpling restaurant for a treat. I will never forget what I experienced that day. A group of Red Guards took charge of the restaurant and used a loudspeaker to announce a new rule: no one should serve; to do so was to allow exploitation. This meant everyone should clean up their own dishes. In addition to the long line for the customers to get the dumplings, there was now a long line for them to get to the kitchen sink to wash the dishes. I dutifully washed the bowl I used with a feeling of profound pride that I was participating in the revolution and on the side of the Red Guards. Is this the next step in the American woke's effort to ensure equity?

Cancel culture is running rampant and has become ubiquitous in today's culture. Yet, it was not that long ago when "cancel culture" as a term made it into the American lexicon. In 2019, the Macquarie Dictionary, an authoritative source on Australian English, named "cancel culture" the "word of the year." Here is the reason given: "A term that captures an important aspect of the past year's Zeitgeist...an attitude which is so pervasive that it now has a name, society's *cancel culture* has become, for better or worse, a powerful force."[1]

It has indeed become a powerful force, a force aiming at transforming the traditional Western culture to a Marxist or woke culture. Cancel culture has become one of America's leading and most dangerous pandemics that can ultimately be our nation's undoing. Cancel culture is one of the core elements of the Marxist Cultural Revolution.

Mao also carried out his "cancel culture," although it is called by another name: Destroy the Four Olds, or *po si jiu*. The Four Olds stands for old ideas, old traditions, old customs, and old habits. In other words, the entire preexisting Chinese culture.

Destroying the Four Olds didn't start with the 1966 launch of the Great Cultural Revolution. As early as 1949, at the beginning of his reign, Mao and the CCP devised ways to weaken traditional Chinese civilization. This continued for seventeen years leading up to the Cultural Revolution. This was to be Mao's final attempt to destroy the remnants of the old China.

With the Land Reform in 1949, the CCP began exercising its

most destructive power in wiping away traditional culture. Not only did the CCP confiscate land and property from the landlords, it also physically eradicated the country gentry who had served as the de facto guardians and transmitters of the traditional culture and values for centuries. The history and traditions that had been preserved for centuries by these "guardians" was completely taken away by the CCP in just a few short years.

Mao stated in his 1940 published work *On New Democracy* that Confucianism was an obstacle to the new culture and new ideas. "There is no construction without destruction, no flowing without damming and no motion without rest; the two are locked in a life-and-death struggle."[2]

The goal of Destroy the Four Olds was to cancel the old to usher in the Four News. Hidden in the cloak of these four new Marxist and Communist ideas, traditions, customs, and habits was something much more radical: Maoism.

Following the first Red Guard rally in Beijing's Tiananmen Square on August 18, 1966, the Red Guards did not waste time launching the Destroy the Four Olds campaign. This was the beginning of the Mao-style cancel culture.

The Red Guards began their fanatic destruction with the abolishment of traditional names for anything that was considered to be feudalistic or not in line with the Cultural Revolution. They set out to revolutionaize names of institutions, streets, parks, brands, stores, popular dishes, and eventually personal names.

Many streets got new names like Anti-imperialism Road, Anti-Revisionism Blvd, or Revolutionary Street.

The Red Guards renamed the very school where the concept of Red Guards was born, Tsinghua University Middle School.

Tsinghua means "pure China." The school was very aptly renamed to Red Guards Fighting School.[3]

One of Beijing's best-known hospitals, Beijing Xiehe Hospital (also known as Peking Union Medical College Hospital) came out of its visit from the Red Guards known as the Anti-imperialist Hospital. Ironically, the hospital was founded in 1921 by the US "imperialist" Rockefeller Foundation.[4]

The Red Guards' ambition to change names gave rise to what we, as Americans, know and enjoy as "Peking duck." The original name of this upscale resturant and its most famous dish is Quanjude Roast Duck restaurant, with decades-old history. *Quanjude* can be loosely translated as "accumulated virtues"; definitely not a revolutionary name. The Red Guards smashed the restaurant signboard and renamed it Peking Duck Restaurant. They held struggle sessions against the owner and gave him the sentence of exile to the countryside to raise pigs.[5]

I remember the time of name changing very well, as it hit my home city of Chengdu. One of the most popular steets in the city's busiest shopping district had a lovely name, Chunxi Road, which meant "spring splendor." That road was renamed, simply, Anti-imperialism Road. "Anti-imperialism" was the most popular new name of the day.

Even personal names fell prey to cancel culture. Traditionally, Chinese parents chose auspicious words for their children, such as *virtue, pure, fortune, longevity,* or *luck*; but in order to be politically correct and fashionable, young people changed their traditional names to revolutionary names. My name, Xi, which means "west," can refer to "Western imperialism" and even as young as I was, I knew that I certainly didn't want to be carrying that name around with me. So I asked my parents to change it. But they wouldn't have any part of that, wisely choosing instead to convince my peers that I had been named after the city Xi'an, where I was born.

While I kept my name, many of my classmates chose to change theirs to be more revolutionary, e.g., red, bravery, guard, or fighter. One boy changed his name to Dangsheng, which means "birth by the Party." Without any legal process required for changing your name, picking a new name was an easy way to *virtue signal* your compliance with the Revolution.

Not all personal name changes were made so voluntarily and easily. There was a story about a former factory owner in Shanghai who was subjected to a struggle session because of his name and his desire to keep it. His name was Yangmin, which can sound like "feed the people." But because he was deemed a capitalist and therefore an exploiter of the people, he was ordered to change his name by switching the characters from Yangmin to Minyang, which now sounded like "fed by the people."[6]

By now the idea of name change should be familiar to most Americans, since we have our own version of the name-change campaign, carried out by American Red Guards.

As part of the Destroy the Four Olds campaign, many historical sites and cultural relics were destroyed. In Beijing alone, 4,922 of the 6,843 cultural relics—more than 70 percent—that had been registered in China's first cultural relic census of 1958 were destroyed or damaged.[7]

In November 1966, members of the Red Guards gathered en masse in Beijing's Tiananmen Square and vowed to annihilate the Qufu Temple of Confucius in Shandong Province, where Confucius was born and grew up more than two thousand years ago, and where his descendants had lived. Several days later, the Red Guards moved into the site. Their mission was to destroy statues of Confucius, commemorative stele in the temple, and the family mansion. In tandem with local workers, the Red Guards proceeded to desecrate and lay waste to the family cemetery, digging up more than two thousand graves, looting their contents, and hanging naked corpses from surrounding trees.[8]

Unlike Beijing and other ancient cities, Shanghai was and still is a modern commercial city. When the Red Guards in Shanghai joined the destructive bent of the cancel culture acts, they headed to the city's busiest commercial districts of Nanjing Road and Huaihai Road. They smashed the signboards of many famous and old stores and forbade the selling of high-end products such as the fine bread from Lao Dachang, the "butter cream" from Taishan Restaurant, and the shrimp noodles from Canglang Pavilion. Cafés, billiards, and jewelry and antique shops were ordered to close.[9]

It is heartbreaking for me now to have seen the monuments to our history being torn down in my own hometown of Chengdu. One such destruction was Huang Cheng Ba, which had stood in the city's very center for at least four hundred years. Huang Cheng Ba was nicknamed Small Forbidden City because it was modeled after the Forbidden City in Beijing, built by the son of the Ming dynasty's first emperor. Although it's been decades since I last saw Huang Cheng Ba, I can still picture its walls as well as its Tiananmen-like tower. I am grateful for having a visual memory, because Huang Cheng Ba was torn down to make room for the Long Live the Victory of Mao Zedong Thought Exhibition Hall, accompanied by a giant statue of Mao.

Most of the statues in China at the time of the Great Cultural Revolution were religious figures in temples and other places of worship. The sanctity of those statues did not protect them from the destructive hands of the Red Guards who sought to wipe society clean of traditional culture. Anything held dear by the people of China was even more of a target to the Red Guards, as was demonstrated when they stormed the Summer Palace in Beijing to tear down a giant statue of Buddha and knocked off the heads of other statues of Buddha along their path.[10] Countless Buddha statues all over China were beheaded or totally destroyed, lost forever as part of the Chinese heritage.

On August 26, 1966, the Destroy the Four Olds campaign reached Tibet. The Red Guards, made up of both Han Chinese and Tibetans, raided Jokhang Temple in Lhasa, the most sacred temple in Tibet.[11]

Four days before the attack on the Jokhang Temple, more than two hundred Hui (Chinese Muslim) students rebelled and took over the Niujie Mosque in Beijing. The students presented orders to the imams (Muslim prayer leaders): 1) hand over all the Quran, 2) no superstitious activities (meaning religious activities) allowed, 3) reform the imams through physical labor, and 4) ban Muslim robes.[12]

You may ask why the Muslim students would attack their own religion. Because these Muslim students had also been indoctrinated by the CCP, and now they were Red Guards who believed in nothing but Marxism.

Not satisfied with the destruction in public places, the Red Guards soon launched the home raid (*chao jia*) campaign to turn their focus to private homes where more Four Olds were suspected to be hidden. With the assistance of the CCP-directed neighborhood committees, the Red Guards had no problem locating their targets. Once they were at such a targeted home, the Red Guards would barge inside and ransack the home, grabbing anything they considered old.

As a young girl, I witnessed a chaotic scene of an entire neighborhood raided by Red Guards in Chengdu, and there was little that homeowners and their family members could do but watch helplessly, knowing if they resisted, they would probably be beaten and taken away for further punishment. The whole street was littered with items confiscated from homes—old furniture, antique vases, old family photos, old books...*everything*. In addition to the visual memory of this event, I will never forget the sounds of homeowners' crying and wailing, along with the sounds of their precious possessions being smashed or taken away.

A friend told me what happened to his family in Beijing. A group of neighborhood kids, no more than twelve years old, started their own "raid" operation. They went door to door to "raid." When they found nothing old at his home, they cut off his sister's hair instead. Why? Just because they could. The kids understood that they were automatically granted power by simply claiming to be Red Guards or Little Red Guards.

These home invasions occurred in vast numbers, with tens of thousands taking place over just several weeks. After the first Red Guard mass rally in Tiananmen Square in mid-August 1966, they raided more than 114,000 homes in Beijing alone in about a month's time. Almost simultaneously, a total of 84,222 homes were raided in Shanghai between August 23 and September 8. By the end of September, 12,000 homes in Tianjin had been ransacked.[13]

The Home Raid proved to be a massive looting campaign in

the name of a political ideology. Much ended in the pockets of the Red Guards and the Party leaders in charge of campaigns.

Too many families not only lost their long-held treasures, but also their personal items, including family photos, records, correspondences, manuscripts, and religious items. All were irreplaceable. Home Raid, although brief, was tied to some of the most notorious violence and thievery in the history of the world.

The Red Guards looked at the home raids as a "victory" to be celebrated. In October 1966, the Capital Red Guard Revolutionary Rebellion Exhibition was held in Beijing to display the bounty seized during the hunt for the Four Olds.[14]

But Mao was not pleased by the "victory" the Home Raid had achieved. He viewed it as a distraction from his real target. The rebel Red Guards eventually understood Mao's true intentions, so they shifted their aim for raids from the Black Class to the soon-to-be Black Class—those distrusted CCP bureaucrats Mao didn't like.

Some of the raided homes of those CCP new ruling class members were left open to the public to demonstrate their privileged lives. As a young girl, I once went to see an "open house" of a high-level official and was stunned by the incredible luxury these people lived in. While my family of five lived in a one-and-a-half–room unit, sharing a toilet and kitchen with four other families, this official lived in a mansion that offered four or five levels of living quarters for just his family and servants. I was in awe as I walked through the maze of luxurious rooms. I remember thinking that this official must be a bad guy, just like those bad landlords and capitalists in the movies who were able to live a life of luxury by exploiting the poor.

It is imperative for people to understand, especially American youth, that Communism's claim of *equity for all* is a myth. In China, the Communist liberators of the oppressed quickly became the new ruling class with privileges. Communists simply wiped out the old privileged class and replaced it with the new privileged class: themselves.

In 1966, everyone in my city of Chengdu was commanded to turn over anything considered to be any of the Four Olds. I remember my mother searching our home and came up with an old bottle of perfume. She promptly turned it over to the authorities. The Red Guards were determined to not miss *anything*.

There were plenty of other categories of cancelations to go around.

Fashion Canceled

Fancy clothes and fancy hairstyles, such as perms, were deemed "bourgeois" and banned. As a young girl, I knew that three styles were allowed for females: short cut, two short ponytails, and two short or long braided pigtails. Two short ponytails was pretty much my only hairstyle growing up, and fortunately I was never coerced into doing something different because I had the correct hairstyle. I did, however, witness Red Guards forcefully cut off a girl's hair because she dared to have a different style. In many cities, Red Guards set up "hair-fixing stations" to reinforce the ban.

The Red Guards of Maoism Middle School (renamed from Beijing 26th Middle School) published the "100 Rules for Destroy the Four Olds," which included a list of canceled items regarding fashion. On the list were jeans, skinny pants, pointed shoes, Western or Hong Kong–style fashion, jewelry, perfume, and cologne—everything that a girl or woman concerned for her appearance would want to own.[15]

The only desirable and luxury fashion was the army uniform; every boy or girl, young man or young woman, dreamed of owning one, although most had to settle for an imitation army uniform. The majority of people had access to only gray, dark blue, or black Mao-style clothing.

Femininity Canceled

Mao denounced femininity, proclaiming it to be too bourgeois and therefore not fit for revolution. He wrote in a poem that Chinese women preferred carrying weapons to wearing makeup. With that, female beauty was canceled. Men and women dressed and acted alike, and thus were indistinguishable from one another. Women were basically regarded as no different from men.

Before there was Superwoman, there were Mao's Iron Girls, who supposedly could do anything men could do and "hold up half a sky." This was Mao's expression of female power. During an address to the graduating class at the Coast Guard Academy in 2021, Joe Biden used Mao's remark about gender equality, admittedly borrowing from Mao's comments by saying, "Women hold up half the world."[16] Are you catching the drift of what's going on here? An American president in the twenty-first century invoking the words of one of the most brutal and powerful Communist dictators in the world as if they were his own.

During the ten years of the Cultural Revolution, Madame Mao maintained a unisex appearance, becoming the role model of what a Chinese female should look like: unisex.

Books Canceled

This included the banning and burning of both Chinese publications and foreign works. The few libraries that existed prior to the Cultural Revolution were closed and collections cleared. As an alternative to libraries, there used to be "little picture book" reading stations on many street corners. One could pay one or two cents to read a book at the station. I can remember reading *Snow White* and *Cinderella*, which are some of my precious pre–Cultural Revolution childhood memories. All of them were shut down and abolished, never to come back.

A large number of ancient books in private collections could be found in the Jiangsu and Zhejiang regions of China, an area rich in literary tradition. Of course, the Red Guards took notice of this. They confiscated numerous thread-bound ancient books of the Ming and Qing dynasties in the city of Ningbo alone. Instead of burning them, the Red Guards made sure the books were pulped (for recycling), altogether weighing in at more than eighty tons![17]

Allowed reading was reduced to Mao's *Little Red Book*, four volumes of Mao's works, plus works by Karl Marx, Lenin, and Stalin. New books published for juveniles were all about Communist heroes.

Common Sense Canceled

While staying busy Destroying the Four Olds, the Red Guards and many young students showed a determination to "dare to think, dare to speak, dare to act, and dare to rebel." Their examples of extremism, stupidity, and lack of common sense were boundless. Here are two examples:

- They demanded that the traffic police use Mao's *Little Red Book* in place of batons to direct traffic.
- They demanded that traffic lights be changed. Since RED was the color of revolution, it would now be the color designating GO, and GREEN would now mean STOP.

This is what happened when reckless youngsters were allowed to be in charge. The reversal of the meaning of colors at traffic lights caused countless traffic nightmares and was eventually stopped.[18]

If woke Social Justice Warriors in America had had their way, they would have canceled the "white man" icon that indicates when it is safe to cross the street. Why? Because some can even construe waiting for this safety symbol as akin to waiting for a white man to give permission to cross the street.[19]

* * *

The Red Guards would eventually expand beyond targeting traditional Chinese culture by targeting even the CCP culture that was no longer up to Mao's new political code. This included hundreds of movies and shows as well as countless songs and books that had been created since 1949.

There were more than six hundred movies made in China from 1949 to 1966. More than four hundred of those films were deemed counterrevolutionary "poison weeds" and were no longer allowed to be shown. Only a handful of those not deemed as "poison weeds" were permitted to continue being shown.[20]

Song of Youth was a popular novel published in 1958 and made into a popular movie. It tells the story of how young patriotic Chinese intellectuals in the 1930s grew to become Communist revolutionaries under the guidance of the CCP. However, both the novel and movie were denounced as big "poison weeds" because there was too much bourgeois sentiment. Both the book and the movie were banned, and the author Yang Mo was canceled.[21] It is the American version of "not woke enough."

What happened to Yang Mo and her work happened to almost all Chinese writers and their works during the Cultural Revolution. Many of them were not only canceled, but were prosecuted, exiled to labor camps, or even killed.

The old saying holds true for all dictators and many in positions of power: "Do as I say and not what I do." Mao proved to be a hypocrite when it came to the Four Olds.

When traditional Chinese operas were banned, Mao Zedong watched a set of specially filmed performances in his private residence. Lower-level Party leaders could watch foreign movies barred from public view, rationalized as "study." Zhu De, the politically inactive onetime commander of the Red Army, passed the Cultural Revolution watching movies by Abbott and Costello, those well-known American comedians of the 1940s. I can't help but be reminded of the hypocrisy of the American progressive elites who, for example, fly private jets to meetings to plot how to convince the rest of us to give up fossil fuels, gas-powered cars, or even gas stoves. I am also reminded of BLM founders acquiring multimillion-dollar mansions for themselves.

While Mao urged the Red Guards to Destroy the Four Olds, he held on to his love for old ideas and old culture that would help him to maintain power. Apart from reading Marxist works, such as *The Communist Manifesto*—which he claimed to have read more than one hundred times[22]—one of the books he read most often was *Zizhi Tongjian* (in English: *Comprehensive Mirror for Aid in Government*), an ancient chronicle of Chinese history from 403 BC to 959 AD detailing the rise and fall of sixteen dynasties, fortunes and misfortunes of all the emperors; as well as court infights and political intrigue. Mao loved this particular book and claimed that he read the lengthy work seventeen times.[23] It is easy to see why: He wanted to learn how emperors over time maneuvered in the power game and won.

Many scholars regard Mao as the combination of Karl Marx and Emperor Qin, the first emperor who united China and the most notorious tyrant in Chinese history. Mao was truly a Communist emperor. If he honestly disliked old tradition, he would have stopped the revolutionary masses from chanting "Long live Chairman Mao," an old, out-of-date, feudalistic tradition for the Chinese subjects to address their rulers. But it was only appropriate, since Mao was indeed the true ruler over the Chinese people.

Marxism has proven to be highly adaptive. It quickly attaches itself to the host culture and mutates to something more potent and sinister. In China, it is feudalistic totalitarianism. In America, it is Freud and liberalism, which has now mutated into identity ideology and woke-ism. Basically, it is Marxism with Chinese characteristics, and Marxism with American characteristics, respectively.

The Cultural Revolution also aimed to cancel people: people of the Black Class, people of authority, people of the expert class, and people with *wrong* thoughts.

When I was about ten, I was hospitalized after a bike accident. While in the hospital, I befriended a janitor who cleaned my ward. She was an older woman, always smiling and quick to comfort me with kind words. I would eventually learn from a nurse that this janitor had at one time been one of the highest-ranking doctors in the hospital. She had been canceled for being a reactionary academic authority, simply because of her education and training predating the revolution. She had been tagged with a label given to professionals and intellectuals—a status that made them enemies of the Mao regime and its exercise of cancel culture.

I was not surprised when I learned her story. My school principal was canceled. The mayor of my city was canceled. The governor of my province was canceled. And the president of China was canceled.

Cancel culture in America is just another version of Destroy the Four Olds. It aims to cancel traditional American values and founding principles. In fact, the progressives want to dismantle more than American culture; they want to undo all of Western civilization.

Start with the avowed Marxists who have been leading the BLM movement. These are not your civil rights activists and advocates from recent decades—they are Marxists looking to tear down this country and build back with progressivism, which is just a name disguising Marxism, socialism, or Communism. They have infiltrated all our institutions through their "long march." They are the ones pushing cancel culture across the board.

Douglas Murray, in his book *The War on the West*, explains how the progressives are looking to lay waste to—that is, cancel—the entirety of Western civilization. In his introduction, he writes: "In recent years it has become clear that there is a war going on: a war on the West. This is not like earlier wars, where armies clash, and victors are declared. It is a cultural war, and it is being waged remorselessly against all the roots of the Western tradition and against everything good that the Western tradition has produced."[24] The key phrase in Murray's intro segment is *all the roots*. Both Chinese and American cultural revolutions want to uproot traditional cultures. Period.

The old world the progressives want to destroy is the so-called "white world," because *white* is synonymous with *Western*. *Whiteness* is at the root of American founding. This *whiteness* is best demonstrated by a "white chart" that was posted on the website of the Smithsonian's National Museum of African American History and Culture.[25] Although it has since been removed after an outcry, it serves as a perfect summary of what the progressives intend to destroy:

- Rugged individualism
- Nuclear family structure
- Emphasis on scientific methods
- Eurocentric history
- Protestant work ethic
- Christianity
- Status, power, & authority
- Materialism
- Future orientation

- Time: rigid time schedules and time is money
- Eurocentric aesthetics
- White-centric holidays
- Eurocentric Justice
- Competition

Although many of us have heard of Critical Race Theory, it's likely many have not heard of Critical Whiteness Studies, which Barbara Applebaum, an educator at Syracuse University writing for Oxford Research Encyclopedias, describes as "a growing field of scholarship whose aim is to reveal the invisible structures that produce and reproduce white supremacy and privilege."[26] The University of Kansas now offers an "Angry White Male Studies" class to examine the "rise" of the "angry white male" in the United States.[27] University of Chicago planned to offer a course entitled The Problem of Whiteness.[28] This seems to be a fast-growing field of study for students, many of whom acquire student loans to study.

Robin DiAngelo, author of *White Fragility*, writes that "a positive white identity is an impossible goal. White identity is inherently racist; white people do not exist outside the system of white supremacy."[29] That sounds a lot like DiAngelo is saying that being born white automatically makes a person a racist. And that sounds a lot like what Mao said about being born into the Black Class automatically makes a person the enemy of the state.

Canceling whiteness is a euphemism for canceling Western civilization. Yes, America was founded by white settlers and is rooted in Western civilization.

America is the first nation in all of human history built on the foundation that acknowledges ALL humans are created equal and free, and that their inalienable rights were bestowed upon them by

God—not from kings, emperors, or the government. It is because of this fundamental belief that America fought a bloody civil war to eradicate slavery, an institution as old as recorded history and not exclusive to those with black skin tone. It is also because of this fundamental belief of individual freedom that America has abolished slavery and has been a magnet for freedom-loving people all around the world since its founding.

People in countries under Communism such as Russia, China, Cuba, and Eritrea reject Marxism and Communism; they do it wherever they are and wherever it is implemented. People in countries under Communism or socialism don't see the bearded man Karl Marx as white, they see him as evil!

Obviously, the BLM Marxists don't mind that Karl Marx was white. They were attracted to his evil ideology because it provides the playbook for how to tear down a society.

One of most public and visible cancel culture actions in America is the toppling of monuments and statues. Unlike in China, where most statues are in temples or monasteries, in Western countries, monuments and statues are usually found in public spaces and the heart of a city or town. The action of tearing down these structures created fear-driven spectacles that have the effect of demonstrating the progressives' power that they are in control of our culture and our history.

Former President Trump asked, "So this week, it is Robert E. Lee...I wonder, is it George Washington next week? And is it Thomas Jefferson the week after? You know, you really do have to ask yourself, where does it stop?" The liberal media mocked Trump. In 2017, the *New York Times* quoted John Fabian Witt, a professor of history at Yale University, who stated that "Mr. Witt called Mr. Trump's warning of a slippery slope a 'red herring.'"

There have been, after all, no calls to tear down the Washington Monument."[30]

Fast-forward to 2020 after the death of George Floyd, the toppling of statues reached a fever pitch. Statues were pulled down left and right. Exactly as Trump predicted, the woke mobs went after any statues. Among those torn down or defaced were statues of George Washington, Thomas Jefferson, Abraham Lincoln, Teddy Roosevelt, Frederick Douglass, Christopher Columbus, and the Virgin Mary.[31]

In 2017, I made a trip to Richmond to visit some historic sites, where I ran into a local art professor. We struck up a conversation about the statues. At that time, Charlottesville, where the statue toppling movement had started, still seemed far away. This professor did not give much thought to the possibility that the mobs would eventually make their way to Richmond. I visited Richmond again in the summer of 2022. The celebrated "Monument Avenue" has now become the "Monumentless Avenue," as all the monuments and statues were assaulted and removed. The crowning spectacle of all the toppling of statues in America is no doubt that of the removal of Robert E. Lee's statue on Monument Avenue.

Since then, a coalition called Reimagine Monument Avenue has been formed. Some suggested a "social justice trail" be created instead. (The page has since been taken down.)[32] That is exactly what the Red Guards would have done. Tearing down the past, the history, and the memory of a nation to replace it with the symbolism of Marxist ideology.

As these aforementioned statues are being removed from public squares, new statues of the likes of the *martyred* George Floyd, Breonna Taylor, and BLM protestor Jen Reid (a UK BLM activist whose protest photo with raised arm went viral) are going up in their place.

While there are no consequences for the woke mobs tearing down the old statues, the New York City Police Department Hate Crimes Task Force in 2021 charged thirty-seven-year-old Micah Beals of Manhattan with second-degree criminal mischief for vandalizing a New York City statue of George Floyd.[33] Let's not forget that Floyd was a career criminal!

It is indeed a world turned upside down.

Just like the Red Guards, the woke mobs understand the power that names have to remind people of virtue, of shared values, of their heroes, and, most of all, their history. These names must be erased, too, to make room for progressives' virtue, value, and heroes.

In northern Virginia, where I live, two public schools that were named after our founding fathers and native Virginians, Thomas Jefferson and George Mason, were renamed Oak Street Elementary School and Meridian High School, respectively.[34] In Detroit, hometown of the celebrated neurosurgeon and former Republican presidential candidate Ben Carson, the school board voted to change the name of the Benjamin Carson High School of Science and Medicine. The reason? Having Ben Carson's name on the high school is "synonymous with having Trump's name on our school in blackface," a board member claimed.[35]

Streets and highways have fallen victim to name changers as well. A section of 16th Street in front of the White House in Washington, DC, is now ceremonially named Black Lives Matter Plaza.[36] What's next? How far will the name change go? Will it go so far as to change the name of the White House to the Black House?

Again, just like in the Chinese Cultural Revolution, the changing of names has taken place with various well-known American food brands as well. Some popular food brands that are looking to make changes to steer their products away from racial stereotypes include the popular Aunt Jemima syrup and Uncle Ben's rice. They both deserve retirement, as NBC News put it, because they're racist myths of happy Black servitude.[37] To the progressives, Aunt Jemima and Uncle Ben should be angry and raise their fists like the BLM rioters. Replacing the happy Uncle Ben and Aunt Jemima on American store shelves now is the "blond" drag queen RuPaul for Cheez-It. RuPaul is shown very happy on the cracker box.

Classic books many Americans grew up with that are now deemed racist have been banned, including *The Adventures of Tom Sawyer*, which I enjoyed reading so much in college in China. The latest added to the list of cancelations are Dr. Seuss's works, which I used to read to my son when he was little. There is irony to this. When parents demand pornographic books be taken out of school libraries, the left complain that their free speech is violated. Stacy Langton, a mother of six, became a national figure for fighting against and exposing the Fairfax school board for stocking graphic pornography books in the school library. The two books Langton brought to the school board meeting are *Lawn Boy* by Jonathan Evison and *Gender Queer: A Memoir* by Maia Kobabe.[38] Not on the parents' side is the American Library Association, which claims to fight against "censorship" to include *ALL* books in library collections, *except* those they don't like.

Any person or group that poses a threat to the agenda of the progressives is at risk for cancelation. Strong men who abide by traditional gender roles are now considered dangerous and said to be suffering from toxic masculinity. The only cure is—yes, you guessed it—cancelation.

Toxic masculinity is no longer simply defined by a notion that implies "manliness." It perpetuates domination, homophobia, and aggression, especially toward women. The common saying "boys will be boys" is no longer indicative of an innocent stage to be coached through during boyhood but believed to be, instead, a toxic and dangerous threat that must be swiftly neutralized. "Experts" suggest parents intervene early by providing their young boys with only gender-neutral toys so that they don't foster those threatening male traits![39]

Toxic masculinity is a buzzword used to create division and push an agenda. It is also a tactic used to neutralize any threat or resistance to that agenda and to create a population that is more pliable and easier to control.

During the Cultural Revolution in China, the CCP approached the idea of gender definition and sexuality from the other side of the coin, doing all it could to cancel femininity. Today, the CCP has taken the task again to cancel out femininity, this time, not in women but in men. They aim to reengineer grown-up "sissy men" to become real men, men with "toxic masculinity." It was reported in September 2021 that regulators of the Chinese government, exercising its usual heavy-handed, domineering ways, have banned effeminate men from appearing on television or video streaming sites. The reason is simple: toxic masculinity is good for Xi Jinping's military and global ambitions.[40]

Nonbinary/gender-fluid activists think they are demonstrating the ultimate freedom to be whatever they choose to be. I am afraid their "freedom" is just one of the progressives' tools for tearing down tradition. Once absolute power is in hand, those in power will allow us to be only that which they want us to be, as demonstrated by the CCP.

A gift from American Marxists to cultural Marxism is the erasure of women. We are in a bizarre era where individuals either cannot or will not define a "woman" because of the woke mob. The question "what is a woman" could not be answered by then–US Supreme Court nominee, Justice Ketanji Brown Jackson. Jackson found this question too difficult to answer because she "is not a biologist." Responding to this absurdity, Republican Senator Marsha Blackburn said: "The fact that you can't give me a straight answer about something as fundamental as what a woman is underscores the dangers of the kind of progressive education that we are hearing about."[41]

Sensitivities and confusion around gender are so pervasive that many proactively state their preferred pronouns, as I experienced at my former workplace. This is yet another tactic progressives use to dominate the culture and identify who is with them and who is the enemy.

It is with a sigh of relief that I am no longer in the woke machine that exists in corporate America, because the crime of misgendering anyone in 2022 is a dangerous and serious offense. Schools, too, are a hotbed for gender ideology. Public schools in Virginia's Fairfax County may now expel elementary students for "maliciously misgendering" people. That's not the worst of it, either. Anyone charged with "malicious misgendering" of fellow students could be subject to charges equivalent in scope to assault and battery.[42] At a middle school in Wisconsin, three students were accused of "sexual harassment" for using biologically correct pronouns in addressing another student.[43]

American Marxists created identity Marxism, which goes a long way in destabilizing American culture and furthering division within communities and families. I am not sure how gender identity Marxism would work in China, however. The word *nan* and *nv* in the Chinese language are used for both sex and gender.

When Mao canceled femininity, he made China a genderless society, while America's progressives are trying to create endless genders, which is really nothing more than another version of the goal to achieve "genderlessness."

Based on Dictionary.com's definition, we are told that cancel culture targets famous people or corporations via social media. What must be understood is that it is not actually the individual or company that is being canceled. It is the idea behind that person or corporation.

In 2020, while most corporations aligned their brands with BLM, donating millions of dollars to the organization for the right to carry the BLM logo on their websites, products, or merchandise, one company did not jump on the bandwagon. As a result, Goya Foods became the target of the woke mob and of threats of cancel culture. Not only did Goya's CEO, Robert Unanue, not bow to the corrupt BLM organization, but he let it be known that he supported President Donald Trump. Unanue and Goya quickly became a target of the progressives' vicious attacks.

Soon after one well documented attack, Unanue gleefully announced on Michael Berry's radio show that Marxist Congresswoman Alexandria Ocasio-Cortez was named "employee of the month" at Goya Foods after her call for a boycott of the company resulted in a 1,000 percent increase in sales.[44] AOC's efforts to inflict damage upon a company rooted in her own Latin culture backfired beautifully.

The cultural cancelations have even touched bestselling Harry Potter author J. K. Rowling. She riled many of her fans with social media posts supporting a British woman fired from her job after posting tweets that were perceived as transphobic. For this offense, she was banned from attending 2021's Harry Potter anniversary special.[45]

The progressives believe all conservatives, Republicans, and libertarians should be canceled as racists and white supremacists.

If there is any poetic justice in this, it is that it is not safe even for those on the left. Cancel culture is a monster. Once created and unleashed, it will eat everything in its path, including itself. It does not see the left vs. the right. Cancel culture does not discriminate and the pendulum may swing in any direction at any time. We are seeing more and more of the progressives being canceled for not being *woke enough*.

Tom Hanks, a popular movie star and ally of the left, was under attack by cancel cultural mobs. Reason? He may not be a racist, but he is definitely not an *anti-racist*. According to Eric Deggans, an NPR TV critic, Hanks has made a career out of playing righteous white men. In his editorial, Deggans asserts that the actor should become an "anti-racist" in order to redeem his sin.[46] I can visualize Deggans putting a tall cone hat on Hanks and presiding over a struggle session for the actor while holding high Kendi's book *How To Be an Antiracist* in place of Mao's *Little Red Book*.

Not even Ellen DeGeneres was safe from cancel culture. This iconic darling of entertainment's LGBTQ community saw the tides turn on her in 2020 when her reputation as the nicest and most generous television talk show host was challenged by disgruntled employees who accused her of fostering a hostile work environment that was riddled with instances of sexual harassment. Both Ellen and *The Ellen DeGeneres Show* were canceled.[47]

Nothing can stop the woke mob from going after people to cancel, not even the first Black president, Barack Obama. A Chicago school district wanted to rename Thomas Jefferson Middle School after the forty-fourth president. But the immigration activists would not allow it. They pointed out that Obama deported more undocumented immigrants than any president in history. They called Obama an "oppressor" and "Deporter in Chief."[48]

Bright Sheng knows something about the cancel culture in Mao's China, as well as in today's America. Like me, Sheng also lived through the Cultural Revolution, during which the Red Guards took away his family piano during the Home Raid. He also experienced cancel culture in America on the University of Michigan campus where he was professor of music composition. In November 2021, a group of students demanded that the school administration fire Sheng for creating a classroom space they described as "unsafe."

What made them feel unsafe was a movie Sheng showed in class that illustrated how a play was adapted for the opera. It was the 1965 version of Shakespeare's *Othello*. The legendary actor Laurence Olivier wore blackface to portray the character of Othello, a choice that was controversial even back in the '60s.

When confronted by the school's administration regarding the students' outrage, Sheng offered a profuse apology, admitting he now understood it had been a mistake for him to screen it for the class. An apology was not enough for these gravely offended students, who acted as if they had been traumatized by the experience.[49]

It's scary to think that a group of intolerant and thin-skinned college students can have such a profound effect on the career of a professor who unintentionally offended them while trying to open their minds to impart various cultural insights related to the arts. Not the other students, nor the administration, nor his colleagues, were brave enough to say what was not right or just. For Sheng, this was a reminder of dark times spent under a Communist regime in China, a history that those woke students and professors know little about.

In the conclusion of his book *The War on the West*, author Douglas Murray writes:

> Today the West faces challenges without and threats within. But no greater threat exists than that which comes from people inside the West intent on pulling apart the fabric of our societies, piece by piece. By assaulting the majority populations in these countries. By saying that our histories are entirely reprehensible and have nothing good to be said about them. By claiming that everything in our past that has led up to our present is irredeemably riddled with sin and that while these same sins have beset every society in history, the debtor should knock at only one door. And most importantly by those who pretend that a civilization that has given more to the world in knowledge, understanding, and culture than any other in history somehow has nothing whatsoever to be said for it. What is anyone to say or do in the face of such myopic, omnipresent hatred?[50]

How chilling Murray's description is! What he describes is taking place in America and in the West exactly how it happened in China more than fifty years ago. Mao convinced the Red Guards and the Chinese people that there was nothing good in China's three-thousand–year history.

I am a fan of Glenn Loury and follow his podcast. Loury is an African American intellectual, a Merton P. Stoltz Professor of Economics at Brown University, and a senior fellow at the Manhattan Institute. His work focuses on affirmative action, the Black family, and Black patriotism.[51]

I have heard him say in many episodes of his podcast that he is a man of the West.

In an April 2022 interview with *Chronicles Magazine*, Loury was quoted as saying:

I agree that elites have lost confidence. It's not just that they don't any longer embrace and propagate this sense of pride or ownership of the Western civilization that we inhabit. They don't even recognize what it is and what is unique about it. My God, slavery is a constant of human experience for thousands of years! What's new is emancipation en masse as a result of a movement for human rights. That's a completely new idea in human history before the 18th century. And where does it come from? We could go through the pedigree, and certainly Christianity is going to be part of that. That's 2,000 years plus of the evolution of our social and moral thought, but we [society at large] don't want to embrace the Christian foundations of our civilization.[52]

What he said is so true. In that sense, I will say that I have become a woman of the West, because I embrace the Western values of natural rights and individual liberty. When white people are told to be ashamed of the culture that has produced them, and to denounce their whiteness, I say that I am happy to be called "white adjacent," a slur the progressives assigned to successful Asians. I will not allow anyone to cancel me.

CHAPTER 8

Destruction of Family

On November 3, 2021, the day after the election, I was invited by Fox News for an interview to discuss Republican candidate Glenn Youngkin's victory in the tight gubernatorial race for the increasingly blue state of Virginia. I became emotional and choked up—on national TV! At that moment, all the memories came back: the countless rallies, door knocking, standing in cold rain for nine hours handing out sample ballots at the polling station, and the agony of waiting for the final result…It was such a hard-fought battle that when I learned about the victory, not just for the office of governor but also for that of lieutenant governor and attorney general of Virginia, I cried.

What was his winning issue? Parental rights in education. Since my speech at the Loudoun County School Board in June

2021, I have had the opportunity to meet with and talk to count-less parents across the country. They all shared the same concerns: "They are coming after our children" and "They want to break up our family."

Their fear is real and justified. Marxists are coming after our children. Marxists want to break up our family. This is not a hidden agenda. This is openly declared in Karl Marx's *Communist Manifesto*: "Abolition [*aufhebung*] of the family!" They mean it. They have done that in the USSR, in China, and anywhere they manage to get a foothold. Now they are doing it in America.

In traditional Chinese society, the long-established idea of the family as an institution was regarded as something sacred. In such family units, extended and multigenerational, the head of the family—mostly a senior male figure—exercised profound influence and commanded the loyalty of the clan. The importance of this in Chinese society was not only to organize kinship through inherent blood relations, but also to establish ethical relationships with filial piety at the core. That in turn became the foundation for traditional Chinese virtue. It had worked for so long, dating back two millenniums.

The original Chinese character for the word *filial piety* is *xiao*, or 孝, which depicts a child helping an elderly person walk. Filial piety is an important part of Confucian teaching. It preaches that people should love, obey, and care for their parents; respect them by virtue of good conduct to maintain a positive reputation for the family, for the reason that an ethical and harmonious family is the foundation of an ethical and harmonious society. Yet, filial piety was never taught to us either in school or home under Mao. During the Cultural Revolution, it was regarded as part of the Four Olds to be condemned.

This concept of traditional family was first assailed by the May Fourth Movement in 1919. It can be described as a progressive student movement, marked by a protest by thousands of college students at Tiananmen Square in Beijing against the government's weak response to the Treaty of Versailles, which permitted Japan to retain Shandong territories that had been surrendered to Germany after the Siege of Tsingtao (aka Qingdao) years earlier.

The student-led demonstration ignited protests across the country, which bolstered Chinese nationalism. The movement eventually evolved into a New Cultural Movement, which rejected traditional Chinese culture and welcomed Western ideas, especially science and democracy. One of the new ideas was the promotion of the Western nuclear family model and the rejection of the traditional Chinese model. By the time the CCP came into power in 1949, the nuclear family had become commonplace, at least in urban areas.

The May Fourth Movement was significant. It produced many of the future leaders of the Chinese Communist Party (CCP), laying the groundwork for Mao's eventual surge to power and fueling his obsession for eliminating the old/traditional and replacing it with the new, effectively tearing apart a nation—and millions of Chinese families—in the process.

Mao, however, obviously saw something he liked in the traditional model of extended and multigeneration family, where a patriarch was in charge of an entire clan. He saw himself as that patriarch and the entire Chinese nation as his clan. Mao took advantage of this aspect of the traditional family concept and imposed it as a new family model to redirect the loyalty and obedience away from individual families and over to himself and to the Party: the "revolutionary big family." It sounded like a grandiose description of something new and exciting, when actually it signaled destruction and devastation for the Chinese family as traditionalists knew it.

The CCP's adoption of the revolutionary big family philosophy was a classic case of manipulation of the masses. The CCP reengineered language to help convince or persuade the Chinese people to embrace this new kind of family. In so doing, the Chinese people would supposedly be nurtured, cared for, loved, and protected as one gigantic, tightly knit family. I often heard my mother use this term whenever she recalled her days as a young Communist in the CCP army.

With Mao's proclamation of a new revolutionary big family, there was a new patriarchy fulfilled by Mao and the Party. The children were now bound by strict loyalty to their "big family" father/mother, who effectively replaced their biological parents. The head of the big family had the sole authority to decide what was good for every family member—even when the family members numbered in the hundreds of millions.

A very similar thing is going on in America today, in which the progressives are working hard and progressing in making the idea of abolishing the nuclear family more palatable. We will examine it in more detail in the second half of this chapter. In fact, these American Marxists are adopting Mao's revolutionary big family approach. The template is right there in front of them, put in place in China before and during its Cultural Revolution.

Here's a segment of what openDemocracy.net has published on its website, an opinion piece entitled "Family Abolition Isn't about Ending Love and Care. It's about Extending It to Everyone." In the commentary, the author argues that "societies which rely on the fact that the family has to be the only site of loving and caring relationships are inherently unequal and undermine solidarity."[1] Just like Mao arguing in favor of the revolutionary big family, "extending love" really means letting the state be the parents.

The indoctrination of the revolutionary big family and the people's commune campaign (which I discuss later) did unimaginable damage to Chinese families. The Cultural Revolution shredded the remaining fabric of the family. Many families became deeply divided, with members turning against one another—well beyond the level of political divisiveness we see in America today, where conservative family members and their left-leaning kin are in resolute dispute. In China, such political differences within families, especially during the Cultural Revolution, became so intense as to be matters of life and death in many instances. No story was more horrifying than that of Zhang Hongbing. Below is a recounting of the horror based on an interview of Zhang by the *Global Times* in 2016.[2]

At the age of sixteen in 1970, Zhang, along with his father, denounced his mother, Fang Zhongmou, to local government officials. This was in response to her criticism of Chairman Mao, which took place in the privacy of their home. But there was no privacy/secret in the Mao-engineered world—certainly not for "enemies of the state," such as Fang. Note here that Zhang had joined the Red Guards at the age of thirteen, which inspired him to change his name to Hongbing, which means "red guard." This was done with the support of his parents.

In 1966, Zhang's only sister died unexpectedly. Meanwhile, his father was subjected to nearly two years of criticism and struggle sessions amidst charges that he had followed a "bourgeois reactionary line."

After Zhang's father was finally released, Fang, the mom, was put through brutal struggle sessions as well. She suffered severe psychological and emotional anguish. Almost totally broken, Fang was heard calling Mao a "traitor" while praising Liu Shaoqi, the former Chinese president who had been purged by Mao. Fang's proclamations led to an argument with her son. Zhang, with his father's backing, reported his mother to local officials, which led to her arrest.

In April 1970, less than two months after her arrest, Fang was executed.

As much as Zhang was haunted by his role in contributing to his mother's death, he said years later that, at the time, it was an easy choice to make—out of deference to his real parent, Mao. He had an obligation to his "father" to report anyone who questioned or criticized the "Great Leader," whether the perpetrator was a stranger or a parent. This was mainstream thinking among the young, at least during the Cultural Revolution. Zhang's story was a symbol of the Cultural Revolution era, when the nuclear family was not only under attack but also subject to internal division, with family members turning against each other in defense of Mao.

Horrifying as this story is, it was by no means an isolated incident. There were countless instances of children turning against their parents and/or turning them in for supposedly anti-Mao misdeeds, including former high-ranking government officials. After President Liu Shaoqi was purged by Mao in December 1966, Liu Tao, his daughter, posted a big-character poster of her own entitled "Rebel against Liu Shaoqi. Follow Chairman Mao to Carry on Revolution for a Lifetime." And she wasn't finished! A week later, she and her younger brother Liu Yunzhen posted another poster, this time displaying the message, "Look at Liu Shaoqi's Ugly Soul."

Clearly, they tried hard to demonstrate that they had placed their loyalty to Mao above family. As Liu Tao said, "If my family doesn't want me, I know the Party and people want me!"[3] Isn't it ironic that Zhang's mother died in defense of Liu Shaoqi while Liu's own children openly denounced him?

This was expected of family members after years of Communist indoctrination. Such action was known as *hua qing jie xian*, which meant to "draw a clear line" to display loyalty to the Party. It became part of the cultural norm.

Everyone was expected to report on whoever was suspected of being a "counterrevolutionary." The purpose was to separate oneself from the "class enemy," even if the "enemy" turned out to be one's own parents or children.

The new ruler of China, Xi Jinping, and his family were also victims of the Cultural Revolution. His father, a high-ranking CCP official, was purged by Mao in the early '60s, which placed him and his entire family into the category of Black Class. At the young age of thirteen, Xi Jinping was targeted by rebel Red Guards and deemed an "active counterrevolutionary" because he was heard complaining about the Cultural Revolution. He was condemned in a struggle session with five adults. His mother had to sit in the audience and raise her fist, shouting along with the slogan "Down with Xi Jinping."[4] One day, according to Xi Jinping, he slipped out of the juvenile detention center for children of purged CCP officials. He ran home and told his mother he was hungry. Instead of giving him food, his mother reported him and had him sent back to the authority.[5]

My father never stopped working on "drawing the line" from his Black Class mother. I never heard him talk about her and learned nothing from him about his childhood stories. My grandmother was a shame to us, and we tried to hide the fact that we were related to her.

My father kept many of the family's private papers, including the very first written evaluation given to me at age of three by the preschool I attended. In the "moral development" section, I received a positive evaluation from my teacher because I understood that Chairman Mao was our great leader, that he lived in Beijing, that he loved us as his children, and that I wanted to be his good child.

You can see that children were being brainwashed at a very young age, as early as three years old in my case. The goal of Mao and the CCP was to program us into believing that *they* were indeed our parents—our caregivers and providers. And it worked, showing itself in everything that we did and said, including the songs we were taught to sing, with lyrics such as, "Sky is vast. Earth is vast. Neither is as vast as Party's benevolence. Father is dear. Mother is dear. Neither as dear as Chairman Mao."

The CCP's mind-bending indoctrination of Chinese children and adults was indeed appalling. It hit me what I had really been through as a child when I watched the student protest in Tiananmen Square in 1989 while I was attending college in Florida. As I was glued to the TV screen, I was completely confident that the People's Liberation Army (PLA) soldiers called to the scene would not open fire on the demonstrators. Growing up, we believed what we were taught: PLA soldiers were the sons and brothers of the people (*ren min zi di bing*). How would it ever be possible that our sons and brothers would fire upon members of their big revolutionary family? But that was exactly what happened.

The CCP had two complementary actions going on at the same time. While they were hard at work promoting the revolutionary big family, they were also busy undermining the nuclear family. The idea was to give prominence and power to the former while pulling out all the stops to try to weaken and destroy the latter.

Some of the groundwork for such a reversal of what would define "family" in China had already been put in place several years before the start of the Cultural Revolution. That was the people's commune campaign of 1958–1962, which was a political push to collectivize all land that had been redistributed to peasants from the landlords. This operation was implemented to have all rural areas in China converted into communes (not at all to be confused with the American hippie communes that cropped up in the 1960s). The purpose of such a movement in China was to pave the road to socialism and thus eradicate private ownership of property once and for all. But there was really more to it. And the ulterior motive was a formidable push to collectivize and destroy *families*.

Hong Kong–based Phoenix Television broadcasted a documentary series in 2013 entitled *Utopia Experiment* that told the story of the disastrous CCP people's commune based on what took place at the Chayashan commune in Henan Province. Chayashan was China's first commune and was eventually singled out as a model to be emulated throughout the country. The documentary offered a rich source of valuable historic footage, photos, and interviews that provided a compelling story involving those who were instrumental in pioneering the commune campaign in Chayashan and beyond.

In episode three, "The Climax—The Short-Lived 'Happy Life,'"[6] we can watch former commune members recounting how every aspect of their lives was collectivized as if they were cattle: collective dining, collective kindergarten, and collective schooling where children lived away from parents, and men and women among the working force lived a collective life in separate dorms. The Chinese government made it all sound so wonderful, promising the communal residents all kinds of freebies through the CCP's mouthpiece *Red Flag* magazine (1958, issue eight). It listed "ten freebies": free food, free clothing, free childbirth and childcare, free funeral and burial, free wedding, free education, free housing, free heating, free haircuts, and free movies, etc."[7] This documentary series was an excellent production. I wish it would be translated and made available to the American audience.

As you might have guessed, these ten "freebies," and others not listed, all comprised empty promises no different from many other exciting and beautiful things that Mao and the CCP promised to the Chinese people. The food, for instance, was not free. It was collected from every household and shared by all. It lasted until it ran out and then the famine hit, after which all the other freebies vanished. People compare Mao's socialism to a picture of a delicious meat pie hanging in the sky. You can see it but will never be able to reach it.

With traditional families, meals were normally shared by family members seated together, having what Americans refer to as "quality family time." But during the people's commune campaign, private meals were replaced by "big collective dining" (*da shi tong*). Every household was required to hand over not only its grain and livestock, but also cooking utensils, tables, and stools to the commune's mass dining halls to be shared by everyone there. Some had to walk as far as two miles for their meals, as these were peasants living in scattered villages. One of the men interviewed for the documentary said that the only thing he could remember that he did not have to share with others was his toothbrush.

It was true that the free dining, free childcare, free schooling, and free dorms from the communal living supposedly liberated women from all their usual domestic chores in theory, but it did not actually translate into a steady diet of restful days for them. Those "liberated" women were now forced to join the labor force and work in the fields alongside men. As you might now surmise, the communes were nothing more than Communist plantations.

Not everyone at the time was fooled by the CCP's lies and twisted promises about how the communes and their forced collectivized living would benefit everyone. Writing in 1959, in just the second year of the people's commune campaign, Zhou Jingwen, author of *Ten Years of Storm*, said that he believed the main purpose of collective life was to break apart the family structure. This would allow the government to control the people more easily and effectively. By destroying family structures millions of times over, the CCP was aiming to isolate individuals, alienate couples, and separate children from their parents at an early age. Thus, they would become slave labor for the CCP, with children destined to become property of the Party from the day they were born.[8]

Mao's totalitarian-like affection for communal living brings to mind the proclamation that "it takes a village to raise a child" made popular by Hillary Clinton in her book entitled *It Takes a Village* some thirty years ago. Hillary Clinton advocated government-driven social reforms for the well-being of children. It appeared that she was virtually ripping a page out of Mao's playbook of collectivism, essentially saying that there was really no such thing as individual success or achievement, and that any such accomplishment was actually the work of a "village" pulling together and supporting the community. Totalitarian minds think alike.

One day I was on my way to a store during the time I was writing this chapter, and I noticed a sign for a new preschool about to open called Village, with the word *Gateway* scrawled above it in smaller type. My immediate reaction was that this school had to be inspired by Hillary's pet phrase. Yet another example of how Americans are embracing collectivism without realizing it.

As described by another author, Cheng Yinghong, who saw Mao and the CCP for what they really were, "Mao dreamed of a new society based on the 'new village' (a notion directly inspired by utopian socialists and Russian populists) in which raising children, along with many other family functions, would be operated by the community."[9]

History has shown the world over and over how so many socialist ventures have been abject failures, victimizing people and leaving a country in tatters, chaos, or teetering on ruins. However, no one who has ever advocated for socialism has gotten the memo. They don't have a clue: this…stuff…doesn't work—it never lasts. The people's commune and Great Leap Forward, launched simultaneously by Mao and the CCP, resulted in catastrophe, leading to the Great Chinese Famine (1959–1961). Collective dining was, mercifully to the people, eventually phased out. It makes one wonder, though, how this communal collective dining could even be called that when the peasants were collectively starving. Yet the commune survived and lasted until 1983. I know a little bit about this exact kind of communal collectivism; I lived and worked in one during my three-year reeducation by the peasants from 1975 to 1978. The only lessons I learned were the ones that demonstrated how lousy and horrible socialism was. Those Americans with a favorable attitude toward socialism cannot possibly have a clue what they are striving for.

One of George H. W. Bush's presidential campaign issues when running for reelection in 1992 was family values. It was a sticking issue of the times. The state of the family was sad then. Not much has changed since. It is even sadder now. Here's a statistic revealing what America as a whole feels about traditional family and family values: according to Pew Research Center, as of 2022, the United States has the world's highest rate of children living in single-parent households.[10]

We know that Karl Marx wanted to abolish capitalism—whether you support or reject capitalism, we all can agree that was what Marx had as one of his chief goals. What might not be all that clear to many Americans is that abolition of the family was also part of the grand Marxist plan. Marx believed that the foundation of the bourgeois family was based on capital and private gain, the purpose being to preserve wealth for the rich. While family ties among the proletarians were transformed into simple articles of commerce and instruments of labor, Karl Marx predicted that when capital vanished, the bourgeois family would disappear along with it.[11]

American Marxists faithfully follow Marx's socialist ideals in their desire to destroy the nuclear family and, with it, to wipe away capitalist ideology. They view capitalists as evil—nothing more than selfish, greedy money hoarders who have zero empathy for those less fortunate.

Marxists regard the purpose of the bourgeois nuclear family as twofold: first, to protect the capital/wealth within itself, and second, to promote capitalist ideology to protect the former. The unique function of family as the promoter of the "ideology apparatus" is what the progressives want to destroy. What is the ideology they refer to? American traditional values!

What the American Marxists pretend not to see is that the institutions of marriage and family provide important human goods such as affection, procreation, and parenthood. But they understand that marriage is in itself an exercise of freedom that provides a foundation for securing a self-governing people. Scott Yenor, writing for the Heritage Foundation, sums it up nicely: "Marriage and family life provide invaluable education in and preparation for the responsibilities of self-governing citizenship. Without this moral education, people are poorer, more dependent, and less equipped to become citizens."[12] The progressives want to destroy family, precisely because they understand its paramount importance.

What follows is a summary of how American families have been assaulted.

1960s: Counterculture and Radical Second-Wave Feminism

First, let us remember the first wave of feminism in America, which came ashore in the mid-1800s and lasted into the early 1900s. It focused on equal rights for women, including suffrage (the right to vote in political elections) and "was interrelated with the temperance and abolitionist movements,"[13] as noted in 2008 by Dr. Martha Rampton, an emeritus professor at Pacific University in Oregon.

Let's move ahead to the second wave of feminism, also as defined by Rampton, which started in the 1960s: "This wave unfolded in the context of the anti-war and civil rights movements and the growing self-consciousness of a variety of minority groups around the world. The New Left was on the rise, and the voice of the second wave was increasingly radical."[14] It is more appropriate to say that it became extremely *radical*. These feminists' goal was no longer equality but the abolition of capitalism and private property for the lofty goal of "liberating" women who were "household slaves," and represented the "proletariat" within the family.[15] In the second wave of feminism, not only men and patriarchy were under attack, but also marriage, motherhood, gender, and the institution of family.

Avid feminists are not just writing about bringing down the American family, they seem to be relishing it. Kathie Sarachild (1943—) in her younger years was a leader and key figure in the radical feminist movement. In 1968, she changed her name to Sarachild as an act to denounce patriarchy while at the same time honoring her mother, Sara.[16] This reminds me of the Chinese Red Guards' name-changing campaign. In 1969, Sarachild proposed that women should "use marriage as the 'dictatorship of the proletariat' in the family revolution. When male supremacy is completely eliminated, marriage, like the state, will disappear."[17]

This is no random sociological phenomenon: It has a planned purpose. Author Alice Echols, a professor of history and contemporary gender studies at the University of Southern California, wrote this in her 1989 book *Daring to Be Bad: Radical Feminism in America*: "Radical feminism did exactly what its opponents accuse it of: it played a key role in subverting traditional values and destabilizing the family."[18]

It has clearly become a Marxist movement orchestrating the descent into rejection and deconstruction of the traditional American family.

What is going on with the deconstruction of the family in America invites comparisons with more than just China. We can also place the American radical progressives' views on family alongside those of the Soviet Communists and see what we get, as Ella Winter, author of *Red Virtue: Human Relationships in the New Russia,* does here: "The home has been regarded by Soviet theorists as one of the most insidious of the institutions that foster individualism. It ties the woman, aggravates the greed for money and private possessions, fosters ideals of self-interest, is opposed to society."[19]

The Soviet attitude toward the educational influence of family is that, Winter writes, "our children are not only members of a family unit. They are members of a classroom, a school, a Pioneer, a Comsomol group, a community. And these, not the family, should play the vital and predominant role in training and shaping them."[20]

If by now you are not asking from where these hardcore feminists are getting their beliefs and premises, you might at least be asking: Are they for real? Yes, they are, very much so, and the America of the twenty-first century is providing them with the fertile soil that makes plowing these fields for the spread of Marxism (or ideological manure) so fruitful for them. Radical feminism has contributed more than any other radical movements to the destruction of American families.

How the American Government Became "The Father" (Great Society)

While radical feminists had long been attacking American families, President Lyndon Johnson bore the responsibility for his Great Society (1964–1965), which effectively dismantled fatherhood by replacing the role of fathers with the federal government. Note that, by then, Mao had been pulling off the same "I'm your daddy" stunt in China for more than a decade.

The link between family breakdown and the welfare system is clear. When the government steps in to play the role of the bread-winner, there is no incentive for women to be married and no incentive for men to stay home to take care of the children. Under this umbrella of "progressivism," everyone is free to do as they please, as long as our Federal Father approves and is willing to foot the bill. Welfare, naturally, creates generational dependency and poverty. And that's the goal. When the population is dependent and poor, they fall automatically under the control of the state.

The ramifications are obvious; recent history tells us so. For one thing, broken families produce broken children. Many of the mass shooters that have popped up in recent years share one familial trait—they have grown up without a father in their home. Here's what Utah Senator Mike Lee said in the aftermath of the 2022 mass shooting at Robb Elementary School in Uvalde, Texas, where nineteen defenseless children and two adults were gunned down by a crazed killer: "Why is our culture suddenly producing so many young men who want to murder innocent people?...It raises questions like, you know, could things like fatherlessness, the breakdown of families, isolation from civil society or the glori-fication of violence be contributing factors?"[21] But the progressives try to convince Americans that toxic masculinity and guns are the culprit.

Denzel Washington, the great American actor and an African American himself, blames Black crime on the lack of father fig-ures: "If the father is not in the home, the boy will find a father in the streets. I saw it in my generation and every generation before me, and every one ever since. If the streets raise you, then the judge becomes your mother and prison becomes your home."[22]

The numbers help tell the story. According to Statista, a global statistics portal, in 1980, 18.4 percent of all women in the United States who gave birth were unmarried. As of 2021, the percentage of births to unmarried women had increased to 40 percent.[23] If we are to believe the progressives, that is part of what they define as "progress" in a progressive country, right? More single moms.

Indoctrination: Turning Children against Parents

Because schools have been teaching progressive ideologies for decades, many parents continue to find a growing ideological divide between themselves and their children that goes well beyond which clothes to wear to school or their preferences for music. Any parents, including me, who failed to pay attention to this dramatic change in this ideological divide got their wake-up call in 2020 during the BLM/Antifa riots—and that's what they were, *riots*. During the pandemic, with many classes being taught online via virtual apps such as Zoom, parents were able to see with their own eyes and hear with their own ears exactly what was being taught to their children.

Progressive schools hold tremendous sway over millions of our public-school students—and no doubt some private-school children as well. Some children have cut ties with their parents, just like what happened during China's Cultural Revolution. This is an especially painful reminder to those of us who are survivors of Communism and its anti-family ideologies of what this world can become—and is further becoming.

Do not make the fatal mistake of denying or downplaying any of this. A day is coming when it will become common for American children to start reporting their parents to government authorities for possible "hate crimes" that exist only in someone's prejudicial PC mentality. Let me make clear the essential warning here: Episodes of the Chinese Cultural Revolution are already being replayed here in America.

One case involves a young man in Texas tipping off the FBI about his father, who was subsequently charged in the January 6 Capitol riot case. Jackson Reffitt, eighteen, had informed law enforcement several weeks before the Capitol incident that he believed his father, Guy W. Reffitt, was planning something but he was not exactly sure what, later telling the *New York Times*, "He would always tell me that he's going to do something big."[24]

To go with the "son against the father" story, here is one of a daughter against the mother: Therese Duke lost her job after her eighteen-year-old daughter identified her in a viral January 6 video on Twitter by retweeting it with the comment "hi mom remember the time you told me I shouldn't go to BLM protests bc they could get violent…this you?" according to the *Newsweek* report.[25]

In May 2020, an apparently emotionally distraught "Izabella," reportedly fifteen, took to TikTok to launch this rant against her parents, her eyes red and soaked with tears: "I literally hate my family so much. It's just. They just tried to argue with me that George Floyd—like, they just tried to tell me that he deserved that 'cause he did something wrong, and that it was okay. That is not okay. And it's just making me so upset. I don't know. I do not wanna live here. I hate livin' in Louisiana. I hate livin' around these racist f-cks. Like, I just wanna leave." Just two days after Izabella had posted her verbal assault against her parents, her

TikTok following went from fewer than a hundred to seventeen thousand.[26]

The ideological divide between parents and children spares no one, not even the rich and famous. Elon Musk, the richest man in the world, blames the "neo-Marxists" for the fact that his eighteen-year-old daughter wants nothing to do with her über-wealthy dad. "It's full-on communism...and a general sentiment that if you're rich, you're evil," Musk told the *Financial Times* on October 7, 2022.[27]

The roles of parents and children have been reversed! Parents across America are left having to tiptoe on eggshells when discussing sensitive topics in and around the household. Now we have children taking on the role of "educating" their "backward," "racist" parents about social justice, just like those kids in the USSR and China.

Transgender ideology, too, as it is now being pushed in so many schools, has smacked parents in the face almost overnight, out of nowhere it seems. Children as young as pre-K students are now being introduced to ideas such as boys can be girls and vice versa and men can have babies. The transition is presented as being just as simple as taking some pills and undergoing surgery.[28] This ideology aims only to push the bounds of our societal norms and, in doing so, can harm children's minds and their bodies. Children are told the school and government will back them if their parents object to such ideas, and many will conspire to keep the information from the parents. In such cases, children essentially become the property of the government-led schools, who then become the parent-like authorities left to decide what is best for children.

We hear more and more horror stories of schools grooming children behind parents' backs. In Spreckels, California, a mother initiated legal action in January 2022 against her daughter's middle school, accusing two teachers of manipulating her daughter, then eleven, into identifying herself at the school as a boy, without her mother's knowledge. The two "groomers" at the time were directing the school's Equality Club—which also became known as UBU (You Be You). They reportedly had "planted a seed" within the girl when she was in sixth grade that she was bisexual, before later suggesting to her that she was now transgender.[29]

It is disturbing that the battle is not simply between parents and groomers in government schools. Some woke parents are on board with the transgender ideology to try to transition their underaged children to the opposite sex. One such case is a Texas mother who has, against the will of the father, determined to transition her nine-year-old son, James Younger, to a girl. The battle is still waging on in court between the mother and father as of the beginning of 2023.[30]

Transgender ideology turns children against parents and parents against children. In the process, families are weakened or destroyed.

* * *

Family provides the building blocks of a society—as we have discussed here, both proponents and opponents of the traditional nuclear family would agree with that premise. This is a widely held acknowledgment across religions and cultures. If one wants to destroy a society, one has to destroy its building blocks. The following are three quotes from great men of wisdom and insight, which make compelling yet concise arguments for preserving the traditional family:

- Confucius: "The strength of a nation derives from the integrity of the home."
- Ronald Reagan: "The family has always been the cornerstone of American society. Our families nurture, preserve, and pass on to each succeeding generation the values we share and cherish, values that are the foundation for our freedoms."
- Dr. Billy Graham: "When the family is destroyed, the society eventually disintegrates."

Several decades of relentless attacks on American families by the Marxist radicals have left us with an American family landscape that has been radically changed. A question that was frequently and rhetorically asked of parents in the 1960s and 1970s was: "Do you know *where* your children are?" A more appropriate question to ask today's parents might be: "Do you know *what* your children are?"

CHAPTER 9

Destruction of Religion

O ne of my first impressions of Bowling Green, Kentucky, where I began my life in America in 1986, was that there was a church on almost every corner. This absolutely amazed me. I saw it as a visual evidence and statement that Christianity is an intricate part of this country and its people.

Throughout my subsequential travels to so many countries and so many civilizations, I have also seen that churches, temples, and mosques are always conspicuous parts of their townscapes and landscapes. The fact is that we know of no world civilization that was built on atheism.

I came to realize later that China, too, used to be dotted with religious buildings before the CCP took over in 1949. The most common ones were the ancestral temples (*ci tan*). They could be seen in almost every town and village where people enshrined and worshipped ancestors or sages, and where Confucianism was taught and passed down from generation to generation. I did not see any while living under Mao because they were either destroyed or converted into secular uses.

When I first came to America, I attended church services with my friend Pat Nave. In a way, it reminded me of the weekly mandatory political studies I endured my whole life in China where the Party leader, like a priest, would read aloud the latest Party instructions and demand that we, the congregation, study and carry them through. Regular confession was a part of that study where we were required to criticize and self-criticize. It dawned on me that Communism is truly like a religion itself, although we were taught to believe that Communism is against religion.

* * *

Growing up, I had no exposure to religion, prayer, or worship. I was not even aware that any religion existed other than Buddhism, as there were Buddhist temples and monasteries in and all around my city. I remember visiting those places, thinking of them more as recreational parks than houses of worship. In fact, some of them were converted into recreational parks. I was taught that religion was nothing more than superstition and that religion was the *opiate* of the people. Although I had no idea what religion was about, I was sure that it was something bad because the CCP had taught me so.

In addition to calling for the abolition of private properties and nuclear families, the *Communist Manifesto* also explicitly calls for the abolition of religion, all morality, and eternal truth. In order for Marxist ideology to establish its roots in a civilization, it has to first dig up and throw away the people's spiritual and religious foundations. If anything or anyone is to be worshipped, it would be Marxism and the Party; they are to be the indisputable "higher power" over the entire nation.

Throughout the ages, many of the world's major religions have made their way to China and made their marks on the development of Chinese civilization. China also produced its own indigenous religion, known as Taoism. At its core, Taoism preaches living in harmony with nature, although the very foundation of traditional Chinese civilization was founded on Confucianism.

Buddhism came to China via India around two thousand years ago. Over the centuries, it became the most influential foreign religion in the country. Its impactful presence is evident in the many Buddhist temples and shrines spread throughout the country, and Buddha has become the most revered deity to the Chinese people. Buddhist teaching has been integrated into Chinese culture and ethics, along the way converging with Taoism and other Chinese folk beliefs to produce a form of Buddhism laced with Chinese characteristics. Taoism's authority for the people is rooted more in culture than it is in religion; the best-known Taoist principles of yin and yang represent the two interdependent yet opposing forces that govern nature.

Islam is the second most influential foreign religion. It found its way into China via the major trade route of the Silk Road between China and Europe via central Asia. The most well-known Muslims in China today are the Uyghurs, who have recently caught the attention of the world after becoming the target of genocide by the CCP.

Christianity was introduced in China as early as 700 AD, although it wasn't until many missionaries arrived in China during the nineteenth and twentieth centuries that Christianity established a foothold in the country. Henry Luce, founder of *Time* and *Life* magazines, was born in China to missionary parents.

While I was in my twenties teaching in Chengdu in 1985, I met an elderly American woman—she was close to eighty years old—who was teaching English at a local medical school. She told me she was born in Sichuan to an American missionary in a remote town bordering the Tibetan region. It stunned me that an American missionary would give up the comfort and security of living in America to take his family to such a desolate place to preach Christianity. This woman told me that she really wanted to go to see her birthplace despite the expectation it would be an arduous journey, even in the 1980s.

Despite China's long legacy of open arms to a variety of religions, homegrown or imported, Mao and the CCP were openly hostile to faith-based religion. They saw any denomination of religion as a rival to the Communist ideology and something they simply couldn't tolerate, so they were going to do something about it.

This power-based hostility toward religion and faith practices had been in place well before the Cultural Revolution. Since 1949, nonstop political campaigns had been chipping away at all faith-based religions and their institutions through one major campaign after another. Even the slowest learners realized that if they wanted to survive, they had no choice but to abandon all faiths. We were taught we were atheists, when in fact, I eventually came to realize that what we were being taught was how to be Communist believers. Communism was our new religion.

Confucianism

Despite the lack of agreement among scholars about whether Confucianism is a religion or philosophy, no one doubts that it has had a dominant effect in shaping the Chinese civilization, its morality, and its ethics. The Chinese have revered Confucius for more than two thousand years, whose teaching can be summed up in the expressions of *ren* and *li*, with the former translated as benevolence, or humanity, while the latter refers to aspects of life such as virtue, manner, ritual, etc.

Confucianism was never made known to us in school or at home. The first time I learned about it was in 1974 when I was in high school. My mother came home one day, saying something unimaginable had occurred, but she wasn't allowed to reveal what it was. Being a Party member, she had been given the shocking information before it was disclosed to the public. Weeks went by before I and millions of my fellow countrymen finally learned through the news that Lin Biao, Mao's handpicked successor, had been killed in a plane crash in Mongolia while en route to Russia. This was after his alleged attempted coup against Mao had failed.

That was a shocking wake-up call for many Chinese people. They suddenly realized that Mao was not the all-knowing and all-seeing figure who had conned us into worshipping him as our god. Mao's problem in the eyes of awakened people was they now perceived him as a flawed leader; he had picked the wrong person—a traitor—to be his successor. I didn't see it that way, though; I was oblivious, still sold out to Mao. As a high school senior, I unconditionally accepted Mao's version of the story, that Lin Biao was a hidden enemy of the people and that we needed to further intensify the class struggle.

Soon after that, Mao launched his last campaign, the Anti–Lin Biao, Anti–Confucius Campaign. It was not clear to me then, and still baffles me to this day, what it was about Lin Biao that linked him to Confucius, or vice versa. It was during this campaign that I was first exposed to Confucianism. I was taught that Confucius was a reactionary figure who had taught feudalistic values with the intent to instill obedience in people instead of a revolutionary mindset. That explained why Mao condemned Confucianism—it ran counter to his revolutionary goals.

One of Confucius's classic works was known as the *Three Character Classic*, which describes what it takes to be a moral person. The book was written in three Chinese characters per line to make it easier for children to understand and be taught from it. In traditional China, the *Three Character Classic* was something that all educated Chinese people learned to memorize and recite. Instead, I learned to recite the "scripture" of Mao's *Little Red Book*.

I would eventually come to know that Confucius is among the pantheon of the greatest thinkers in human history; he is revered by people around the world, especially in East Asia and Southeast Asia. That explains why Mao detested Confucius so much that he would inspire his Red Guards to act on his behalf to ravage the Confucius Temple of the great Chinese sage.

I described the Red Guards' attack on the Confucius Temple in Chapter 6. This act was the equivalent of something as unimaginable as Jews destroying the Wailing Wall in Jerusalem or Muslims destroying the Kaaba in Mecca. Since those turbulent years, the CCP has deceitfully tried to present itself to the world as the heirs of Confucius, opening Confucius Institutes around the world. It's crucial to see through their political charade. The world needs to know that the CCP is *not* the heirs of Confucius but the heirs of Western-imported, evil Marxist ideology.

Christianity

Mao was more hostile to Christianity than any other religion. He understood that Christianity had the power to influence and organize its followers and also had a close connection with the West and the outside world. He regarded Christianity as a tool for Western imperialist aggression against China, and considered Christianity the biggest threat to his regime. But there is a more profound reason for Mao's hostility toward Christianity. Christianity fundamentally challenges the very premise of Communism, which holds the belief that the state has power over individuals and the state determines what is true and what is right. The CCP understood that Christianity is their mortal threat. I will discuss this in more detail in this chapter.

An anti-Christian movement in China began as soon as the CCP took over China. What eventually became known as the Three-Self Patriotic Movement started taking root following the 1949 triumph of Communism in China. The movement grew when Mao and the CCP launched a series of measures aimed at taking over control of churches from the hands of foreign missionaries by changing the political loyalties of Chinese Christians to CCP adherence.

The term "three selfs" stands for self-governing (independent of the influence of foreign Christian groups), self-sufficient (independent of financial support from foreign governments and Christian groups), and self-evangelizing (independent of foreign

Christian groups in terms of preaching and interpretation of scriptures).[1] The churches would now be guided by and answer only to the CCP. In summary, the purpose of the Three-Self Movement was to transform churches in China into "Chinese churches" by cutting off their ties with the outside Christian world. They would now be isolated and under the CCP's control.

It didn't take long for the CCP to put church leaders to the test. In 1950, the CCP launched the first denunciation meeting in Beijing. Participating church leaders were asked to expose "crimes" of the American imperialists committed against China and the Chinese using Christianity. The named missionaries for the denunciation were American missionary Frank Wilson Price (1895–1974), Elijah Coleman Bridgman (1801–1861), and the English missionary Robert Morrison (1782–1834). The meeting was considered a success, and it was used as a model for similar meetings introduced to the rest of China. The denunciation meeting looked very much like the Cultural Revolution struggle sessions.[2] The only difference was that the targets were white men, either dead or absent.

The CCP was far from finished "cleaning up" China's churches. Its next step was threefold: 1) require all church leaders to participate in CCP's "church" through political studies, 2) insert CCP political studies in all seminaries, and 3) take over Christian publications.[3] They meant business. The CCP's efforts greatly weakened the churches. By the time of the Cultural Revolution in 1966, most of the churches were closed and the buildings converted into warehouses, factories, office spaces, or meeting halls.[4]

During the Cultural Revolution, the surviving church leaders and members, even those CCP cadres in charge of religious organizations, were all prosecuted. Many had their homes raided and were struggled against. Some were exiled, beaten, tortured, or killed, and plenty of suicides added to the numbers. In Guangzhou, for instance, the Red Guards demanded a pastor to shout, "Down with God!" When he refused, the Red Guards "branded" the top of his head with a red-hot iron![5]

What is illuminating about faith and religion in China is the opposing perspectives between Christians and Communists. Father de Jaegher, a Catholic missionary who lived among the Chinese Communists in their "liberated" area during the 1940s, gave an account of part of a conversation he once had with Chang Kuo-Chien, a Communist cadre, on the subject of morality. Speaking to De Jaegher, Chang stated:

> You are a Christian. You are in favour of the Cross. I am a Communist. I am in favour of the hammer and sickle. Your Jesus Christ, I understand, came on earth to save all humanity by His death on a cross; you preach that He sacrificed Himself for everyone. Well, we Communists have the same aim, with this one difference: The Christians speak about heaven; we don't. The Communists want to liberate the workers from Capitalistic oppression and make a happy society out of a bad society. Our means are different from yours. Where the Christians have failed we will succeed. The Christians try to persuade men by inner understanding, but this cannot succeed. The Communists use the persuasion of political, military, and economic means to attain their aim and they cannot fail.[6]

That is a great illustration of the difference between Christianity and Communism: one wins and the other subjugates the hearts and souls of people, respectively.

Buddhism and Islam

All religious groups suffered tremendously from prosecution and destruction during the Cultural Revolution. And like every other assault on people and their communities, it was relentless, and it was brutal. Buddhism, as the most popular faith, was definitely the Red Guards' main target. They tore down temples, smashed statues, burned scriptures, and forced monks and nuns to return to secular life. In addition, a struggle session for the monks and nuns was a must.

On August 24, 1966, the Red Guards, after ransacking Jile Temple in the city of Harbin, held a struggle session for a group of monks there. A cameraman happened to be on-site and took photos of the scene, which allows us to have a rare glimpse of the madness. One photo shows the monks lined up holding a banner saying, "What Buddhist scriptures? They are nothing but a dog's fart!" In the background are the temple walls covered with Red Guard posters denouncing Buddhism and praising Mao and the CCP.[7]

There were no exceptions for Chinese Muslims. Many mosques were shut down or defaced, copies of the Quran were destroyed, and religious activities were prohibited. Some mosques in Qinghai were converted into pig farms as ordered by the Provincial Party Committee, which then enforced a requirement that Muslims hand over two pigs per household each year as part of their taxes. There is one exception. The largest mosque in the Ningxia Hui Autonomous Region survived the destruction because of a sign on the front door indicating that the mosque was requisitioned by the Red Army in 1936 and therefore became a "revolutionary holy shrine."[8]

Falun Gong

It wasn't just organized, institutionalized religion and faith practices that the CCP has been targeting—they see any kind of exercise of spirituality as a threat to be quashed. By the time the decade-long Cultural Revolution was over, all religions had been decimated. Even Maoism as the new religion had been discredited. All that remained, for the most part, was a huge spiritual vacuum and barren ground that was no longer bearing spiritual fruit. It was against this backdrop that by the early 1990s a spiritual leader emerged in China by the name of Li Hongzhi. He brought into existence what had become known as Falun Gong, with *falun* referring to "the wheel of law" and *gong* being a word synonymous with "martial art."

According to its official website, Falun Gong is a spiritual practice rooted in Buddhist tradition in which a devotee aspires for self-improvement through the study of teachings as well as gentle exercises and meditation.[9] The public's response to Falun Gong was phenomenal. The number of its followers grew quickly and widely throughout the country, its popularity sweeping across China.

Initially, the motivation for many followers was the health benefits offered through the practice of Falun Gong. However, they quickly embraced its moral teachings of truth, compassion, and tolerance, all of which were in direct opposition to Communist decrees and doctrines. In its heyday, Falun Gong had millions of followers that included wives of the members of the CCP's Standing Committee of the Political Bureau.[10] But health benefits and connections to the CCP wives weren't going to save Falun Gong. Not when the CCP was unwilling to tolerate it, instead regarding it as a formidable rival for the hearts and souls of the Chinese people.

What ensued, starting in 1999, was arguably the CCP's most brutal, vigorous, and sustained campaign yet. Untold numbers of practitioners were jailed, tortured, and/or killed. The reports have finally reached the West that organs from Falun Gong members had been harvested.[11] I personally know a few Falun Gong practitioners who have been jailed and have friends who went "missing." They firmly believe that those missing were victims of forced organ harvest.

The Falun Gong movement gained popularity outside China as well. Its practitioners became the most resolute anti-CCP activists, collectively forming the most formidable resistance that the CCP had faced since 1949. The Falun Gong–backed media outlet *Epoch Times* eventually emerged as a significant force against the CCP, as well as a strong conservative voice in the West, earning a spot on the radar of the *New York Times*, drawing the powerful left-leaning newspaper's wrath, which usually is a good sign that one is doing something right as a conservative voice. Both the CCP in China and the progressives in America hate the *Epoch Times*. That says a lot! Read it for yourself:

> For years, *The Epoch Times* was a small, low-budget newspaper with an anti-China slant that was handed out free on New York street corners. But in 2016 and 2017, the paper made two changes that transformed it into one of the country's most powerful digital publishers. The changes also

paved the way for the publication, which is affiliated with the secretive and relatively obscure Chinese spiritual movement Falun Gong, to become a leading purveyor of right-wing misinformation.[12]

In spite of more than twenty years of a heavy-handed crackdown, and after successfully putting all religious organizations under its control, the CCP has failed to eradicate Falun Gong. Practitioners inside China still hold on to their belief, knowing full well that they face imprisonment and death if caught. Outside China, the movement is still growing. The CCP finally has met its match!

* * *

Despite their differences, all these religions teach and promote benevolence and love for one's fellow man, which form the basis of any morality. After decades of relentless attacks by the CCP, the moral foundation of Chinese society has crumbled. The following is a glimpse of a society where there is a total collapse of morality.

On October 13, 2011, a two-year-old girl named Wang Yue was run over by two cars in Foshan, Guangdong. The surveillance video captured not only the hit-and-run accident, but also eighteen passersby who saw but chose to ignore the victim lying in the middle of the narrow street. It took ten minutes before a trash collector noticed the toddler and called for help. The girl later died in the hospital.[13]

This shocking incident is very tough for most Americans to comprehend. *How could this happen in any society?* they would wonder. The reality is that this tragedy is not an isolated case.

To explain this strange social phenomenon unique to CCP's China, I have to tell you about a notorious court case in 2006. The case involved an elderly woman who accused a young man named Peng Yu of bumping into her and causing her to fall. After her fall, Peng accompanied the woman to the hospital and later paid for part of her medical treatment. The case centered on the dispute regarding who was responsible for her fall and her injury, and furthermore, her compensation. The judge ruled in the woman's favor. The ruling was largely not based on evidence but on the judge's reasoning that under *normal* circumstances, a stranger would not have been so generous as to help the woman, unless he was guilty: "If you did not bump into her, why did you help her?" The judge's question sent shock waves across the country.[14]

This case has a far-reaching impact in China. The details of the case and the ruling itself are no longer important. What is devastating is the judge's reasoning and his logic that led to his ruling. Sadly, the judge's reasoning was only a reflection of moral decay of the society and his ruling simply affirmed that morality in China has been long lost. Benevolence and love for one's fellow man do not seem to have a place in CCP's China anymore.

In China today, it would be rare for someone to help those in need in public spaces. It is no longer a shocking scene to see injured people or fallen elderly lying in the middle of a busy street with no one giving them a helping hand. It is a sad society for anyone to live in. After over seventy years of Communist rule over the Chinese people, their religious faiths, beliefs, and practices have been dismantled, and social morality has been destroyed and abandoned. Everyone stands to become a victim in the CCP world where sympathy and compassion are lost.

It is Xi Jinping's dream to build China into a superpower. The question is, how would such a superpower stand on the ruins of its moral foundation?

* * *

We know that Mao wanted to destroy all religions. The American progressives have a narrower focus. They want to destroy Christianity. Why? Because Christianity is *core* to the foundation of the United States of America, and it is a significant theme of the US Constitution, despite what the progressives keep trying to tell us. John Adams noted: "The general principles, on which the fathers achieved independence, were…the general principles of Christianity."[15] The keyword is *principles.*

The progressives are determined to attack America's relationship with Christianity by denying the essential role of Christianity in America's founding. They argue that many of our nation's founding fathers were deists who rejected the divinity of Jesus Christ and therefore meant to make America a totally secular nation.[16]

Bill Flax, a contributor to *Forbes*, penned an article entitled "Was America Founded as a Christian Nation?" In it, Flax offered a counterpoint to the left's argument that the Founding Fathers were more deist than Christian: "The Founders disagreed on much, but were nearly unanimous concerning biblical morality."[17]

Flax offers a nuanced but balanced view as to what's going on here: "America wasn't founded as a Christian nation and many of our beloved Forefathers sadly were not, yet America was largely comprised of Believers. Liberty allows us to worship freely or not at all per conscience. America was never meant to be theocratic or homogenous religiously, but Christianity has always been indelible to our social fabric. The Founders, even non-Believers, considered that a blessing."[18]

One of the guiding principles of Christianity is that we are all created by God and equal in God's eyes, regardless of race and cultural background. That is why people from diverse religious backgrounds or no religious affiliation find America not only a welcoming place but a place anyone can pursue their own dreams and prosper. This encompasses a uniquely Christian principle. Throughout Chinese history, rights were bestowed by rulers. The concept of natural rights was and still is alien to many Chinese people today.

How did progressives try to destroy Christianity? Let's count the ways.

Drugs Replaced God

Once again, we go back to the counterculture movement of the 1960s, this time to see how the open war against Christianity got its footing. That brings us to Timothy Leary, renowned LSD guru. In his autobiography, *Flashbacks: A Personal and Cultural History of an Era*, Leary explains the power of psychoactive plants such as the psychedelic mushrooms in Mexico: "It permits you to see vistas beyond the horizons of this life," Leary wrote. "To travel backwards and forward in time. To enter other planes of existence. Even, as the Indians say, to know God." To Leary it is the proof that "drugs are the origin of religion and philosophy."[19]

More from Leary: "We had run up against the Judeo-Christian commitment to one God, one religion, one reality that has cursed

Europe for centuries and America since our founding days. Drugs that open the mind to multiple realities inevitably lead to a polytheistic view of the universe. We sensed that the time for a new humanist religion based on intelligent, good-natured pluralism and scientific paganism had arrived."[20]

That's Leary's contribution to the counterculture against God and Christianity. They were replaced by drugs. Leary consequentially updated Karl Marx's famous assertion from "Religion is the opiate of the people" to "Opiates are the religion of the people!"

Christianity Replaced by Other Religions

I don't know much about popular music (rock, pop, country, etc.), but I am somewhat familiar with the Beatles—the most popular rock band in history. In the late 1960s, they took a trip to India in search of Eastern religious wisdom. Only recently did I come to understand that this much-publicized excursion by the Beatles was an orchestrated part of the counterculture movement in search of a replacement religion for Christianity. It was, in the eyes of some informed observers, just a setup to sway public opinion about Eastern religion, which is nothing like Christianity. As Roger Kimball states in his book *The Long March*: "Finally, there was the bogus embrace of Eastern religion: the chanting, the incense, the pilgrimages to India and Tibet, the I Ching, The Tibetan Book of the Dead, assorted Hindu and Buddhist scriptures—a nauseating goulash of pseudo-spirituality."[21]

Christianity, to a large degree, was being abandoned or outright rejected. Perhaps the most conspicuous move away from Christianity was performed by the legendary sports figure, world champion boxer, Cassius Clay, who, in giving up his Baptist ties for Islam, changed his name to Muhammad Ali in the process.[22]

As a worldwide traveler, I have backpacked my way to and through many countries, with their colorful array of different religions and cultures. I love seeing, experiencing, and photographing the rich cultural diversity the world has to offer. Each trip has reinforced my conviction that America is exceptional—it is the only country in the world to which anyone from any corner of the world can come (legally) and claim to be American. The sad part is that new arrivals are finding a twenty-first-century America that in many ways has lost its way in terms of its once staunch faith-based spirituality and Christian conviction. Communism's influential long-arm reach has made tremendous strides in knocking this country off its Christian bearings and damaging the moral compass.

Call Jesus a Socialist

This bears repeating: As much as Marxists/Communists hate religion, they understand, embrace, and crave the power of religion. Both use the deceptive tactics to lure potential converts.

Mao once made a comparison between Buddhism and Communism. On March 8, 1955, while meeting with the Dalai Lama, Mao said that "the founder of Buddhism, Siddhartha, advocated liberation from suffering for all sentient beings. He spoke on behalf of those who were oppressed in India at the time. Instead of being a prince, he became a monk and founded Buddhism. Therefore, Buddhists and Communists have one thing in common. Both aim at lifting the suffering of oppression for all sentient beings, that is, the masses of the people."[23] The truth is, while Buddhism aims to help people to alleviate suffering, Communism creates suffering. This is evident in the unprecedented suffering brought to the Chinese people by the CCP.

Antonio Gramsci said it best: "Socialism is precisely the religion that must overwhelm Christianity."[24] That's the reason that progressives would quote Bible verses in order to deceive unsuspecting Christians. Peter Dreier was a college professor at Occidental College when he wrote a self-explanatory piece in 2016 entitled "Jesus Was a Socialist" for the ultraliberal *HuffPost*. Here's part of what Dreier had to say:

> As people around the world celebrate Christmas, it is worth remembering that Jesus was a socialist. Of course, he was born long before the rise of industrial Capitalism in the 19th century, but his radical ideas have influenced many critics of Capitalism, including many prominent socialists and even Pope Francis…"No one can serve two masters," Jesus says in Matthew 6:24. "Either he will hate the one and love the other, or he will be devoted to the one and despise the other. You cannot serve both God and Money."
>
> In Luke 12:15, Jesus says, "Watch out! Be on your guard against all kinds of greed; a man's life does not consist in the abundance of his possessions."[25]

What Dreier writes and the fact that many readers just nod their heads in agreement should be a point of concern, but it's also ironic in one respect: the fact that he, who believes in socialism, is quoting Christian scripture, which seems counterintuitive considering how many leftists typically are determined to stomp out Christianity—and, along with it, the Bible—into the ground.

Yet they will eagerly pull out Bible verses to throw in the faces of Christians while trying to make their points.

Historic fact is undeniable. Socialism is not about tending to the needs of the poor. Nor is it about sharing and caring. Socialism is about government taking wealth by force from one group and redistributing it to others until it runs out. Socialism is about subjugating the populace and making them dependent on the government. Socialism is about creating scarcity and poverty. I'm not just throwing that out there without anything to support it—I lived it firsthand growing up for twenty-six years. Nothing much has changed, except now it's happening in America.

DEI (Diversity, Equity, and Inclusion) in Religion

Religious diversity or religious pluralism is just code for the real goal, which is to exclude Christianity from the club. This is done by proclaiming Christianity as one of many religions worldwide—nothing special—and trying to convince others that its traditional role as the foundation of Western civilization should be rejected. What the progressives are doing is similar to them wanting to pack the court with the intention of diluting conservative influence.

President Barack Obama is the champion of religious pluralism. In his first inaugural address in 2009, he said, "We are shaped by every language and culture, drawn from every end of this Earth."[26]

Obama wanted us to believe that America was created through the forces of multiculturalism and religious pluralism. Not true. He wants us to forget that America was founded exclusively on Christian principles and values. Individual liberty and natural rights are rooted in Christianity, certainly not in Islam or

Buddhism. They did not come from other religious traditions—definitely not from Confucianism.

Many citizens across America know bogus religious thought or expression when they see or hear it. That's why some parents sued California when they found out that their public school curriculum included students being required to learn chants to Aztec gods—for real! The rationale appeared to be for "religious justice" since their curriculum claims that Christians committed "'theocide' (i.e., killing gods) against indigenous tribes."[27]

Public schools kicked out the Christian God but invited in other gods. This is a perfect example of how our education system tries to make children turn their back to Christianity. Aztecs were not indigenous to the areas over which they ruled. They were, in other words, colonizers, and brutal ones at that. The Aztec faith shared many aspects with other Mesoamerican religions, including the practice of human sacrifice.[28] Naturally, this historic fact was deliberately hidden from the students.

Dig as deep you want to into the subject of Aztec religion; you won't find anything about the Aztecs that values individual liberty!

Christians Became Oppressors

Elijah Muhammad (1897–1975), leader of the Nation of Islam, argued that "Christianity was a white faith used to delude blacks, a gospel of subservience which taught acceptance of degradation by promising paradise in the afterlife. Whites, those 'blue-eyed devils,' could never be trusted."[29]

The narrative about Christianity being a white man's religion has resurfaced and gained strength in recent years. Why? Because it is politically expedient for Marxists looking to weaken

Christianity. A little knowledge of history might debunk that lie, however. Christianity originated in Asia. It spread from modern-day Israel to Asia Minor and the Mediterranean area, including North Africa. Both Armenia and Ethiopia claimed to be the first Christian state—neither located in Europe. The first Christian monastery, Monastery of Saint Anthony, was founded in Egypt.

No matter; the hits just keep on coming. One of the more curious—I might even say outrageous—was an article published in *The Atlantic* in August 2022 that described the Catholic rosary as an extremist symbol that represented violent, right-wing extremism in the United States.[30]

I see this as a sign of desperation of the progressives. This reminds me of the Red Guards attacking not just religion, but every religious symbol.

Non-Christian religious believers who joined the left's identity campaign made their religion an identity, thanks to intersectionality. While being a Christian adds to the oppressor index in the court of intersectionality, being a non-Christian gains an intersectionality point as someone who is oppressed.

Not everyone can wear their faith, even if it truly is the faith they practice. But Linda Sarsour can. Sarsour, a descendant of Palestinian immigrant parents and a radical anti-Israel activist, admitted that she only wears a hijab in order to make people believe she is a Muslim, therefore, a member of a "marginalized" group. Otherwise, "I was just an ordinary white girl," she said.[31] Sarsour is not alone. She just happens to be one of the few who openly admit it.

Meet also Raquel Evita Saraswati, the former chief equity, inclusion, and culture officer of the social justice organization

American Friends Service Committee. She seems not only transracial, but transreligious. By wearing a hijab, she has transformed herself from a white woman to an Arab and a Muslim.[32]

In the insane world of identity Marxism, a non-Christian religion can make an "oppressor" into an "oppressed." Pure magic!

Frontal Attack on Christianity

The attack on Christianity has become much less subtle and much more frontal and in your face. This has been going on for years, that Christmas has become a target for progressives. They insist that saying "Merry Christmas" to someone is offensive and not inclusive. They say it should be replaced by "Happy holiday(s)." In doing so, they try to cancel out Christianity by putting Christmas out of existence.

Then there's Joe Kennedy, a high school football coach in Bremerton, Washington, whose biggest fault is that he is a Christian who dares to pray in public on a football field before and after games and is sometimes joined by the students. Kennedy was ordered by his school district to stop this practice and was eventually fired from his job. The progressives accused Kennedy's daring act of praying a violation of the Constitutional separation of church and state.

Joe Kennedy sued his school district. His case eventually reached the US Supreme Court, which ruled in his favor in July 2022. Justice Neil Gorsuch wrote in the majority opinion that the prayers "were not publicly broadcast or recited to a captive audience. Students were not required or expected to participate."[33]

The decision caused an uproar in progressive media. *Sports Illustrated* magazine, once the trailblazer of sports journalism and now going full woke, labeled Kennedy "a threat to a bedrock of American Democracy."[34] *Slate* writer Mark Joseph Stern in his article entitled "Supreme Court Lets Public Schools Coerce Students into Practicing Christianity" echoed Justice Sonia Sotomayor's opinion that the students could have felt coerced to join in.[35] The intention of "separation of church and state" is to protect religious freedom by keeping the state out of religion. In Joe Kennedy's case, it was the state trying to keep believers out of religion, just like the CCP in China.

During the COVID pandemic, the state went even further by forcefully closing churches. We have seen liquor stores allowed to stay open because they were deemed "essential" by the government, yet houses of worship were ordered to close, and pastors and preachers were arrested for holding Sunday services.[36]

Anti-Christianity fervor became a part of the 2020 "protests" in America. Based on the *United States Conference of Catholic Bishops* report, there have been at least 168 incidents of arson, vandalism, and other destruction at churches since May 2020.[37] On May 31, 2020, the historic St. John's Church behind the White House in Washington, DC, was set on fire during the BLM protest.[38]

The Supreme Court's overturning of *Roe v. Wade* in 2022 provided another perfect opportunity for the progressives to carry out their Marxist-driven rage and animosity to attack Christianity. In July 2022 in Los Angeles, proabortion activists, for the third weekend in a row, took to the streets in the Hollywood area of LA as part of a Rise Up 4 Abortion Rights rally, in concert with other such protests nationwide, brandishing signs such as, "Stop the Spread of Christianity."[39] This sign sums up the progressives' goal. They are working hard to stop the spread of Christianity.

Infiltration of the Church

As I have indicated earlier, the Communist infiltration in America is complete. That definitely includes the church.

Since the death of Floyd and the subsequent protests and riots in 2022, it has become a common scene to see signs or banners outside churches supporting BLM and other woke movements. These signs are there to declare, either intentionally or unknowingly, either voluntarily or coerced, that those churches are on board with CRT and that they are woke .

However, this is not new. Cultural Marxism has been infiltrating the church as early as the 1960s, only its escalation has been intensified in recent years. In 2018, Pastor Eric Mason called for the church to go woke with his book entitled *Woke Church: An Urgent Call for Christians in America to Confront Racism and Injustice*. In 2019, the Southern Baptist Convention (SBC)—the world's largest Baptist denomination, the largest Protestant denomination, and the second-largest Christian denomination in the United States, according to Wikipedia—passed what is known as Resolution 9, which affirms CRT and intersectionality as analytical tools to understand multifaceted social dynamics.[40] By endorsing CRT, SBC sent a dangerous message to the Christian world and wider society.

Sadly, too many churches choose to be neutral by staying out of the fight. They say that they don't want to be political, and they don't want to be divisive. To these churches, Eric Metaxas, conservative radio host and author of three biographies, including *Bonhoeffer: Pastor, Martyr, Prophet, Spy*, issued a serious warning with his new book entitled *Letter to the American Church*. Metaxas drew parallels of what is going on today in American churches to that of German churches during the Nazi regime. He concluded that the American church will doom America if it chooses to be silent, like the German churches in the 1940s. America needs her own Bonhoeffers, who not only understood the evil of Nazism but also gave his life fighting against that evil.

Thankfully, the pushback within the church against the Marxist infiltration has been gaining strength. One of the prominent fighters is Pastor Voddie Baucham, who was a candidate for the 2023 SBC Pastors' Conference President and currently serves as Dean of Theology at the African Christian University in Lusaka, Zambia.[41] Baucham is an outspoken critic of critical race theory, BLM, and cultural Marxism. In his 2021 book, *Fault Lines: The Social Justice Movement and Evangelicalism's Looming Catastrophe*, Baucham sounds the alarm: "I want this book to be a clarion call. I want to unmask the ideology of Critical Theory, Critical Race Theory, and Intersectionality in hopes that those who have imbibed it can have the blinders removed from their eyes, and those who have bowed in the face of it can stand up, take courage, and 'contend for the faith that was once for all delivered to the saints.'"[42] Pastor Baucham is an excellent educator. I have learned so much from his lectures on CRT and cultural Marxism on YouTube.

* * *

We should have learned by now that Communism is not against religion. Rather, it wants to replace religion. In America, it wants to replace Christianity.

Maoism became a religion. To the Chinese, Mao's *Little Red Book* was the scripture and Mao was a god in human form on earth. Mao had eight hundred million followers—either coerced or brainwashed—in China. Those who refused to follow were sent to labor camps, jail, or their graves.

Wokeness today has become its own particular form of religion, with millions in its congregation. It's a religion seeking to replace Christianity, and they have gained a lot of converts. John McWhorter, a professor of linguistics at Columbia University, is a vocal critic of CRT. In his newly published book entitled *Woke Racism: How a New Religion Has Betrayed Black America*, McWhorter calls woke racism an actual *new* religion, not simply *like* a new religion. He argues that the new woke religion has all the characteristics of a religion, including original sin—"white privilege." Anyone who simply has questions or doubts of this new religion is a heretic and called *racist*.

I totally agree. It is increasingly apparent to me that the woke religion was created as an antithesis of Christianity to undermine the Christian culture. The left cites the Bible with twisted interpretations to preach their narrative. They exploit Christian virtues such as love, kindness, compassion, and charity to either manipulate or force people into accepting or conforming to their new *norms* and new *morality*. They prey on the goodness in people and their disdain for any form of racism and channel it into white guilt. They weaponize the best of human nature to make evil acceptable.

As churches weakened and Christianity was pushed out, the foundation of our shared traditional morality was lost. Judeo-Christian–based morals are being incrementally replaced by a complete absence of morals, or what is called "moral relativism." What is moral relativism? According to the website Ethics Unwrapped, "moral relativism is the idea that there is no universal or absolute set of moral principles. It's a version of morality that advocates 'to each their own,' and those who follow it say, 'Who am I to judge?'[43] In the absence of religion, truth has become subjective. In other words, it became my truth versus your truth, which really means no truth, which means no difference between right and wrong, or between good and evil. Moral relativism is just another face of the progressives' new woke religion.

How is moral relativism practiced? *HuffPost* offers a "how-to" guide in one of its articles, "Step into Your Truth with These 4 Simple Steps," to help individuals find their own truth. Here are *HuffPost*'s four simple steps to moral relativism heaven:

1. Accept who you are at this moment.
2. Acknowledge who you are.
3. Define your truth.
4. Live loudly and proudly (because your personal truth is just that: truth).[44]

We can interpret it this way: when we are perfect the way we are and when you define your own truth, who needs God?

When truth becomes how one chooses to define it, lies can simply become someone else's truth. In this new religion, if the aim is to advance progressive causes, it is okay to lie, to cheat, to break the law, and even to kill. To put it simply: by any means necessary. The progressives are not shy of declaring their goal: to fundamentally transform America and to abolish capitalism.

"Any means necessary" applies perfectly when it comes to stopping Donald Trump from gaining power. Sam Harris, author of the best seller *The End of Faith*, shared this belief. In an episode entitled "Trump, Religion, Wokeness" from a popular podcast called *Triggernometry*, Harris stated that it was absolutely warranted for Twitter to shut down the *New York Post*'s account for reporting the Hunter Biden laptop story, and that he wouldn't care even if Hunter Biden were to be found to have "the corpses of children in his basement."[45]

The sad reality is that it is exactly what the progressives have been doing and will continue to do. Without a moral compass, the Marxist "any means necessary" doctrine will only lead us to institutional breakdown, lawlessness, chaos, and the destruction of America.

Founding Father John Adams made it very clear: "Our constitution was made only for a moral and religious people. It is wholly inadequate to the government of any other."[46] That is to say, only those people with the moral and ethical makeup to willfully abide by the Constitution will feel obligated to honor it. When the people reject Christianity and its morality, the tie is severed between the people and the Constitution. Our Constitution can remain intact. But if the people that this Constitution was created for are no longer moral and religious, the Constitution will cease to function.

Progressives have been unable to change and dismantle the Constitution—yet. They have, however, made great strides in changing millions of people by indoctrinating them with Marxist ideology and undermining Christianity.

That is the ultimate goal of the progressives: destroy America by destroying the morality of the people by destroying Christianity, by any means necessary!

CHAPTER 10

Making of the New Man: Ideological Indoctrination

It was late at night, but I had to write a confession letter to submit to my teacher the following day. It was my mother's order. I was in fifth grade, and it was all because of my misdeeds in school two days prior.

A classmate reported to the teacher that I skipped classes the day before to go see an Albanian movie with another girl, for the third time. What attracted me to this movie was not its boring storyline: An urban doctor overcomes her reluctance and decides to go and serve the poor in rural areas. Instead, it was the fashion worn by the people in the movie. Women had fancy big hairdos and wore miniskirts. This was so foreign and fascinating to me.

The following day, I talked about the hairstyles, the skirts, and the makeup with other girls in the class. That was how I got myself into trouble. The teacher came for a home visit that night, and she brought the snitch with her. She warned my mother—and my mother totally agreed—that I, usually a good student, was under a bad influence and this needed to be swiftly corrected. It was a serious matter, not only because I skipped class, but also because of why I did it. My mother promised the teacher she would see that I wrote the confession (*jian tao*) that night.

By then, I was familiar with the formula of a confession through the endless political study sessions we had in school: admit my wrongdoing, find out the root cause for the problem (*si xiang gen yuan*), and make an action plan to correct the problem. The root cause, of course, was that the bourgeois remnants still existed in me, which made me susceptible to be attracted to the bourgeois way of life. The cure would be more devotion to studying Mao Zedong Thought so that I would stick to the revolutionary tradition of hard work and simple living. I accepted my punishment and sincerely felt ashamed of myself that I had disappointed my parents, my teacher, and the Party. I was a perfect example of an indoctrinated youth.

Indoctrination in Mao's world was known as Thought Reform (*si xiang gai zao*) and the creation of the "New Man." In the words of Lin Biao, Mao's handpicked successor, what Chinese people needed was unified thought, revolutionary thought, correct thought—and that was Mao Zedong Thought. In his speech to the Central Cultural Revolution Group on August 8, 1966, Lin Biao said: "It is easy to confiscate the property of Capitalists, but it is not easy to transform people's minds and souls. It needs to go through a major shock, such as the hydrogen bomb and the atomic bomb this time, which will shake people's hearts." Mao did not launch this nuclear ideological war against the Chinese people in 1966. He started it when the CCP took power in 1949.

Nowhere is there a better example of how this worked in Communist China than in a person named Puyi (1906–1967). Puyi was the last emperor of China, first put on the throne at the age of three, later branded a criminal by the CCP, sentenced to ten years in prison, and, in time, subjected to years of Thought Reform that turned him into a true believer in Communism and a staunch advocate for its mission to take over the world.

You might have heard of him: It is Puyi's life story that is depicted in the classic 1987 film *The Last Emperor*.

Puyi stayed on the Chinese throne for only three years before the Xinhai Revolution overthrew China's thousand-year-old dynastic system. Puyi was later installed as a puppet emperor of Japanese-occupied Manchuria (1932–1945) in northeastern China. After the Japanese were defeated, the Soviet Red Army took Puyi captive and kept him as a prisoner until the CCP took power in 1949, at which time he was repatriated to the CCP.[1]

The CCP immediately declared Puyi a war criminal and sentenced him to ten years in prison, where he would involuntarily receive Thought Reform reeducation designed to transform him from an enemy of the people to a "citizen"—into a New Man.

In his memoir *The First Half of My Life* (translated in English as *The Last Manchu*), Puyi detailed his journey of becoming a New Man, and it remains one of the best testaments of how the CCP conducts its Thought Reform program.

A CCP Thought Reform guidebook entitled *The Key to Intellectuals' Thought Reform: The Issue of Standpoint* details step-by-step instructions. It states that one of the most important goals of Thought Reform is to eradicate bourgeois individualism and replace it with "collectivism." The following is a six-step process that is designed to transform an individual, even one deemed an enemy of the state, into a New Man:

Step one: Studying Marxist-Leninist ideologies.

Step two: Physical labor together with putting down one's own airs (seeking humility) by eating, living, and working with the workers and peasants to better understand and know the feelings of working-class people.

Step three: Participating in actual class struggles.

Step four: Obeying the CCP and accepting its leadership unconditionally.

Step five: Engaging in criticism and self-criticism. This meant conducting self-criticism without any reservation, accepting the criticism of others without resistance, and criticizing the mistakes of others without hesitation.

Step six: Making this a lifelong commitment and continuing the revolution.[2]

This CCP formula for Thought Reform is what Puyi described in his book, detailing how his reeducation was successfully achieved. He was conditioned to understand that the ideal of Communism is to "transform the world; that is, to transform society and human beings."[3] In order to transform himself, Puyi had to study Communist theories to seek and acknowledge the root of his problem: class origin. As an emperor, he was the chief representative of the landlord class. Puyi managed to please the CCP by breaking away from his class origin and all of his past to embrace life as a socialist New Man after taking all the prescribed six steps.

Puyi received a CCP special pardon in 1959. At the end of his book, Puyi remarked, "While I tried to deceive them, while I used all kinds of shameful tactics to resist them, while I exposed my own ignorance, incompetence and stupidity, and while I no longer had the will to live, these Communists had firm belief that I could be reformed and had patiently guided me toward being a new man."[4]

Such is the power of indoctrination, CCP style! Whether Puyi was truly reformed in his heart or not, we will never know. What we do know is that his book gave the CCP a resounding propaganda victory. The brainwashing process that Puyi went through was something ALL Chinese had to go through, whether they belonged to a stratum as high as a former emperor or as low as village peasants.

This process is described as "*tuo tai huan gu*" or *rebirth*. Rebirth is not an event. It is an ongoing process, because it takes a lifetime to completely eradicate any residual influence from the old culture and to resist its never-ending encroachment.

I've talked a lot in this book about the devastation and chaos wrought by the Red Guards. Now it's time to talk about how their minds were shaped and brought into loyal submission to Mao. I quote African American abolitionist Frederick Douglass, who famously said, "It is easier to build strong children than to repair broken men."[5] The reverse is also true. It is easier to build weak children than to break strong men.

Political brainwashing in Mao's China was ubiquitous, especially in schools, media, and entertainment. For children, classroom education was the primary target of indoctrination, which was to be expected. It is much easier to shape young minds by banning old traditional ideas and fairly easily replacing them with competing Marxist ideas that met with little to no resistance.

After seventeen years (1949–1966) of government school indoctrination, the Red Guards' revolutionary mentality had successfully molded the young minds. They were ready for Mao's call for battle. Read this from a former Red Guard member: "In our mind, the world consisted of 'oppressor' and 'oppressed,' the former being our enemies and the latter our brothers, sisters, and friends. Our ideal and our historical mission was to eliminate all of that, both in China and abroad: all the phenomenon of oppression, exploitation, and slavery. Perhaps it was a Utopian ideal and pursuit, but we were utterly sincere."[6]

If you want to capture the minds of the students, you need to control those of the teachers first. That's the strategy the CCP took to gain total control of the schools on what they called the "battlefield over thoughts." The CCP moved deliberately with a plan of developing a complete Thought Reform system first in the "liberated regions" under their control before they took it mainstream throughout China after 1949.

The CCP prioritized its perfected Thought Reform programs on teachers in primary and secondary schools. By controlling and indoctrinating the teachers, the CCP could easily transform schools into Party-controlled government schools. The CCP reoriented teachers' philosophy of instruction away from traditional concepts and perspectives and toward Marxist ideology. And if teachers and staff didn't comply, they were quickly singled out and fired while being deemed "unreformable." At the same time, the CCP recognized those desired activists among the ranks of the faculty and trained them to be leaders and administrators. Everyone else was forced to undergo mandatory training that consisted of daily political studies, intensive training camps, summer training programs, group studies, and self-study combined with group meetings for the purpose of sharing study results. Training was a serious business, as trainees were subject to random inspections of their study notes and tests were held when necessary to ensure no one was simply going through the motions. Political studies became institutionalized, and the practice continues to this day.[7]

As a quick but highly troubling aside, two recent Project Veritas reports have revealed that "weeding out" conservatives in American schools is now happening, and it has been going on for a number of years.[8]

In 1952, the CCP issued a report stating, "This year before the start of the Autumn semester, about 90% of the teaching staff in higher education and about 70% of the teaching staff in secondary schools in the country have completed the work of ideological transformation and institutional clean-up."[9] Great news for the CPP and Communism, bad news for independent thinkers remaining among the country's education "intellectuals." Note that it took just two years for the CCP to reach their goal of transforming teachers!

The plan was working, and a foundation had been laid. Teachers who had been thoroughly reformed would carry out the CCP's indoctrination plan. Not only has that plan remained in motion seventy years later, but efforts have also been intensified under the dictatorial leadership of current leader Xi Jinping.

What's particularly revealing about the CCP's government school since 1952 is its textbooks. A study of elementary school textbooks that were in use from 1957 to 1964 revealed just how openly and pervasively political and behavioral values were being taught as part of the mass indoctrination of young people. Instructional classroom themes included devotion to the new society, benevolence of the new society, glorification of Mao, the evils of China under the Nationalists, social and personal responsibility, and achievement and altruistic behavior. Thusly, the ideal socialist person would have an unquestioning belief in their Communist leaders and the socialist state, and they were to stand ready to make self-sacrifices for their sakes.[10]

Edward Hunter, writing in *Brain-Washing in Red China: The Calculated Destruction of Men's Minds* in the early 1950s, offered his own assessment of the revised narratives of the CCP-approved textbooks: "The history books are by far the most impressive of all the textbooks that the new regime has put out. By comparison, other subjects, such as literature and science, have been carelessly treated. Because of the perhaps decisive role that the teaching of history occupies in the indoctrination of the new generation—the fighting generation—a rather extensive survey is warranted."[11]

The history I learned in Mao's government school was fictitious history. Over three thousand years of Chinese history was reduced to the depiction of class struggle between oppressors (the landlords) and the oppressed (the peasants). All the peasant uprisings failed until the Chinese Communist Party, armed with a winning Marxist ideology, led the peasants to permanent victory. It was the CCP who liberated the Chinese people from the oppression of imperialism, feudalism, and capitalism, and finally set the Chinese people free—or so we were taught.

Here, we turn to George Orwell, who, in offering timeless perspective, famously said: "Who controls the past controls the future: who controls the present controls the past."[12]

In order to create Mao's New Man, a new role model was needed. Lei Feng was forged as the ideal New Man, and the "Learn from Lei Feng" campaign was launched in 1963. As far back as I can remember, Lei Feng was the iconic figure I was supposed to look up to and the model I should follow.

Lei Feng was a member of the People's Liberation Army (PLA). He and his family had supposedly suffered a great deal from oppression by landlords in old China. That was the reason Lei Feng had boundless love for Mao and for the CCP, and boundless hatred for the class enemies. Lei Feng was portrayed as a selfless person who took joy in serving the people with heart and soul. During his short life of twenty-two years, Lei allegedly performed endless good deeds. Songs, movies, and books were created to praise him and encourage the masses to follow Lei Feng's example to become the Communist New Man.

The truth is that what Mao and the CCP wanted most from all Chinese people (including me!) was to emulate Lei Feng's mindless loyalty. It is not difficult to see how Lei Feng's spirit made the genesis of the Red Guards possible. While being encouraged to conduct "good deeds" on behalf of the state, as guided by Lei Feng's spirit, the youths were being molded and conditioned to serve as loyal robots for Mao and the Party. The Learning from Lei Feng campaign was crucial to the formation of the political culture of the Red Guard generation. For the New Man, Chinese people were being called to submit their unconditional love for Mao while holding unconditional hatred for "class enemies" as defined by Mao. That was the essence and purpose of the Red Guards.

One of the reasons Mao launched the Cultural Revolution, as you know by now, was to assume power from the CCP apparatus, which he considered no longer under his direct control. This included education. To Mao, the existing CCP educational system was not radical enough. He believed that it was instead being run by reactionary "bourgeois academic authorities" as well as unreformed bourgeois intellectuals in leading positions. They focused on teaching academics without putting politics front and center. Mao wanted to radicalize the entire educational system. In his May 7 Directive of 1966, Mao stated: "Education needs to be revolutionized, and the phenomenon of bourgeois intellectuals ruling our schools can no longer continue."

Soon after the Cultural Revolution was launched, schools were closed. That deprived me of two years of schooling. In some parts of China, schools were closed for much longer. Upon returning to school formally in 1968, our curriculum was very limited. For more than a year we had just one textbook, which was Mao's *Little Red Book*.

At least five billion copies—that's correct!—of Mao's *Little Red Book* were printed at a time when the total population in China was eight hundred million.[13] Many families received multiple copies. My family owned several copies. I, like so many in my generation, had no other books to read either at home or at school. During the Cultural Revolution, there was a shortage of almost everything imaginable, except for one thing—Mao's *Little Red Book*!

Our education would no longer be restricted to the classroom. We would be learning in real life. In other words, our education was mandated to be in total accordance with the Thought Reform guidelines, which included physical labor. Physical labor is a necessary part of Thought Reform, as Communism believes that "work makes one free." Every semester, we would spend a month working in the fields or the factory, or performing military training to learn from workers, peasants, and soldiers. That was the best way to learn and understand Mao Zedong Thought, by productive labor—or so we were led to believe. To me, it amounts to progressive student activism programs.

This is the legacy of Mao's radicalization and destruction of the education system. According to the CCP's 1982 census, there were more than 230 million illiterate and semiliterate people in China, nearly a quarter of the country's total population,[14] which effectively wiped out much of the progress made in the previous years before the Cultural Revolution. The abandoning of academic education and research reverted China back to the stone age, a sad reality that the majority of Chinese were not aware of until China was opened to the West.

The leaders of the Cultural Revolution banned all of the textbooks that were in existence, criticizing them as infested with bourgeoise elements and lacking emphasis on Mao Zedong Thought. It's been more than fifty years, but I can still remember a few things I learned from my pre–Cultural Revolution textbooks. One of them was a line from a reading textbook: "Water is running in a little creek, *hualala*." It is a line describing nature and its sounds. I still recall it because it was beautiful in its simplicity and easy to visualize.

It is, however, not the sort of thing they wanted to teach students when their mission was to radicalize. Paulo Freire, a Marxist Brazilian educator and author of *Pedagogy of the Oppressed*, agreed with Mao. The only reason to teach words and language to students should be to raise their critical consciousness, including their revolutionary and class consciousness. "Whether one calls this correct thinking 'revolutionary consciousness' or 'class consciousness,' it is an indispensable precondition of revolution," Freire wrote.[15]

Once the new textbooks and new curriculum of the Cultural Revolution arrived in schools, a quick glimpse revealed what the new theme of schooling would be: Mao Zedong Thought. It was now incorporated into every school subject, whether it be reading, math, science, languages, etc. Politics was running the educational system, top to bottom.

While writing this chapter, I discovered on the internet some scanned pages from a math book of that era. Here is an example: "Before liberation, poor peasant Uncle Liu rented 4 *mus* [0.66 acres] of land from the landlord. Every year he had to submit to the landlord 12 *dous* [approx. 3.3 bushels] of grain per *mu*. How many *dous* of grain did the landlord exploit from Uncle Liu each year?" The page also included an illustration depicting Uncle Liu telling a group of young people about his "bitterness" from the past. Mao's portrait was in the center of the page, and above it was a Mao quote: "Never forget class struggle."

Here's another sample of a Cultural Revolution–era math problem: "With boundless love for Chairman Mao, international sailors visited 'Chairman Mao is the Reddest Sun in Our Heart' exhibition. There was a total of 1,184 sailors in eight days. What is the average number of visiting sailors per day?"

My English textbook was nothing more than a book of political slogans such as "Long live Chairman Mao," "Long live proletariat dictatorship!" etc. Obviously, it provided nothing in the form of real and everyday English.

In Imperial China dating back to 600 AD, there was a civil-service examination system, which was quite democratic.

Many talented students, regardless of family background, could pursue admission into the civil service of the imperial courts. This became a long-held Chinese belief that through standard examinations, children of any family background would have a chance to succeed. This was the old Chinese system of meritocracy. The British government adopted a similar testing system for screening civil servants across the board throughout the United Kingdom in 1855, and the United States after 1883.[16] But this tradition of Chinese meritocracy had to be destroyed as part of the Four Olds.

To thoroughly transform the Chinese education system also meant to install Mao's version of affirmative action. College admissions were halted when the Cultural Revolution broke out in 1966. They resumed in 1970, but entrance examinations were eliminated and replaced with a quota system and with "the method of recommendation," in which admission preference was given to the children of workers, peasants, and soldiers. Qualification was determined by Party leaders based on the candidates' good political thinking and rich work experience. Prior education level and academic competency was not relevant. According to data from the most prestigious Beijing University, among its 1970 enrollment of 2,665 students, 171 were from high school, 2,142 from junior high school, and seventy-nine from primary school.[17] Interestingly, the current Chinese CCP leader Xi Jinping is a worker-peasant-soldier college graduate.

These worker-peasant-soldier college students were not going to university just to study. They were also given a mission of "going to universities, taking control of universities, and transforming universities with Mao Zedong Thought."

Mao's goal was to produce "Red Intellectuals," or what he called "Redness and Expertness" (*yu hong yu zhuan*). He wanted his new "expert" class to be foremostly loyal to the Party and the Communist cause. Mao's experiment failed. "Worker-peasant-soldier college student" became a derogatory term. Their degrees were not acknowledged in China after the Cultural Revolution.

Although the ten years' loss of real academic learning left China in the dust behind the West in the areas of science and technology, it did succeed in producing more loyal followers of Mao, the socialist New Man.

* * *

Back to America. In order to understand what has happened to America's system of education, we have to understand the difference between traditional education and progressive education.

Traditionalists, according to Martin Cothran, director of the Classical Latin School Association and editor of *Classical Teacher* magazine, believe schools are academic institutions with a purely academic purpose. And that purpose, he says, is to develop the mental ability of students and more generally to pass on the Western cultural heritage to the next generation. It is also to make well-rounded citizens who can think critically in seeking wisdom and to live a fruitful life by understanding one's nature as a human being. Progressives, by contrast, regard schools as social service agencies, whose purpose is to prepare students for the social, political, and economic realities of modern life. This includes job-skills training, certain forms of social indoctrination, and even some psychological conditioning.[18]

The difference between classic and progressive education in America is a striking parallel to the difference between a traditional Confucius-based education and the CCP's education. The former views the purpose of education as character building, for each individual to strive to be what Confucius called *junzi*, or a noble person. The latter weaponizes education to produce successors for its Communist cause. As young students, we were taught that we would all be a little shiny screw for the socialist machine to happily shine wherever the Party put us.

Cothran also points out that traditionalists typically are parents and older teachers, while progressives are comprised mostly of educational professionals trained by progressive teachers colleges.[19] These professionals are what we now call the "expert class," probably known as such because progressive educators believe they are the only ones capable of determining what is right for schools, curriculums, and students. Do you want to know what the "experts" from the National Education Association proposed lately? They asserted that educators should use the term "birthing parent" instead of "mother,"[20] and that CRT should be taught to our children.[21]

Summing up the difference is easy: educational traditionalists strive to prepare future well-rounded citizens, while progressives seek to groom future activists and future revolutionaries. One truth can't be denied: all public schools and increasingly more private schools are controlled by progressives. The reason is simple. These progressives come from the pipeline of the progressive teachers colleges—the indoctrination mills that have been in operation since the 1940s.

John Dewey (1859–1952), a renowned educator and professor at the Teachers College at Columbia University (1904–1930), was a key figure in helping turn American public schools into progressively run government schools. Dewey also played a key role in making Columbia University the home of the Frankfurt School

Marxists and helping them to put down cultural-Marxist roots in America.[22] He is the father of progressive education. This is what he had to say in summing up the purpose of education in America: "I believe that education is the fundamental method of social progress and reform."[23]

Gloria Ladson-Billings and William F. Tate, authors of *Education Research in the Public Interest: Social Justice, Action, and Policy*, wrote this about Dewey: "Dewey's pragmatism was a project to design the child by eliminating past traditions in order to construct a modern self, an individual whose modes of reflection and participation were directed toward actions for the future."[24]

What are the past traditions that Ladson-Billings and Tate spoke of? They are Western civilization and Christianity. Mao also wanted to eliminate past tradition, which for centuries defined and guided Chinese civilization. Both Dewey and Mao had something available with which to replace the past tradition—Marxism! Both the CCP and the progressives, in indoctrinating educational systems, took (and are taking) aim at creating and shaping the future New Man for China and for America, respectively.

Lei Feng was designated the icon of Mao's New Man in the CCP's bold propaganda. To many American and Western youths, the present-day icon of the New Man is Che Guevara (1928–1967); an Argentine Marxist revolutionary, physician, writer, and guerrilla leader; who still today remains a romantic icon and a martyr in the realm of American Marxism. To many Americans, the real stories of Che—and they weren't always honorable or heroic—were lost. What is left is the part that claims Che gave up his privileged life and sacrificed his life while fighting for the oppressed.

Gerard J. DeGroot, author of *The Sixties Unplugged*, said this about Che: "Since Che maintained that leaders would have to come from the educated class, this explains his appeal to middle-class students in the developed world. He implied, to the delight of radicals everywhere, that a few committed activists could change the world."[25]

Progressive educators have a hero of their own, also from Latin America: Paulo Freire (1921–1997), a radical Brazilian educator whose *Pedagogy of the Oppressed* has been extremely influential. Freire believed that "there's no such thing as neutral education. Education either functions as an instrument to bring about conformity or freedom."

Freire's "conformity" is Christian Western tradition, and his "freedom" is the revolution to change the world. His core belief is that the function of education should be to create revolutionaries. In his foreword to Freire's *Pedagogy of the Oppressed*, Richard Shaull describes Freire's education philosophy as one in which education should inspire "the practice of freedom, the means by which men and women deal critically and creatively with reality and discover how to participate in the transformation of their world. The development of an educational methodology that facilitates this process will inevitably lead to tension and conflict within our society. But it could also contribute to the formation of a New Man and mark the beginning of a new era in Western history."[26]

Dr. James Lindsay, a foremost critic of CRT and Marxist ideologies, claims schools in America have, in fact, become Paulo Freire's schools. A Freire school, Lindsay says, aims to raise students' consciousness of class, race, or identities, and to prepare them to be future revolutionaries.[27]

Project Veritas has uncovered numerous indiscretions of the left that they would rather keep hidden. One Project Veritas scoop showed California high school teacher Gabriel Gipe, his classroom adorned with—among other things—Mao's portrait and an Antifa flag, bragging on camera that he could turn students into "revolutionaries" within 180 days.[28]

Through their takeover and remaking of education in the American classroom, the progressives have successfully changed what was a Christian culture to a Marxist culture. Let's now look at how they have done it.

In the Name of "Separation of Church and State"

In their determination to invoke their own form of "separation of religion from state" by removing any reference to God from the classroom, progressives have ushered in a new religion known as Marxism.

Here's what W. Cleon Skousen, author of *The Naked Communist*, has to say about that: "As teachers we are not to teach a particular faith, but parents are within their rights when they insist that the classroom is not [to] be used by those few teachers who seek to destroy faith."[29]

Today in American public schools, Christianity has been replaced with the new religion of Marxism, and among its tenets are multiculturalism; identity ideologies; intersectionality; social justice; diversity, equity, and inclusion (DEI); green politics…all in all, the religion of woke ideologies.

Teachers' Thought Reform

This takes us back to John Dewey, who, for about a quarter of a century (1904–1930), taught in Columbia University's Teachers College as a leading "philosopher" and "educator." The Teachers

College became the training center for future Marxist educators. By 1950, it was estimated that a third of principals and superintendents of large school districts were being trained there. Many of these left the college with radical ideas about reality, government, society, family, and economics, all of which had been passed down from Dewey and the Frankfurt School.[30]

Keep in mind that statistic about principals and superintendents is from more than seventy years ago. Obviously, a lot has happened since then, and you can safely bet that a segment of academia much greater than a third has since dug in deep with the progressives. The same goes for teachers getting their degrees from colleges and universities offering heavy doses of Marxist ideology. Those who managed to survive that indoctrination with their minds still clear and objective get their second chances to join the ranks of the devoted progressives by making their way through in-depth wokeness training required by school boards. There's no escaping it. Like the CCP, the radical left has to reeducate teachers through wokeness training to make sure everyone is brought up to speed for the indoctrination campaign.

This includes my state of Virginia. As reported by the *Washington Examiner* in November 2021: "Teacher training materials in Virginia provide instructions for incorporating critical race theory into the classroom, and the state's education department website specifically recommends books promoting the framework."[31]

There are plenty of outside resources and consulting services for indoctrinating teachers and therefore helping them indoctrinate children. Panorama Education is one such service that provides support for teaching Marxist-inspired CRT and social-emotional learning (SEL). The service has contracts in more than fifty of the one hundred largest school districts in the US. Guess who cofounded this company? US Attorney General Merrick Garland's son-in-law, Xan Tanner.[32]

Teaching Children to Hate America

To create a new culture, our children need to denounce their past and heritage. That is the mission of the progressives. The way to do this is to teach these students to hate America, and the progressives do it through writing and teaching fake history, such as Nikole Hannah-Jones's *The 1619 Project: A New Origin Story*, a 2021 release that was unsurprisingly launched by the flagship of left-wing media, the *New York Times*. It is a project that stretches thin the bounds of balanced historical scholarship, yet it was awarded the 2020 Pulitzer Prize for Commentary. *1619* rewrote American history, stating that the real beginning of America was not in 1776 but in 1619 when the first slave was brought ashore. Now *The 1619 Project* has entered America's classrooms. If this is the history curriculum for today's students, you can't blame the students for loathing America and for wanting to join the force to destroy it.

Before *The 1619 Project* was the 1980 book *A People's History of the United States* by Howard Zinn. Just like the CCP, Zinn reduced the history of the United States into a story of oppressor versus oppressed. Here's one take on the premise of Zinn's book, posted online by his publisher, The New Press: "Howard Zinn's *A People's History of the United States* has turned history on its head for an entire generation of readers, telling the nation's story from the viewpoints of ordinary people—the slaves, workers, immigrants, women, and Native Americans who made their own history but whose voices are typically omitted from the historical record."[33]

Someone once told me that the word *people's* in the title of a book is a giveaway that the authors are Marxists. It is so true! The word *people* (or *renmin*) is what I grew up with in Communist China. The CCP's China is called the "People's Republic of China" (Taiwan's formal name is the "Republic of China"), the army is known as is the "People's Liberation Army (PLA)," the "legislature" is the "National People's Congress," the court is the "People's Court," the police are the "People's Police," and the Chinese yuan is the "People's Money" (or *renminbi*). The only park in Chengdu, where I grew up, was named People's Park. Communists and Marxists surely "love" the people, because they own the people. Will we soon live in the "People's United States of America"?

History is of paramount importance to both the CCP and the progressives. That's why they want to keep the students from learning the real history. In February 2023, Virginia Democrats rejected a bill that would require schools to teach the history of Communism. Their reason? It may encourage anti-Asian sentiment![34] In April 2023, 673 professors from University of North Carolina signed a public letter opposing legislation that would require university students to take courses on America's government and founding documents, claiming that it violates "academic freedom"![35]

I and millions of Chinese students were indoctrinated to believe the CCP's lies, because the only history books available to us were created by the CCP. The progressives aim at the same result using the same tactic.

Implementing Marxist Programs

Long before CRT was exposed to parents and the public, it had been taught (not as a course) and practiced in government schools through Freire's pedagogy. Thanks to journalist and CRT critic Christopher Rufo's work and to the pandemic, which afforded parents a rare opportunity to see with their own eyes through online classrooms what was being taught to their children, CRT is becoming a household term for the wrong reasons. CRT is so pervasive in government schools that it has sneaked its way into our math textbooks the same way Maoism encroached on China's math textbooks, except in China it wasn't so secretive.

One state that gets it is Florida, whose citizens in early 2022 rejected 41 percent of new math textbooks that promote Marxist ideologies. Below is from a sample page of a rejected math textbook:

What? Me? Racist? More than 2 million people have tested their racial prejudice using an online version of the Implicit Association Test. Most groups' average scores fall between "slight" and "moderate" bias, but the differences among groups, by age and by political identification, are intriguing. In this section's Exercise Set (Exercises 103 and 104), you will be working with models that measure bias...[36]

I don't see any difference between the indoctrinating math textbooks used by Mao and by the woke ideologues. Do you?

Quietly sneaking into school curriculum everywhere is something new called social-emotional learning (SEL). SEL is defined by the Virginia Department of Education as "the process through which all young people and adults acquire and apply the knowledge, skills, and attitudes to develop healthy identities, manage emotions and achieve personal and collective goals, feel and show empathy for others, establish and maintain supportive relationships, and make responsible and caring decisions."[37]

Doesn't this sound attractive, or at least harmless, like all other agendas pushed by the left? I am fortunate to have met Lisa Logan. She is a young mother of three and a fellow activist who started researching SEL when it was going to be taught at her child's school. She eventually became an expert on what SEL is really about and started her activism to stop it from being taught in school. She explained to me that "while many of the attributes taught through SEL *sound* wonderful—empathy, perspective taking, social awareness, etc.—they are being used as both a smokescreen and a springboard to introduce topics to and have conversations with students about societal issues related to critical theories in order to get them to adopt a critical consciousness. Subjects like CRT or Transgenderism are easily inserted into SEL lessons which use cult grooming tactics to manipulate students' innate sense of compassion to get them to become social justice advocates."[38] She continued, "The lessons in SEL programs are designed to get students to question the worldview fostered by their families and adopt a new one that believes that race, class, and sex are social constructs—or ideas made up by society—to oppress specific groups of people." On March 9, 2023, Lisa was invited to give a speech on SEL to delegates at the United Nations Commission on the Status of Women CSW67.

There is no mistake. Marxist programs are being relentlessly pushed to our school-age children.

Abandoning Meritocracy in the Name of Diversity, Equity, and Inclusion

Here again, we see the progressives following Mao's path to destroy meritocracy. Meritocracy is one of the reasons that America is great, because it encourages *individuals* to strive for their best. Meritocracy is color-blind and identity blind. It rewards individuals based on their effort and talent. Meritocracy is the essence of the American dream, which has been proven time and again by individuals for generations, including immigrants like me.

Meritocracy is synonymous to freedom and antonymous to authoritarianism. That is exactly the reason progressive educators have aimed to destroy meritocracy and replace it with *diversity, equity*, and *inclusion*. This is best demonstrated by the racially conscious admission policies implemented by Ivy League universities such as Harvard and elite high schools such as Thomas Jefferson High School in Virginia. Progressive educators have been trying to abandon standardized tests by deeming the tests racist and biased in favor of a *quota* system. Their argument is that ethnic minorities usually score much lower than the national average. However, their argument was easily debunked by the fact that Asian Americans' average scores are much higher than the national average, including that of whites. Asians have become a problem for the progressive DEI narrative. To overcome this predicament, the progressives conveniently classify Asians as "white adjacent" with *white privilege*. The sinister net effect is that Asians have been singled out as a target for discrimination and punished for their academic success. DEI is the antithesis of our cherished American Dream.

Kenny Xu, son of immigrant parents from China, has been a brave fighter for defending meritocracy. His influential book *An Inconvenient Minority: The Attack on Asian American Excellence and the Fight for Meritocracy* makes compelling counterarguments against the progressives' Marxist and racist agenda, which destroys meritocracy and, therefore, our freedom.

Lowering the Standard and Dumb Down the Education

In his book *Battle for the American Mind*, Pete Hegseth quotes C. S. Lewis: "Education is essentially for freemen and vocational training for slaves." Hegseth references the Lewis quote to illustrate how John Dewey took aim at ending the Christian paideia to reduce schools to mere locales for vocational training.[39] But contemporary schools have even failed at functioning as vocational schools. They fail because many of the students coming out of government schools don't even have the *basic* skills (the "three Rs"—reading, writing, and arithmetic) to be able to function as self-sufficient individuals. Without being able to read at even, let's say, the tenth-grade level or perform basic math, they are helpless slaves, totally dependent on the state; and that's exactly the way the state wants it.

The progressives tried to make us believe that lowering educational standards is another way to achieve *equity*. What is the difference between Mao's equity and the progressives' equity?

Nothing. Both aim at dumbing down children so they can better submit to being the progressives' tools for the Marxist-driven revolution.

It's already happening here in America and will continue to spread. Beginning in 2020, the state of Washington no longer requires students to pass standardized tests in order to graduate from high school.[40]

The equity narrative these Marxist educators have been pushing is nothing more than the disastrous experiment Mao implemented in China. The result will be the same: total wrecking of the most valuable resources any nation can have, the human resources, and transforming America into a nation with young people who could hardly read, write, or do math, and so are easy to control.

* * *

As noted earlier, the Red Guards were the prototype for the New Man during the Chinese Cultural Revolution. Mao had seventeen years (1949–1966) to produce his vision for the New Man, while it has taken decades for American Marxists. But now their effort has borne fruit. We now finally have our own American Red Guards.

American Red Guards, as I detailed in Chapter 5, are activists in search of a cause, and they are also victims in search of an identity. They are revolutionaries in search of something—anything—to rebel against.

Conservatives accuse government schools of teaching students *what* to think versus *how* to think. The present-day reality is actually worse than that. Indoctrinated youths are no longer allowed to think for themselves. They simply respond to stimuli. Our youths are so conditioned that they only need to be "triggered" with words or terms such as *Trump, MAGA, pro-life, anti-trans,* or *police shooting of an unarmed Black man* before they act on a knee-jerk response for which they have been conditioned. Off to the streets they go with raised fists and slogans of "Hey, hey, ho, ho, (fill in the blank) has got to go." The mobilization is as simple as sending out a tweet.

Founding Father James Madison wrote that our Constitution requires "sufficient virtue among men for self-government. To each new generation the virtues without which free societies cannot survive: basic honesty, integrity, self-restraint, concern for others and respect for their dignity and rights, civic-mindedness, and the like."[41]

Where does the new generation learn these virtues? The answer should be exactly like it used to be at one time, but sadly is no longer. It should be found in the traditions of *family, church,* and *school.* These are mind-shaping institutions that define future generations.

The progressives have successfully assaulted and undermined all three institutions of family, church, and school, as outlined in these three last chapters, and they will continue to do so unabated unless citizens and public officials of sound mind stop them.

The progressive goal is singular: to make America a nation of their New Man (and, yes, that applies equally to women as well) who embrace woke ideologies and who abandon Christian principles and American traditional values, ultimately putting the will of the state ahead of the rights of the individuals.

If we want to restore and keep our Republic, we need good

citizens instead of activists, and we need John Adams's "moral and religious" citizens.

Hope is not all lost. Progressive education in America started its takeover in the 1930s. It has taken progressives almost a century to get to where they are today, yet they have failed to indoctrinate all of us. The story of John David Rice-Cameron is an encouraging one. He is the son of Susan Rice, who is one of the prominent progressives, former US ambassador to the UN, advisor under both Clinton and Obama, and currently a member of Biden's Domestic Policy Council. Against all odds, Rice-Cameron is a conservative. Here is a direct quote from the October 15, 2018, *Washington Post* article: "Rice-Cameron is not just a conservative but the head of the Stanford College Republicans and a proud supporter of President Trump. His ambition is to 'Make Stanford Great Again.'"[42] Rice-Cameron demonstrates to us that progressive brainwashing is not insurmountable.

There is another encouraging success story of deprogramming. Annabella Rockwell received her education from the elite Mount Holyoke College in Massachusetts. Through four years of progressive indoctrination, "she was 'brainwashed' into believing she had been a lifelong victim of patriarchal oppression and had a duty to fight on behalf of other victims: women, people of color and LBGTQ folks." It is her mother whose determination and relentless efforts to bring back her daughter that saved her. Now Annabella works as a fundraiser for the leading conservative advocacy group PragerU, through which she shares her powerful story.[43]

Indoctrination is not just about pushing bad ideas and deception on unsuspecting people, but also suppressing and demonizing good ideas. We need to bring back those good ideas to our schools and public squares. We need to restore what the progressives have been trying to destroy, the foundational values of America, all of our real history, and a nationwide adherence to and reverence for our Constitution. The conservative movement against woke-ism is, in essence, a *restoration* revolution.

A Warning

Through my interactions with my audience both in person and online, I have often heard questions to the effect of, "Is Mao's Cultural Revolution simply an unfortunate event in the past?" "Is China not better and freer now?" and "Isn't China now a capitalist country?"

These are important questions and deserve expanded answers. To do that we need to go back to the years right after Mao's death.

Mao's Cultural Revolution pushed China to the brink of total collapse. Upon his death in 1976, the country was not only bankrupted economically but also ideologically. People were totally disillusioned by Maoism and by his brand of socialism. This posed the greatest threat to the power of the CCP it has ever faced.

It was against this backdrop that Deng Xiaoping rose to power in China in 1977. Deng had been the voice of reason and pragmatism within the CCP. For that, he was purged by Mao three times as a right-wing "capitalist roader" because he wanted to focus on improving China's economy, and that contradicted Mao's class-struggle Party line. As the new leader, Deng abandoned Mao's class struggle and replaced it with his famous new doctrine: "Black cat or white cat, if it can catch mice, it's a good cat," which means that the focus should be on improving China's economy by bringing in capitalism, or "any means necessary." Deng, as a veteran "capitalist roader," understood that capitialism was the hope to save the CCP, for the time being.

Deng's economic reform kickstarted China's new economy, which opened up China to the world, and courted Western capital and investment. He had something that the Western corporations drooled over: cheap labor, with little or no human rights, and little governmental regulations. Over the past twenty years, we witnessed unprecedented economic growth in China. Today, China stands as the second-largest economy in the world.

Deng was remembered as the greatest CCP "reformer." However, it is important to bear in mind that he only wanted economic reform, not political reform. Period! He was firm that Marxism-Leninism and Mao Zedong Thought should remain the CCP's guiding principles. Deng was the one who ordered the bloody crackdown on the Tiananmen Square student prodemocracy movement in 1989. He had zero tolerance for any challenge to the CCP's power!

The West chose not to see that fact. They wishfully believed that capitalism and a free market would bring China more freedom. Former President Bill Clinton was certainly convinced. It was Clinton who brought China into the World Trade Organization (WTO). In his March 9, 2000, speech on the China Trade Bill, Clinton said: "By joining the WTO, China is not simply agreeing to import more of our products; it is agreeing to import one of democracy's most cherished values: economic freedom. The more China liberalizes its economy, the more fully it will liberate the potential of its people—their initiative, their imagination, their remarkable spirit of enterprise. And when individuals have the power, not just to dream but to realize their dreams, they will demand a greater say."[1]

Clinton was not totally wrong. China's opening up itself to the world indeed brought in the ideas of freedom and democracy. The Chinese people wanted a greater say in how things should be run, and they wanted greater accountability of their government. The sad reality is that they got neither.

China's unprecedented economic growth under former President Jiang Zemin inevitably brought about unprecedented corruption. Those in power enriched themselves at the expense of the people they rule over. People disdained these corrupt CCP bureaucrats and called them "tigers" and "flies." *Tigers* refer to those in high positions of central and provincial governments; *flies* to those in local governments.

The CCP was corrupt from head to toe. Its rulers were widely seen by the masses as captialistic exploiters and oppressors depicted by the CCP's ideological grandfather, Karl Marx. The CCP's legitimacy was again greatly threatened. Many Chinese people openly expressed their longing for a strong man like Mao to bring about "social justice." Their wish came true and their calls were answered in 2013 by none other than Xi Jinping, who was seen as the new Communist messiah promising to save China by saving the CCP.

Xi Jinping launched his anti-corruption campaign to wipe out "tigers" and "flies." In so doing, he vowed: "We must uphold the fighting of tigers and flies at the same time, resolutely investigating law-breaking cases of leading officials and also earnestly resolving the unhealthy tendencies and corruption problems which happen all around people."[2]

Xi Jinping did carry out his vows. His anti-corruption campaign was victorious with wide popular support from the masses. But people soon realized that those "tigers" and "flies" he fought against and succeeded in purging turned out to be his political rivals. Xi Jinping has cleverly managed to secure unchallengeable power by achieving what Mao's main goal for his Cultural Revolution had been: to remove political enemies and challengers.

Following Mao's blueprint for the Cultural Revolution, Xi Jinping has moved to the ideological realm in order to reshape the Chinese "hegemony" with Xi Jinping Thought. He is creating his own brand of socialism: "Socialism with Chinese Characteristics *for a New Era*." Welcome to the Chinese Cultural Revolution 2.0.

On January 5, 2018, Xi Jinping stated the following in a speech at a political meeting for newly selected CCP officials:

Belief in Marxism, socialism and Communism is the political soul of and the spiritual pillar for Communists. We often say that if the foundation is not strong, the ground will shake. Shakable belief will also shake the ground. The same logic applies to the disintegration of the Soviet Union, the collapse of the Communist Party of the Soviet Union (CPSU), and the upheaval in Eastern Europe. The CPSU seized power when it had only 200,000 members, defeated Hitler when it had 2 million members, but lost power when it had nearly 20 million members. I asked the same question before: Why no real men came out to fight in that turmoil? Why? Because the ideals and beliefs were gone.[3]

Xi Jinping takes it to task to restore and strengthen Communism by destroying the *new* Four Olds of Western-style democratic ideas and values, and by denouncing the new Black Class of today's Chinese millionaires and billionaires. Xi Jinping also takes it to task to replace the United States as the world leader with his "Community of Common Destiny for Mankind" initiative; in other words, CCP-style globalism.

After decades of engaging with the CCP, we see that Western-style democracy has been defeated in its infancy in China, while Chinese-style authoritarianism has been exported and is gaining ground in the West. The pandemic brought that reality closer to Americans. While China is becoming less and less like the West, the West is becoming more and more like China.

In China, Xi Jinping has revived Mao's Cultural Revolution. In America, the progressives have launched the second phase of the counterculture revolution. The Chinese Marxists and the American Marxists share the same goal, same standpoints, same tactics, and even the same vocabulary. And they are working on destroying capitalism and, with it, our freedom.

That's why I say it's time to put Communism on trial!

Few would argue against the evils of slavery, Nazism, or Fascism. No one would openly defend these evil systems and ideologies without being denounced. In fact, people have zero tolerance for those who were involved with the Nazis' crimes, even if it involved working as a secretary in a death camp. In December 2022, a ninety-seven-year-old woman, a former Nazi death camp secretary, was convicted by a German court.[4] And rightfully so.

Yet, that is not the case with socialism and Communism, which are responsible for arguably more horrific crimes against humanity. Bernie Sanders openly claims that he himself is a socialist. The same is true for AOC and the "squad," although they put an attractive adjective in front of the word *socialism*: *democratic* socialism.

The Communist Party USA (CPUSA) was founded in 1919, two years after the Bolshevik Revolution of 1917 and two years before the launch of the Chinese Communist Party. More than a hundred years later, CPUSA is still in operation and growing. In December 2021, Senator Richard Blumenthal attended the event to celebrate the 102nd anniversary of the founding of the Communist Party USA in Connecticut to offer his congratulations and present the awards! He did, however, express his regret for doing so afterward.[5]

Why is Communism not condemned in America and in the West in the same manner that Nazism was rebuked? The reason Nazism and Fascism have become synonymous as forms of evil is because their crimes and ideologies were tried and condemned in the court of international law. We need Nuremberg-type trials for the biggest murderers in human history: Lenin, Stalin, Mao, and Pol Pot. We need Nuremberg-type trials for Communist ideology. It is this ideology that is responsible for more than one hundred million deaths![6] Ideology does kill.

The work has indeed already started. In May 2022, Florida Governor Ron DeSantis signed a bill into law, designating November 7 Victims of Communism Day. That bill dedicates at least forty-five minutes of instruction on Victims of Communism Day to teaching students about the evil and danger of Communism.[7] We need to educate not only the schoolchildren but also the entire population on the danger and threat of Communism to America.

* * *

It is all about power. It is about gaining power by first *destabilizing* a society through cultural subversion and upheaval, as demonstrated by Mao's Cultural Revolution, and its present-day reiteration in the form of a Woke Revolution here in America. It is also about maintaining power by secondly *stabilizing* the Marxist hegemony to exact complete control over its people, as demonstrated by Xi Jinping in today's China.

In other words, this Woke cultural revolution in America is the elites' pathway to their ultimate destination: the so-called "China Model," a ruthless totalitarian regime armed with surveillance and AI technology that will control every move of individuals 24/7. Once absolute power is established, the elites will redefine morality and social norms that we all will have to live by. I can assure you that these new moralities and social norms will have nothing to do with the Woke ideology they are pushing today. It's only a means to an end. I can also assure you that our freedom will be taken away and we will all be brought under total subjugation by the state no matter whether you are on the left or the right.

Dear reader, this has been my warning.

ACKNOWLEDGMENTS

A very special thanks to Mike Towle.

I also would like to extend my appreciation to Kevin Higgins, Elicia Brand, and all the great people I've met both in person and online in the past two years who have given me support and encouragement.

NOTES

Chapter 1: Leaving the Kitchen Table

1. Brown, Lee. "Mom Who Survived Mao's China Calls Critical Race Theory America's Cultural Revolution." *New York Post.* June 10, 2021. https://nypost.com /2021/06/10/mom-who-survived-maos-china-blasts-critical-race-theory/.

2. Ruiz, Michael. "Virginia Parents, Teachers Group Accused of 'Racketeering,' Intimidating Conservative Parents." *Fox News.* March 17, 2021. https://www.foxnews .com/us/virginia-parents-teachers-group-accused-of-racketeering-intimidating -conservative-parents.

3. Ruiz, Michael. "Virginia Mom Who Survived Maoist China Eviscerates School Board's Critical Race Theory Push." *Fox News.* May 18, 2021. https://www.foxnews.com /us/virginia-xi-van-fleet-critical-race-theory-china-cultural-revolution-loudoun.

Chapter 4: Two Cultural Revolutions

1. Ding, Li and Yu Mo. "Chronology and Photo Gallery of the Chinese Cultural Revolution." *Voice of America.* May 17, 2016. https://www.voachinese.com/a /china-cultural-revolution-timeline-20160516/3333434.html.

2. Culver, John. "The Unfinished Chinese Civil War." The Lowy Institute. September 30, 2020. https://www.lowyinstitute.org/the-interpreter/unfinished-chinese-civil -war.

3. Kraus, Richard Curt. *The Cultural Revolution: A Very Short Introduction.* (Oxford: Oxford University Press, 2013), 8.

4. "Circular of the Central Committee of the Communist Party of China on the Great Proletarian Cultural Revolution." *Marxists Internet Archive.* May 16, 1966. https://www.marxists.org/subject/china/documents/cpc/cc_gpcr.htm.

5. Cavendish, Richard. "Stalin Denounced by Nikita Khrushchev." *History Today* 56, no. 2. (February 2006). https://www.historytoday.com/archive/months-past /stalin-denounced-nikita-khrushchev.

6. Heywood, Andrew *Political Ideologies: An Introduction*, 7th ed. (New York: Red Globe Press, 2021), 4.

7. Cole, Nicki Lisa. "The Frankfurt School of Critical Theory: An Overview of People and Theory." *ThoughtCo.* Updated October 15, 2019. https://www.thoughtco .com/frankfurt-school-3026079.

8. Cole, "The Frankfurt School."

Notes

9. George, Janel. "A Lesson on Critical Race Theory." *American Bar Association*. January 11, 2021. https://www.americanbar.org/groups/crsj/publications/human _rights_magazine_home/civil-rights-reimagining-policing/a-lesson-on-critical -race-theory/.

10. RT. "Elon Musk Reveals Biggest Threat to Modern Civilization." *Global Village Space*. December 22, 2021. https://www.globalvillagespace.com/elon-musk-reveals -biggest-threat-to-modern-civilization/.

11. Harrington, Bobby. "The Long March through the Institutions of Society." *Renew.org*. Accessed May 26, 2022. https://renew.org/the-long-march-through-the -institutions-of-society/.

12. Kimball, Roger. *The Long March: How the Cultural Revolution of the 1960s Changed America*. (San Francisco: Encounter Books, 2000), 173.

13. Kimball, *The Long March*, 199.

14. Steinbuch, Yaron. "Black Lives Matter Co-Founder Describes Herself as 'Trained Marxist.'" *New York Post*. June 25, 2020. https://nypost.com/2020/06/25 /blm-co-founder-describes-herself-as-trained-marxist/.

15. "(1964) Malcolm X'S Speech at the Founding Rally of the Organization of Afro-American Unity." *BlackPast*. October 15, 2007. https://www.blackpast.org /african-american-history/speeches-african-american-history/1964-malcolm-x-s -speech-founding-rally-organization-afro-american-unity/.

16. Williams, Alexandria S. "From W.E.B. Du Bois to the Panthers: A History of Black Americans in China." *RADII*. February 27, 2019. https://radiichina.com /from-w-e-b-du-bois-to-huey-newton-a-history-of-black-americans-in-the-early-prc/.

17. Gao, Yunxiang. "W.E.B. and Shirley Graham Du Bois in Maoist China." *Du Bois Review: Social Science Research on Race* 10, no. 1. (2013): 59–85.

18. King, Martin Luther Jr. "Communism's Challenge to Christianity." *Martin Luther King Jr. Research and Education Institute*. August 9, 1953. https://kinginstitute .stanford.edu/king-papers/documents/communisms-challenge-christianity.

19. Thorkelson, Nick. "Angela Davis on Protest, 1968, and Her Old Teacher, Herbert Marcuse." *Literary Hub*. April 3, 2019. https://lithub.com/angela-davis -on-protest-1968-and-her-old-teacher-herbert-marcuse/.

20. Davis, Angela. *Angela Davis: Autobiography*, (New York: International Publishing, 1988), 214.

21. "Angela Davis & BLM Co-Founder Alicia Garza in Conversation across Generations." *Democracy Now*. https://www.youtube.com/watch?v=_gqGVni8Oec. Accessed April 29, 2023.

22. "Angela Y. Davis." *UC Santa Cruz*. Accessed May 2, 2022. https://humanities .ucsc.edu/academics/faculty/index.php?uid=aydavis.

23. Kimball, *The Long March*, 129.

24. Maher, Bill. "If You're Part of Today's Woke Revolution, You Need to Study the Part of Revolutions Where They Spin out of Control." Twitter, February 4, 2023, 12:23 a.m. https://twitter.com/billmaher/status/1621741159201800192.

Notes

Chapter 5: Born Guilty: How an Ideology Divides

1. Colton, Emma. "Loudoun County Mom Says 6-Year-Old Asked Her If She Was 'Born Evil' Because She's White." *Fox News.* October 31, 2021. https://www .foxnews.com/us/loudoun-county-mom-6-year-old-born-evil-because-white.

2. Song, Yongyi. *Reassessing Mao's Land Reform: Critical Perspectives on Communist China's First Wave of Political Campaigns* Vol. 1. (Hong Kong: Tianyuan Shuwu, 2019), 454.

3. Dikötter, Frank. *The Tragedy of Liberation: A History of the Chinese Revolution 1945–1957,* 1st ed. (New York: Bloomsbury Press, 2013), 67.

4. Song, *Reassessing Mao's Land Reform,* 54.

5. Snow, Edgar. *Red Star over China: The Classic Account of the Birth of Chinese Communism.* (New York: Grove Press, 1968), 114.

6. Swain, Carol M. and Christopher J. Schorr. *Black Eye for America: How Critical Race Theory Is Burning Down the House.* (Nashville: Be the People, 2021), 9.

7. DiAngelo, Robin. *White Fragility: Why It's So Hard for White People to Talk About Racism.* (Boston: Beacon Press, 2018), 27.

8. Downey, Caroline. "MSNBC Guest on Winsome Sears: 'There Is a Black Mouth Moving but a White Idea Running on the Runway of the Tongue.'" *Yahoo News.* November 5, 2021. https://www.yahoo.com/now/msnbc-guest-winsome-sears -black-131046950.html.

9. Carras, Christi. "White Celebrities Partner with NAACP to 'Take Responsibility' for Racism." *Los Angeles Times.* June 11, 2020. https://www .latimes.com/entertainment-arts/story/2020-06-11/i-take-responsibility-video -white-celebrities-naac.

10. Sanders, Bernie. "At the end of the day, the 1 percent may have enormous wealth and power. But they are just the 1 percent. When the 99 percent stand together, we can transform society." Twitter, August 11, 2019, 3:02 p.m. https:// twitter.com/berniesanders/status/1160627442102333440.

11. Higgins, Charlotte. "The Age of Patriarchy: How an Unfashionable Idea Became a Rallying Cry for Feminism Today." *The Guardian.* June 22, 2018. https://www.theguardian.com/news/2018/jun/22/the-age-of-patriarchy-how-an -unfashionable-idea-became-a-rallying-cry-for-feminism-today.

12. Zambon, Veronica. "What Are Some Different Types of Gender Identity?" *Medical News Today.* Updated January 3, 2023. https://www.medicalnewstoday .com/articles/types-of-gender-identity#fa-qs.

13. Rajkumar, Shruti. "Disabled Community Calls Out Ableism in Coverage of John Fetterman Following Stroke." *Yahoo News.* October 13, 2022. https://www .yahoo.com/now/disabled-community-calls-ableism-coverage-230326084.html.

14. Ortiz, Andi. "'The View' Hosts Slam 'Ageist' Backlash to Biden Gaffe over Dead Congresswoman." *The Wrap.* September 29, 2022. https://www.thewrap.com /the-view-biden-jackie-walorski-gaffe-ageist-response-clip/.

15. Parks, Kristine. "Don Lemon: Republicans Must Be Treated as Danger to Society by Media, Cannot Be 'Coddled.'" *Fox News*. July 14, 2022. https://www.foxnews.com/media/don-lemon-republicans-must-treated-danger-society-media-cannot-coddled.

16. Shaw, Adam. "Flashback: Kamala Harris Compared ICE to KKK in Senate hearing." *Fox News*. August 11, 2020. https://www.foxnews.com/politics/kamala-harris-ice-kkk-senate-hearing.

17. "Remarks by President Biden on Fighting the COVID-19 Pandemic." *The White House*. September 9, 2021. https://www.whitehouse.gov/briefing-room/speeches-remarks/2021/09/09/remarks-by-president-biden-on-fighting-the-covid-19-pandemic-3/.

18. "Kimberlé Crenshaw on Intersectionality, More Than Two Decades Later." *Columbia Law School*. June 8, 2017. https://www.law.columbia.edu/news/archive/kimberle-crenshaw-intersectionality-more-two-decades-later.

19. Blistein, Jon. "Jane Fonda on Ending White Privilege: 'We Have to Try to Change within Ourselves.'" *Rolling Stone*. June 1, 2020. https://www.rollingstone.com/culture/culture-news/jane-fonda-white-privilege-george-floyd-protests-black-panthers-1008299/.

20. Agard, Chancellor. "Kathy Griffin Bloody Trump Pic Defended by Photographer." *Entertainment Weekly*. May 30, 2017. https://ew.com/news/2017/05/30/kathy-griffin-trump-head-photo-tyler-shields/.

21. "Remarks by President Biden on the Continued Battle for the Soul of the Nation." *The White House*. September 1, 2022. https://www.whitehouse.gov/briefing-room/speeches-remarks/2022/09/01/remarks-by-president-biden-on-the-continued-battle-for-the-soul-of-the-nation/.

22. Botelho, Greg. "Ex-NAACP Leader Rachel Dolezal: 'I Identify as Black.'" *CNN*. Updated June 17, 2015. https://www.cnn.com/2015/06/16/us/washington-rachel-dolezal-naacp/index.html.

23. Jamerson, Joshua. "Elizabeth Warren Apologizes for DNA Test, Identifying as Native American." *Wall Street Journal*. Updated August 19, 2019. https://www.wsj.com/articles/elizabeth-warren-again-apologizes-after-release-of-native-american-ancestry-link-11566241904.

Chapter 6: Red Guards: Stormtroopers of the Revolution

1. "The Nation's First Big-Character Poster of Marxism-Leninism." *CPC Central Committee Party History and Literature Research Institute*. January 4, 2013. https://www.dswxyjy.org.cn/n/2013/0104/c244520-20082625.html.

2. Wang, Shenghui. "Review of 'Red Guards' Research since 1992." *Modern China Studies* 3. 2004. https://www.modernchinastudies.org/cn/issues/past-issues/85-mcs-2004-issue-3/876-1992.html.

3. Mao, Zedong. "A Letter to the Red Guards of Tsinghua University Middle School." *Marxists Internet Archive*. August 1, 1966. https://www.marxists.org/reference/archive/mao/selected-works/volume-9/mswv9_60.htm.

4. "Chairman Mao Met with the Red Guards Eight Times." *Mzdbl.cn*. Accessed May 24, 2022. http://www.mzdbl.cn/gushi/gushi5/hongweibing.html.

5. Tushou, Chen. "Remembering Red Guards Big-Linkup in Beijing." *Aisixiang*. January 6, 2014. https://www.aisixiang.com/data/71196.html.

6. "Chairman Mao Met with the Red Guards Eight Times."

7. Rittenberg, Sidney. *The Man Who Stayed Behind*. (Durham: Duke University Press, 2000), 362–363.

8. Rittenberg, *The Man Who Stayed Behind*, 363–364.

9. Li, Shu. "Bloodline Theory and Class Pedigree Theory." *Voice of America*. April 20, 2007. https://www.voachinese.com/a/a-21-w2007-04-06-voa42-63065397/1046364.html.

10. "Yu Luoke." *Baike.com*. Accessed May 23, 2022. https://www.baike.com/wiki/遇罗克?view_id=3ltzfavb7ko000.

11. Yu, Luoke. "Class Pedigree Theory." *Marxists Internet Archive*. January 18, 1967. https://www.marxists.org/chinese/reference-books/minjian-1966-1976/05.htm.

12. Hu, Ping. "Commemorating the 50th Anniversary of Yu Luoke's Martyrdom." *Aboluowang.com*. March 9, 2020. https://www.aboluowang.com/2020/0309/1419820.html.

13. "The CCP Central Committee Agrees with the Ministry of Public Security's Regulations on Strictly Prohibiting the Use of Police to Suppress Revolutionary Student Movements." *WikiSource*. August 22, 1966. https://zh.m.wikisource.org/zh-hans/中共中央同意公安部关于严禁出动警察镇压革命学生运动的规定.

14. "Why Destroy the Public Security Law?" *Coin Dollar Pay*. Accessed May 12, 2022. https://coindollarpay.com/why-mao-destroyed-judicial-system/.

15. Rittenberg, *The Man Who Stayed Behind*, 321.

16. "Letter to Jiang Qing" *Zmdbl.cn*. July 8, 1966. http://www.mzdbl.cn/maoxuan/huibian/geijiangqingdexin.html.

17. Ding, Shu. "Fifty Years of Wrongful Death Investigation in Mainland China." *Creaders.net*. September 3, 2015. https://blog.creaders.net/u/9588/201509/232967.html.

18. "On the Death of Bian Zhongyun Again." *Radio of Free Asia*. September 10, 2008. https://www.rfa.org/mandarin/zhuanlan/xinlingzhilyu/wengebeiwanglu/wegen-09102008144407.html.

19. "On the Death of Bian Zhongyun Again."

20. "Xi Jinping's Two Bitter Weeps." *New Tang Dynasty Television*. May 25, 2016. https://www.ntdtv.com/gb/2016/05/25/a1268155.html.

21. "Retribution for Li Jingquan." *Aboluowang.com*. October 24, 2016. https://www.aboluowang.com/2016/1024/824092.html.

22. "The Sleepless Night When the Red Guards Stormed Zhongnanhai during the Cultural Revolution." *M.hnbllw.com*. Accessed May 5, 2022. https://m.hnbllw.com/duzhewenzhai/2019/0222/64561.html.

23. Lemire, Jonathan and Zeke Miller. "Trump Took Shelter in White House

Bunker as Protests Raged." *AP News.* May 31, 2020. https://apnews.com/article/donald-trump-ap-top-news-george-floyd-politics-a2326518da6b25b4509bef1ec85f5d7f.

24. Li, Shu. "Violence—The Civil War Directed by Mao Zedong." *Voice of America.* July 7, 2006. https://www.voachinese.com/a/a-21-w2006-07-07-voa50-58446607/1088033.html.

25. "Red Guard Violence and Destruction." *Facts and Details.* Updated August 2021. https://factsanddetails.com/china/cat2/sub6/entry-7458.html.

26. Yang, Guobin. *The Red Guard Generation and Political Activism in China.* (New York: Columbia University Press, 2016), 192.

27. "Interview: 'Dear Chairman Mao, Please Think about What You Are Doing.'" *Radio Free Asia.* May 16, 2016. https://www.rfa.org/english/news/china/china-cultrev-05162016173649.html.

28. Li, "Violence—The Civil War."

29. Rubin, Jerry. *Do It! Scenarios of the Revolution.* (New York: Simon & Schuster, 1970), 215.

30. Farber, Samuel. "The Berkeley Free Speech Movement, 56 Years Later." *Jacobin.* September 3, 2020. https://jacobin.com/2020/09/berkeley-free-speech-movement-hal-draper.

31. Park, Madison. "Ben Shapiro Spoke at Berkeley as Protesters Gathered Outside." *CNN.* Updated September 15, 2017. https://www.cnn.com/2017/09/14/us/berkeley-ben-shapiro-speech/index.html.

32. Kifner, John. "Columbia's Radicals of 1968 Hold a Bittersweet Reunion." *New York Times.* April 28, 2008. https://www.nytimes.com/2008/04/28/nyregion/28columbia.html?scp=1&sq=columbia+1968&st=nyt.

33. Kimball, *The Long March*, 112–113.

34. Kimball, *The Long March*, 112–113.

35. Sowell, Thomas. "The Day Cornell Died." *Hoover Digest.* October 30, 1999. https://www.hoover.org/research/day-cornell-died.

36. Kilpatrick, Amina. "Cornell Commemorates Willard Straight Hall Takeover with Permanent Plaque during Homecoming Weekend." *Cornell Daily Sun.* October 6, 2019. https://cornellsun.com/2019/10/06/cornell-commemorates-willard-straight-hall-takeover-with-permanent-plaque-during-homecoming-weekend/.

37. Kaufman, Elliot. "Another Professor, Another Mob." *National Review.* May 26, 2017. https://www.nationalreview.com/2017/05/evergreen-state-pc-mob-accosts-liberal-professor/.

38. Blankley, Bethany. "Campus Speech: Survey Finds 66% of Students Support Shouting Down Campus Speakers." *Center Square.* September 27, 2021. https://www.thecentersquare.com/national/campus-speech-survey-finds-66-of-students-support-shouting-down-campus-speakers/article_3e8d6236-1fa7-11ec-94d4-539d0724c0ef.html.

39. Feldman Barrett, Lisa. "When Is Speech Violence?" *New York Times.* July 14, 2017. https://www.nytimes.com/2017/07/14/opinion/sunday/when-is-speech-violence.html.

40. "About." *Black Lives Matter.* https://blacklivesmatter.com/about/.

41. H., Kat. "Trained Marxist Patrisse Cullors, Black Lives Matters BLM." YouTube. June 20, 2020. https://www.youtube.com/watch?v=1noLh25FbKI.

42. Cullors, Patrisse. "Am I A Marist?" YouTube. December 14, 2020. https://www.youtube.com/watch?v=rEp1kxg58kE.

43. King, Martin Luther Jr. *A Gift of Love Sermons from Strength to Love and Other Preachings.* (Boston: Beacon Press, 2012), 144.

44. King, Martin Luther Jr. "I've Been to the Mountaintop." *American Rhetoric.* April 3, 1968. https://www.americanrhetoric.com/speeches/mlkivebeentothemountaintop.htm.

45. Hua Yang. "Hypocrisy of American Civil Rights." *People's Daily Online.* December 14, 2023. http://world.people.com.cn/n1/2020/1214/c1002-31965801.html.

46. Gonzalez, Mike. "Yes, a Pro-China Group in America Supports a Black Lives Matter Founder." *Daily Signal.* October 20, 2020. https://www.dailysignal.com/2020/10/20/yes-a-pro-china-group-in-america-supports-a-black-lives-matter-founder/.

47. Arora, Rav. "These Black Lives Didn't Seem to Matter in 2020." *New York Post.* February 6, 2021. https://nypost.com/2021/02/06/these-black-lives-didnt-seem-to-matter-in-2020/.

48. Pullmann, Joy. "Study: Up to 95 Percent of 2020 U.S. Riots Are Linked to Black Lives Matter." *The Federalist.* September 16, 2020. https://thefederalist.com/2020/09/16/study-up-to-95-percent-of-2020-u-s-riots-are-linked-to-black-lives-matter/.

49. Manskar, Noah. "Riots Following George Floyd's Death May Cost Insurance Companies Up to $2B." *New York Post.* September 16, 2020. https://nypost.com/2020/09/16/riots-following-george-floyds-death-could-cost-up-to-2b/.

50. "Propaganda Slogans during the Cultural Revolution." *Aisixiang.* October 11, 2004. http://www.aisixiang.com/data/4306.html.

51. Escobar, Natalie. "One Author's Controversial View: 'In Defense of Looting.'" *NPR.* August 27, 2020. https://www.npr.org/sections/codeswitch/2020/08/27/906642178/one-authors-argument-in-defense-of-looting.

52. Shaw, Adam. "Biden Says Antifa Is an 'Idea,' Days after WH Moved to Label It a Terror Group." *Fox News.* September 30, 2020. https://www.foxnews.com/politics/biden-antifa-idea-what-we-know.

53. Nelson, Steven. "Jim Jordan Tells Jerry Nadler to Stop 'Minimizing' Antifa Violence, Calls for Hearing." *New York Post.* September 8, 2020. https://nypost.com/2020/09/08/jim-jordan-tells-jerry-nadler-to-stop-minimizing-antifa-violence.

Notes

54. "Antifa (United States)." *Wikipedia.* https://en.wikipedia.org/wiki/Antifa_(United_States).

55. Ngo, Andy. *Unmasked: Inside Antifa's Radical Plan to Destroy Democracy.* (New York: Center Street, 2021), 82.

56. "Antifa: Trump Says Group Will Be Designated 'Terrorist Organisation.'" *BBC.* May 31, 2020. https://www.bbc.com/news/world-us-canada-52868295.

57. Ngo, *Unmasked,* 127.

58. Ngo, *Unmasked,* 201.

59. McDonald, Mark. "Police Exodus 'Crisis': Officers Are Ditching the Job at a Rate 'Never Seen Before.'" Fraternal Order of Police. https://fop.net/2022/08/police-exodus-crisis-fox news/. Accessed on April 29, 2023.

60. Miller, Joshua Rhett. "Bail Fund Backed by Kamala Harris Freed Minneapolis Man Charged with Murder." *New York Post.* September 8, 2021. https://nypost.com/2021/09/08/bail-fund-backed-by-kamala-harris-freed-man-charged-with-murder/.

61. Ibrahim, Nur. "Did Kamala Harris Tell Jacob Blake She Was 'Proud of Him'?" *Snopes.* September 16, 2020. https://www.snopes.com/fact-check/kamala-harris-jacob-blake-proud/.

62. Fuzzy Slippers. "NYC Drops Charges against Hundreds of BLM/Antifa Rioters, Looters." *Legal Insurrection.* June 19, 2021. https://legalinsurrection.com/2021/06/nyc-drops-charges-against-hundreds-of-blm-antifa-rioters-looters/.

63. Ngo, *Unmasked,* 199.

64. Carlson, Tucker. "Tucker Carlson: Antifa Is the Armed Militia of the Democratic Party and Is Back in Force." *Fox News.* January 23, 2023. https://www.foxnews.com/opinion/tucker-carlson-antifa-armed-militia-democratic-party-back-in-force.

65. Brown, Tim. "List of 269 Companies Supporting ANTIFA, Black Lives Matter." *Conservative Firing Line.* June 9, 2020. https://conservativefiringline.com/list-of-269-companies-supporting-antifa-black-lives-matter/.

66. Rufo, Christopher. "The State of CHAZ." June 16, 2020. https://christopherrufo.com/.

67. Emory, Julie. "One Year Later: The Capitol Hill Autonomous Zone." *The Daily.* September 13, 2021. https://www.dailyuw.com/news/community/one-year-later-the-capitol-hill-autonomous-zone/article_4eb11000-1457-11ec-afe4-f7038defb158.html.

68. Rufo, Christopher F. "The End of Chaz." *City Journal.* July 1, 2020. https://www.city-journal.org/end-of-chaz.

69. Buchanan, Larry. "Black Lives Matter May Be the Largest Movement in U.S. History." *New York Times.* July 3, 2020. https://www.nytimes.com/interactive/2020/07/03/us/george-floyd-protests-crowd-size.html.

70. "Secret $6 Million Home Has Allies and Critics Skeptical of BLM Foundation's Finances." *NPR.* April 7, 2022. https://www.npr.org/2022/04/07/1091487910/blm-leaders-face-questions-after-allegedly-buying-a-mansion-with-donation-money.

71. Loh, Matthew. "A Black Lives Matter Cofounder Used $840,000 of the Group's Funds to Pay Her Brother for 'Security Services.'" *Yahoo News*. May 19, 2022. https://news.yahoo.com/black-lives-matter-cofounder-used-075136722.html CH5-78.

72. Downey, Caroline. "BLM Chapters Sue Organization Head over Alleged $10 Million Theft." *National Review*. September 3, 2022. https://www.nationalreview .com/news/blm-chapters-sue-organization-head-over-alleged-10-million-theft/.

73. Catenacci, Thomas. "John Fetterman Wipes BLM Section from Campaign Site." *New York Post*. September 28, 2022. https://nypost.com/2022/09/28/john -fetterman-wipes-black-lives-matter-section-from-campaign-site/.

Chapter 7: Cancel Culture: War on the Old World

1. "The Committee's Choice & People's Choice Word of the Year 2019." *Macquarie Dictionary*. December 9, 2019. https://www.macquariedictionary.com .au/resources/view/word/of/the/year/2019.

2. Mao, Zedong. "On New Democracy." *Marxists Internet Archive*. January 1940. https://www.marxists.org/reference/archive/mao/selected-works/volume-2/mswv2 _26.htm.

3. "Great Job!" *People's Daily*. August 25, 1966. https://zh.m.wikisource.org /wiki/%E5%A5%BD%E5%BE%97%E5%BE%88%EF%BC%81.

4. Mann, Jim. "Hospital Renamed to Show Chinese Tolerance." *Los Angeles Times*. June 8, 1985. https://www.latimes.com/archives/la-xpm-1985-06-08-mn -7211-story.html.

5. Lin, Hui. "Beijing's Time-Honored 'Quanjude Roast Duck Restaurant' Suffered a Catastrophe during the Cultural Revolution." *Epoch Times*. July 25, 2014. https://www.epochtimes.com/gb/14/7/25/n4208731.htm.

6. Ding, Shu. "Brief Notes on 'Destroying the Four Olds' in 1966." *Aisixiang*. Updated August 23, 2004. https://m.aisixiang.com/data/3904-2.html.

7. Bo, Weihua. *Destroying the Old World—The Upheaval and Catastrophe of the Cultural Revolution; The History of the People's Republic of China* Vol. 6 (1966-1968). (Hong Kong: The Chinese University of Hong Kong Press, 2008), 243.

8. Jaffe, Gabrielle. "China's Enthusiastic Re-Embrace of Confucius." *The Atlantic*. October 7, 2013. https://www.theatlantic.com/china/archive/2013/10 /chinas-enthusiastic-re-embrace-of-confucius/280326/.

9. Bo, *Destroying the Old World*, 237.

10. Lin, Hui. "The Royal Garden of the Summer Palace." *Botan Network*. July 31, 2020. https://botanwang.com/articles/202007/皇家园林颐和园之殇.html.

11. Woeser, Tsering; Robert Barnett; and Susan Chen. "Lhasa in the Cultural Revolution." *Modern Chinese Literature and Culture Resource Center*. November 13, 2020. https://u.osu.edu/mclc/2020/11/14/lhasa-in-the-cultural-revolution/.

12. Bo, *Destroying the Old World*, 232.

13. Ding, Dahua. "The World's Rare Exhibition of the Results of the Red Guards Raiding the House." *The Essence of Literature and History*, no. 1. (2008). http://www.520yuwen.com/book/wsjh/wsjh20080104.html.

14. Ding, "The World's Rare Exhibition."

15. "100 Examples for Destroying the Four Olds." *Cultural Revolution and Contemporary History Research Network's Archiver*. January 22, 2010. https://difangwenge.org/archiver/?tid-742.html.

16. Creitz, Charles. "Biden Appears to Quote Mao Zedong in Coast Guard Commencement Address: 'Women Hold Up Half the World.'" *Fox News*. May 19, 2021. https://www.foxnews.com/media/biden-appears-to-quote-mao-zedong-in-coast-guard-commencement-address-women-hold-up-half-the-world.

17. "During the Cultural Revolution, the Red Guards Burned Books When They Saw Them, and It Was Enough to Keep Only the Xinhua Dictionary." *Phoenix TV*. July 11, 2012. http://phtv.ifeng.com/program/tfzg/detail_2012_07/11/15940084_0.shtml.

18. Yang, Jisheng. *The World Turned Upside Down: A History of the Chinese Cultural Revolution*. (New York: Farrar, Straus, and Giroux, 2021), 122.

19. Kaufman, Davis. "The Unintentional Racism Found in Traffic Signals." *Level*. July 7, 2020. https://www.levelman.com/the-unintentional-racism-found-in-traffic-signals-b2899c34fefb/.

20. Wang, Yiwei. "Criticism of 'Poisonous Weed' Films During the Cultural Revolution." *Medium*. May 28, 2016. https://medium.com/birthday-paper/文革-毒草-电影大批判-钱钢老师课上的生日报㊶-c80fb24f3d8.

21. "Yang Mo's Life Breakout." *China Youth Daily*. July 5, 2011. https://www.chinanews.com.cn/cul/2011/07-05/3156469.shtml.

22. Xu, Zhongyua. "Mao Zedong's Enlightenment from Reading 'Communist Manifesto.'" *Chinese Communist Party News Network*. November 4, 2015. http://theory.people.com.cn/n/2015/1104/c352498-27776751.html.

23. *Mao Zedong Always Kept a Copy of "Zi Zhi Tong Jian" by His Bedside*. (毛泽东床头总放着一部《资治通鉴》). CPCNews.cn. March 19, 2009. https://www.chinanews.com.cn/cul/news/2009/03-19/1609653.shtml.

24. Murray, Douglas. *The War on the West*. (New York: Broadside Books, 2022), 1.

25. Gesualdi-Gilmore, Laura. "'Deeply Insulting': African American Museum Accused of 'Racism' over Whiteness Chart Linking Hard Work and Nuclear Family to White Culture." *The Sun*. July 16, 2020. https://www.thesun.co.uk/news/12142926/african-american-museum-whiteness-chart-protestant-values/.

26. Applebaum, Barbara. "Critical Whiteness Studies" in G. Noblit, ed., *Oxford Research Encyclopedia of Education*. (Oxford: Oxford University Press, 2016), 1–23. https://oxfordre.com/education/view/10.1093/acrefore/9780190264093.001.0001/acrefore-9780190264093-e-5.

27. Miller, Andrew Mark. "University of Kansas Offers 'Angry White Male Studies' Class." *Fox News*. August 6, 2022. https://www.foxnews.com/us/university-kansas-offers-angry-white-male-studies-class.

28. Cason, Caroline. "UChicago Announces 'The Problem with Whiteness' Course." *Campus Reform*. December 2, 2022. https://www.campusreform.org/article?id=20707.

29. DiAngelo, *White Fragility*, 149.

30. Schuessler, Jennifer. "Historians Question Trump's Comments on Confederate Monuments." *New York Times*. August 15, 2017. https://www.nytimes.com/2017/08/15/arts/design/trump-robert-e-lee-george-washington-thomas-jefferson.html.

31. "List of Monuments and Memorials Removed during the George Floyd Protests." *Wikipedia*. Accessed July 15, 2022. https://en.wikipedia.org/wiki/List_of_monuments_and_memorials_removed_during_the_George_Floyd_protests.

32. "Path and Process." *Reimagining Monument Avenue*. https://web.archive.org/web/20220126203432/https://reimaginingmonumentavenue.org/path-and-process/.

33. Treisman, Rachel. "An Actor Has Been Charged with Vandalizing a New York City Statue of George Floyd." *NPR*. October 28, 2021. https://www.npr.org/2021/10/28/1050030939/george-floyd-statue-vandalism-actor-arrested-new-york.

34. DeVoe, Jo. "Falls Church School Board Renames Schools That Previously Honored Thomas Jefferson, George Mason." *Tysons Reporter*. April 29, 2021. https://www.tysonsreporter.com/2021/04/29/falls-church-school-board-renames-schools-that-previously-honored-thomas-jefferson-george-mason/.

35. Creitz, Charles. "Ben Carson Reacts to Name Being Removed from Detroit High School: Ideology Trumping Purpose of Institutions." *Fox News*. December 13, 2022. https://www.foxnews.com/media/ben-carson-name-removed-detroit-high-school-ideology-trumping-purpose-institutions.

36. Barnes, Sophia and Justin Finch. "DC Ceremonially Names Street to White House after Black Lives Matter; Emblazons Name on Road." *NBC Washington*. June 5, 2020. https://www.nbcwashington.com/news/local/dc-paints-black-lives-matter-on-street-near-lafayette-square-street-renamed-black-lives-matter-way/2323647/.

37. Twitty, Michael. "Aunt Jemima and Uncle Ben Deserve Retirement. They're Racist Myths of Happy Black Servitude." *Think*. June 21, 2020. https://www.nbcnews.com/think/opinion/aunt-jemima-uncle-ben-deserve-retirement-they-re-racist-myths-ncna1231623.

38. Paul, Pritha. "Stacy Langton: Virginia Mom Banned from Library After 'Lawn Boy' Porn Controversy." *MEAWW*. November 9, 2021. https://meaww.com/stacy-langton-virginia-mom-banned-from-school-library-after-speech-about-porn-books.

Notes

39. Maas, Megan K. "Gender-Neutral Toys Aren't Enough to Beat Toxic Masculinity—But They're a Start." *Quartz*. December 9, 2019. https://qz.com /1764372/why-gender-neutral-toys-do-and-dont-help-fight-sexism-2/.

40. Frater, Patrick. "China Wants 'Sissy Idols' and 'Effeminate Men' Scrubbed from Entertainment Industry." *Variety*. September 3, 2021. https://variety.com/2021 /global/asia/china-cissy-idols-effeminate-men-entertainment-industry -1235055304/.

41. Dastagir, Alia E. "Marsha Blackburn Asked Ketanji Brown Jackson to Define 'Woman.' Science Says There's No Simple Answer." *USA Today*. March 24, 2022. https://www.usatoday.com/story/life/health-wellness/2022/03/24/marsha-blackburn -asked-ketanji-jackson-define-woman-science/7152439001/.

42. Brown, Jon. "Fairfax Public Schools Consider Rule Suspending Students for 'Malicious Misgendering.'" *Fox News*. May 16, 2022. https://www.foxnews.com/us /fairfax-schools-rules-suspend-students-malicious-misgendering.

43. Lee, Michael. "Wisconsin Middle Schoolers Accused of Sexual Harassment for Using Wrong Gender Pronouns." *Fox News*. May 15, 2022. https://www.foxnews .com/us/middle-schoolers-sexual-harassment-gender-pronouns.

44. Benveniste, Alexis. "Goya CEO Names Alexandria Ocasio-Cortez 'Employee of the Month,' Claiming Her Tweets Boosted Sales." *CNN Business*. December 8, 2020. https://www.cnn.com/2020/12/08/business/goya-aoc-employee-of-the-month /index.html.

45. Myers, Kristin. "J.K. Rowling Banned from 'Harry Potter' Anniversary Special for Past Transphobic Comments." *Blast*. November 17, 2021. https://theblast .com/125437/jk-rowling-banned-from-new-harry-potter-anniversary-special/.

46. O'Brien, Cortney. "NPR Writer Doubles Down, Says He's 'Proud' of Panned Piece Urging Tom Hanks to Be an 'Anti-Racist.'" *Fox News*. June 13, 2021. https:// www.foxnews.com/media/npr-writer-urges-tom-hanks-to-be-an-anti-racist.

47. Abad-Santos, Alex. "How Ellen DeGeneres's Facade of Kindness Crumbled." *Vox*. August 7, 2020. https://www.vox.com/21357113/ellen-degeneres-canceled-mean -backlash-toxic-workplace.

48. Concha, Joe. "WokeWorld Comes for 'Oppressor' Obama: Activists Rip School Being Named after 'Deporter in Chief.'" *The Hill*. April 3, 2021. https:// thehill.com/opinion/immigration/546285-wokeworld-comes-for-oppressor -obama-activists-rip-school-being-named/.

49. Soave, Robby. "Michigan Students Accuse Celebrated Music Professor of Racism for Screening *Othello*." *Reason*. October 8, 2021. https://reason.com/2021/10 /08/bright-sheng-university-of-michigan-othello-racism/.

50. Murray, *The War on the West*, 269–270.

51. "Glenn C. Loury." *Manhattan Institute*. Accessed June 1, 2022. https://www .manhattan-institute.org/expert/glenn-c-loury.

52. Riley, Alexander. "Man of the West: An Interview with Glenn Loury." *Chronicles*.

April 26, 2022. https://chroniclesmagazine.org/web/man-of-the-west-an-interview-with-glenn-loury/.

Chapter 8: Destruction of Family

1. Silverstein, Sophie. "Family Abolition Isn't about Ending Love and Care. It's about Extending It to Everyone." *openDemocracy*. April 24, 2020. https://www.opendemocracy.net/en/oureconomy/family-abolition-isnt-about-ending-love-and-care-its-about-extending-it-to-everyone/.

2. Xie, Wenting. "Son Still Haunted after Sending Mother to Execution during Cultural Revolution." *Global Times*. March 18, 2016. https://www.globaltimes.cn/content/974530.shtml.

3. He, Shu. "Family Relations in the Cultural Revolution Worth Studying." *Secret China*. February 28, 2010. https://www.secretchina.com/news/gb/2010/02/28/336928.html.

4. Chu, Bailiang and Di Yufei. "Xi Jinping, Who Emerged from the Catastrophe of the Cultural Revolution." *New York Times: China*. September 24, 2015. https://cn.nytimes.com/china/20150924/c24revolution/.

5. Bevan, Matthew and Scott Mitchell. "Secrets of Xi Jinping." *Timed News*. June 3, 2021. https://www.timednews.com/news/2021/06/03/5322.html.

6. "The Climax: The Short-Lived 'Happy Life.'" *Yxjedu.com*. Updated April 27, 2022. http://www.yxjedu.com/piaoyi_film20/li_shi/li_shi_2/china_60/rmgs_cys3.html.

7. "From Agricultural Production Cooperatives to People's Communes." *Red Flag* 8. 1958. https://www.bilibili.com/read/cv12656216.

8. Zhou, Jingwen. *Ten Years of Storm: The True Story of the Communist Regime in China*. (Hong Kong: Times Critic Society, 1959).

9. Cheng, Yinghong. *Creating the New Man: From Enlightenment Ideals to Socialist Realities*. (Honolulu: University of Hawaii Press, 2009), 82.

10. "National Single Parent Day: March 21, 2023." *United States Census Bureau*. March 21, 2023. https://www.census.gov/newsroom/stories/single-parent-day.html#:~:text=%E2%80%9CAlmost%20a%20quarter%20of%20U.S.,who%20do%20so%20(7%25)%20%E2%80%A6.

11. Marx, Karl and Friedrich Engels. "Manifesto of the Communist Party" in *Marx/Engels Selected Works*, Vol. 1. (Moscow: Progress Publishers, 1848/1969), 98–137.

12. Yenor, Scott. "The True Origin of Society: The Founders on the Family." *Heritage Foundation*. October 16, 2013. https://www.heritage.org/political-process/report/the-true-origin-society-the-founders-the-family/#_ftn4.

13. Rampton, Martha. "Four Waves of Feminism." *Pacific*. 2008. https://www.pacificu.edu/magazine/four-waves-feminism.

14. Rampton, "Four Waves of Feminism."

15. Echols, Alice. *Daring to Be Bad: Radical Feminism in America*. (Minneapolis: University of Minnesota Press, 1989), 159.

16. Ames, Mollie S. and Elyse D. Pham. "A Radical Weapon." *The Crimson*. October 31, 2019. https://www.thecrimson.com/article/2019/10/31/kathie-sara child/.

17. Sarachild quoted in Sheila Cronan, "Marriage," in Anne Koedt, Anita Rapone and Ellen Levine, eds., *Notes from the Third Year: Women's Liberation*. (New York: Radical Feminists, 1971), 146.

18. Echols, *Daring to Be Bad*, xi.

19. Winter, Ella. *Red Virtue: Human Relationships in the New Russia*. (London: Victor Gollancz, 1933), 146.

20. Winter, *Red Virtue*, 137.

21. Collins, Lois M. "Are Fatherlessness and Societal Breakdown to Blame for Mass Shootings?" *Deseret News*. June 5, 2022. https://www.deseret.com /2022/6/5/23148521/mike-lee-school-mass-shooting-uvalde-fatherlessness-family -structure-gun-violence-dickey-amendment.

22. "Denzel Washington Blames Black Crime on Lack of Father Figures." *Regal Mag*. Accessed July 13, 2022. https://www.regalmag.com/archives/additional -archives/denzel-washington-blames-black-crime-on-lack-of-father-figures/.

23. Michas, Frédéric. "Percentage of Births to Unmarried Women in the United States from 1980 to 2021." *Statista*. March 23, 2023. https://www.statista.com /statistics/276025/us-percentage-of-births-to-unmarried-women/.

24. Pietsch, Bryan. "Son Tipped Off F.B.I. about His Father, Who Is Charged in Capitol Riot." *New York Times*. January 24, 2021. https://www.nytimes .com/2021/01/24/us/politics/jackson-reffitt-father-capitol-riot.html.

25. Slisco, Aila. "Massachusetts Mom Loses Job after Daughter Outs Her as Capitol Rioter: 'This You?'" *Newsweek*. January 13, 2021. https://www.newsweek .com/massachusetts-mom-loses-job-after-daughter-outs-her-capitol-rioter -this-you-1561384.

26. Lustig, Hanna. "Teens on TikTok Are Exposing a Generational Rift between Parents and Kids over How They Treat Black Lives Matter Protests." *Insider*. June 3, 2020. https://www.insider.com/tiktok-george-floyd-black-lives-matter-teens-par ents-racist-views-2020-6.

27. Zilber, Ariel. "Elon Musk Blames 'Neo-Marxists' at Universities for Poor Relationship with His Daughter." *New York Post*. October 7, 2022. https:// nypost.com/2022/10/07/elon-musk-blames-neo-marxists-at-universities-for -his-daughter-not-speaking-to-him/?utm_campaign=iphone_nyp&utm_source =mail_appChapter%207.

28. "Transgender Reveal in Kindergarten Class Leaves Parents Feeling 'Betrayed.'" CBS News. August 22, 2017. https://www.cbsnews.com/news/transgender-reveal -kindergarten-class-rocklin-academy-parents-upset/.

29. Melley, Brian. "Mother: Teachers Manipulated Child to Change Gender Identity." *Associated Press.* January 21, 2022. https://apnews.com/article/business -california-gender-identity-cdb790cc3059e71e22d86b8e7b445361#:~:text =Jessica%20Konen%20said%20two%20middle,the%20idea%20she%20was %20transgender.

30. Farberov, Snejana. "Texas Dad Fears Ex-Wife Plans to 'Chemically Castrate' 9-Year-Old Son." *New York Post.* January 6, 2023. https://nypost.com/2023/01/06 /texas-dad-fears-ex-wife-plans-to-chemically-castrate-9-year-old-son/.

Chapter 9: Destruction of Religion

1. Huang, Xiaobei. "The Underground Church: The Battle between Faith and Political Power: An Analysis of the History of the Origin of China's Underground Church." *Pu Shi Institute for Social Science.* November 12, 2011. http://www .pacilution.com/showarticle.asp?articleid=3180.

2. Zhou, Tuan'en. *History of the Development of Christianity in Contemporary China: 1947–1997.* (Taipei: Chinese Gospel Publishing, 1997), 34.

3. Zhou, *History of the Development,* 49.

4. Zhou, *History of the Development,* 188.

5. Zhou, *History of the Development,* 194.

6. De Jaegher, R.J. *The Enemy Within: An Eyewitness Account of the Communist Conquest of China.* (Homebush, Australia: Daughters of St. Paul, 1967), 194.

7. "Daily Life in the Years of the Cultural Revolution." *Hk.aboluowang.com.* June 29, 2016. https://hk.aboluowang.com/2016/0629/762327.html.

8. "During the Cultural Revolution, the Mosque Became a Pig Farm." *Talkcc .com,* May 19, 2018. https://www.talkcc.com/article/4337475.

9. "Home." *FalunDafa.org.* https://en.falundafa.org/.

10. Liao, Ran. "Disagreement at Top-Level CCP over the Falun Gong Issue." *Falun Dafa Minghui.* March 27, 2010. https://www.minghui.org/mmh/articles /2010/3/27/220486.html.

11. Elks, Sonia. "China Is Harvesting Organs from Falun Gong Members, Finds Expert Panel." *Reuters.* June 17, 2019. https://www.reuters.com/article/us-britain -china-rights/china-is-harvesting-organs-from-falun-gong-members-finds -expert-panel-idUSKCN1TI236.

12. Roose, Kevin. "How The Epoch Times Created a Giant Influence Machine." *New York Times.* October 24, 2020. https://www.nytimes.com/2020/10/24 /technology/epoch-times-influence-falun-gong.html.

13. FlorCruz, Jaime. "China Soul-Searching after Toddler's Death." *CNN.* Updated October 22, 2011. https://www.cnn.com/2011/10/22/world/asia /china-toddler-reaction/index.html.

14. Huang, Haifeng. "What a Tragic Traffic Incident Says about Chinese Social Ethics." *Sixth Tone.* June 16, 2017. https://www.sixthtone.com/news/1000343 /what-a-tragic-traffic-incident-says-about-chinese-social-ethics.

15. "John Adams to Thomas Jefferson, 28 June 1813." *National Archives.* June 28, 1813. https://founders.archives.gov/documents/Jefferson/03-06-02-0208.

16. Morris, Steven. "America's Unchristian Beginnings: Founding Fathers: Most, Despite Preachings of Our Pious Right, Were Deists Who Rejected the Divinity of Jesus." *Los Angeles Times.* August 3, 1995. https://www.latimes.com /archives/la-xpm-1995-08-03-me-30974-story.html.

17. Flax, Bill. "Was America Founded as a Christian Nation?" *Forbes.* September 25, 2012. https://www.forbes.com/sites/billflax/2012/09/25/was-america -founded-as-a-christian-nation/?sh=31844b854e7b.

18. Flax, "Was America Founded as a Christian Nation?"

19. Leary, Timothy. *Flashbacks: A Personal and Cultural History of an Era.* (New York: G.P. Putnam's Sons, 1990), 92.

20. Leary, *Flashbacks*, 109.

21. Kimball, *The Long March*, 201.

22. "Muhammad Ali." *Britannica.* Updated January 25, 2023. https://www .britannica.com/biography/Muhammad-Ali-boxer.

23. Kang, Zhijie. "Mao Zedong's Interpretation and Research on the Three World Religions." *Fo.ifeng.com.* July 23, 2013. https://fo.ifeng.com/guanchajia /detail_2013_07/23/27793729_0.shtml.

24. Kiska, Roger. "Antonio Gramsci's Long March through History." *Acton Institute.* December 12, 2019. https://www.acton.org/religion-liberty/volume-29 -number-3/antonio-gramscis-long-march-through-history#:~:text=In%20Gramsci's %20own%20words%2C%20he,transforming%20the%20consciousness%20of %20society.%E2%80%9D.

25. Dreier, Peter. "Jesus Was a Socialist." *HuffPost.* December 25, 2016. https:// www.huffpost.com/entry/jesus-was-a-socialist_b_13854296.

26. Phillips, Macon. "President Barack Obama's Inaugural Address." *The White House.* January 21, 2009. https://obamawhitehouse.archives.gov/blog/2009/01/21 /president-Barack-obamas-inaugural-address.

27. Blankley, Bethany. "Parents Sue California over Public School Curriculum That Includes Chants to Aztec Gods." *Center Square.* September 8, 2021. https:// www.thecentersquare.com/california/parents-sue-california-over-public-school -curriculum-that-includes-chants-to-aztec-gods/article_cde773f4-10c0-11ec-b1b1 -4bc18ccf6253.html.

28. "Aztecs." *History.* Updated September 9, 2020. https://www.history.com /topics/ancient-americas/aztecs.

29. De Groot, Gerard J. *The Sixties Unplugged: A Kaleidoscopic History of a Disorderly Decade.* (Cambridge, MA: Harvard University Press, 2008), 117.

30. Panneton, D. "How Extremist Gun Culture Is Trying to Co-Opt the Rosary." *The Atlantic.* August 14, 2022. https://www.theatlantic.com/ideas/archive/2022/08 /radical-traditionalist-catholic-christian-rosary-weapon/671122/.

31. Sheva, Arutz. "Before Wearing a Hijab, I Was Just an Ordinary White Girl." *Israel National News*. September 7, 2017. https://www.israelnationalnews.com /news/235179.

32. Oliver, David. "Raquel Evita Saraswati, Rachel Dolezal and the Scandal of Pretending to Be Another Race." *USA Today*. March 2, 2023. https://eu.usatoday .com/story/life/health-wellness/2023/03/02/rachel-dolezal-raquel-evita-saraswati -pretending-race/11323159002/.

33. VanTryon, Matthew. "Supreme Court Sided with Praying Football Coach. What Now for Coaches and Players?" *Indy Star*. July 5, 2022. https:// www.indystar.com/story/sports/high-school/2022/07/05/the-supreme-court -prayer-joseph-kennedy-football-coach/7773084001.

34. Burack, Bobby. "SI Says Praying Football Coach Is Destroying America." *OutKick*. June 13, 2022. https://www.outkick.com/sports-illustrated-joe-kennedy/.

35. "Supreme Court Lets Public Schools Coerce Students into Praticing Christianity." *Slate*. June 27, 2022. https://slate.com/news-and-politics/2022/06 /coach-kennedy-bremerton-prayer-football-public-school.html#:~:text =The%20Supreme%20Court%20has%20long,religious%20%E2%80%9Ccoercion %E2%80%9D%20of%20students.

36. Tiako, Max Jordan Nguemeni and Kelsey C. Priest. "Yes, Liquor Stores Are Essential Businesses." *Scientific American*. April 7, 2020. https:// blogs.scientificamerican.com/observations/yes-liquor-stores-are-essential -businesses/#:~:text=In%20the%20midst%20of%20the,measures%20mandated %20by%20government%20officials.

37. "Arson, Vandalism, and Other Destruction at Catholic Churches in the United States." *United States Conference of Catholic Bishops*. Accessed August 2, 2022. https://www.usccb.org/committees/religious-liberty/Backgrounder-Attacks -on-Catholic-Churches-in-US.

38. Barnes, Sophia. "Historic Church Near White House Damaged amid Unrest; Leaders Pray for Healing." *NBC Washington*. Updated June 2, 2020. https://www .nbcwashington.com/news/local/historic-church-near-white-house-damaged -amid-unrest-leaders-pray-for-healing/2318673/.

39. Rondeau, Olivia. "Hollywood Pro-Abortion Activists Demand End to Christianity and 'Fascist' Supreme Court." *Post Millenial*. July 12, 2022. https:// thepostmillennial.com/hollywood-pro-abortion-activists-demand-end-to -christianity-and-fascist-supreme-court.

40. "On Critical Race Theory and Intersectionality." *Southern Baptist Convention*. June 1, 2019. https://www.sbc.net/resource-library/resolutions/on-critical-race -theory-and-intersectionality/.

41. Chandler, Diana. "Voddie Baucham to Be 2023 SBC Pastors' Conference Presidential Nominee." *Baptist Press*. March 22, 2022. https://www .baptistpress.com/resource-library/news/voddie-baucham-to-be-2023-sbc -pastors-conference-presidential-nominee/.

42. Baucham, Voddie T. Jr. *Fault Lines: The Social Justice Movement and Evangelicalism's Looming Catastrophe.* (Irving, TX: Salem Books, 2021), 230.

43. "Moral Relativism." *Ethics Unwrapped.* https://ethicsunwrapped.utexas.edu/glossary/moral-relativism#:~:text=Moral%20relativism%20is%20the%20idea,Who%20am%20I%20to%20judge%3F%E2%80%9D.

44. Mckown, Rebecca. "Step into Your Truth with These 4 Simple Steps." *HuffPost.* July 8, 2014. https://www.huffpost.com/entry/step-into-your-truth-with_b_5564066.

45. Brown, Lee. "Sam Harris: Censoring the Post's Hunter Biden Exposés 'Warranted' to Beat Trump." *New York Post.* August 19, 2022. https://nypost.com/2022/08/19/sam-harris-defends-silencing-the-post-on-hunter-biden/.

46. Adams, John. "From John Adams to Massachusetts Militia, 11 October 1798." *National Archives.* Accessed April 29, 2023. https://founders.archives.gov/documents/Adams/99-02-02-3102.

Chapter 10: Making of the New Man: Ideological Indoctrination

1. "Puyi." *Britannica.* Updated Feb 3, 2023. https://www.britannica.com/biography/Puyi.

2. *The Key to Intellectuals' Thought Reform: The Issue of Standpoint* (Jilin, China: Jilin People's Publishing House, 1958).

3. Pu Yi, Henry. *The Last Manchu: The Autobiography of Henry Pu Yi.* (New York: Skyhorse, 2010), 317.

4. Pu Yi, *The Last Manchu*, 432.

5. Blow, Charles M. "Fathers' Sons and Brothers' Keepers." *New York Times.* Febuary 28, 2014. https://www.nytimes.com/2014/03/01/opinion/blow-fathers-sons-and-brothers-keepers.html.

6. Yang, *The Red Guard Generation*, 65.

7. Hu, Qingning. ""On Ideological Study Activities among Primary and Middle School Teachers in the Early Post-Liberation Ages—With a Special Focus on the Cases in Jiangsu Province." *Journal of Nanjing University: Philosophy and Social Sciences Edition*, 4. (October 1, 2009).

8. Schemmel, Alec. "NY School Board Launches Probe after Administrator's Remarks about Not Hiring Conservatives." ABC15News. March 9, 2023. https://wpde.com/news/nation-world/ny-school-board-initiates-probe-into-assistant-superintendent-after-remarks-about-not-hiring-conservatives-east-meadow-union-long-island-new-york-david-casamento.

9. Tang, Wen. "The CCP's Thought Remolding of Intellectuals." *Epoch Times.* May 17, 2017. https://www.epochtimes.com/gb/17/5/9/n9124299.htm.

10. Yang, *The Red Guard Generation*, 63.

11. Hunter, Edward. *Brain-Washing in Red China: The Calculated Destruction of Men's Minds.* (New York: Vanguard Press, 1951), 262.

12. Orwell, George. *1984.* Free eBooks at Planet eBook.com. 313.

13. "Little Red Book." *Encyclopedia.com*. Accessed October 12, 2022. https://www.encyclopedia.com/social-sciences/applied-and-social-sciences-magazines/little-red-book.

14. "Ten Years of Civil Unrest in the 'Cultural Revolution.'" www.gov.cn. Accessed April 29, 2023. http://www.gov.cn/18da/content_2247076.htm.

15. Freire, Paulo. *Pedagogy of the Oppressed*. 30th ann. ed. (New York: Continuum, 2000), 149.

16. "Imperial Examination." *Wikipedia*. Accessed August 13, 2022. https://en.wikipedia.org/wiki/Imperial_examination.

17. "Looking Back on the Cultural Revolution (22): The Maoist Educational Revolution." *Voice of America*. April 21, 2007. https://www.voachinese.com/a/a-21-w2007-04-21-voa2-58422912/1084320.html.

18. Cothran, Martin. "Traditional vs. Progressive Education." *Memoria Press*. June 13, 2016. https://www.memoriapress.com/articles/traditional-vs-progressive-education/.

19. Cothran, "Traditional vs. Progressive Education."

20. Grossman, Hannah. "National Education Association Teachers Union Proposes Resolution to Change 'Mother' to 'Birthing Parent.'" *Fox News*. July 6, 2022. https://www.foxnews.com/media/national-education-association-teachers-union-proposes-resolution-change-mother-birthing-parent.

21. Rufo, Christopher F. "Going All In." *City Journal*. July 15, 2021. https://www.city-journal.org/nea-to-promote-critical-race-theory-in-schools.

22. Newman, Alex. "Frankfurt School Weaponized US Education against Civilization." *Epoch Times*. March 10, 2020. https://www.theepochtimes.com/frankfurt-school-weaponized-u-s-education-against-civilization_3137064.html.

23. Gibbon, Peter. "John Dewey: Portrait of a Progressive Thinker." *Humanities* 40, no. 2. Spring 2019. https://www.neh.gov/article/john-dewey-portrait-progressive-thinker.

24. Ladson-Billings, Gloria and William F. Tate. *Education Research in the Public Interest: Social Justice, Action, and Policy*. (New York: Teachers College Press, 2006), 127.

25. DeGroot, Gerard J. *The Sixties Unplugged: A Kaleidoscopic History of a Disorderly Decade*. (Cambridge, MA: Harvard University Press, 2008), 123.

26. Shaull, Richard in Freire, *Pedagogy of the Oppressed*, 34.

27. Lindsay, James. "Paulo Freire's Schools." *New Discourses Bullets* ep. 7. May 19, 2022. https://newdiscourses.com/2022/05/paulo-freires-schools-new-discourses-bullets-ep-7/.

28. Campbell, Neil. "Speaking on Hidden Camera, California High School Teacher Admits Using Classroom to Turn Students into 'Revolutionaries.'" *Vision Times*. September 1, 2021. https://www.visiontimes.com/2021/09/01/sacramento-antifa-high-school-teacher-revolutionaries.html.

29. Skousen, W. Cleon. *The Naked Communist*, 11th ed. (Salt Lake City: The Ensign Publishing Company, 1962), 279.

30. Newman, "Frankfurt School Weaponized."

31. Poff, Jeremiah. "Critical Race Theory Pervasive in Virginia Teacher Training Materials, Contrary to Democratic Claims." *Washington Examiner.* November 9, 2021. https://www.washingtonexaminer.com/policy/critical-race -theory-pervasive-in-virginia-teacher-training-materials-contrary-to-democratic -claims.

32. Patteson, Callie. "AG Garland's Son-in-Law's Education Company Supports Critical Race Theory." *New York Post.* October 13, 2021. https://nypost .com/2021/10/13/critical-race-theory-firm-linked-to-ag-garlands-kin-serves -schoolscompany-co-founded-by-ag-garlands-son-in-law-serves-over-20k-schools/.

33. "*A People's History of the United States*: Abridged Teaching Edition." *The New Press.* Accessed on January 27, 2023. https://thenewpress.com/books /peoples-history-of-united-states-1#:~:text=Howard%20Zinn's%20A%20People's %20History,voices%20are%20typically%20omitted%20from.

34. Betz, Bradford. "Virginia Dems Reject New Communism Curriculum after Teachers Union Said It Could Offend Asians." *Fox News.* February 22, 2023. https:// www.foxnews.com/politics/virginia-dems-rejects-new-communism-curriculum -teachers-union-said-could-offend-asians.

35. Hagstrom, Anders. "673 University Professors Sign Letter Opposing Courses on America's Founding, Constitution." *Fox News.* April 26, 2023. https:// www.foxnews.com/politics/673-university-professors-sign-letter-opposing -courses-americas-founding-constitution.

36. Clancy, Maggie. "Here Are 4 Examples of Math Problems in Textbooks Banned in Florida." *Scary Mommy.* April 23, 2022. https://www.scarymommy.com /parenting/florida-rejected-math-textbooks-critical-race-theory-examples.

37. "Virginia's Definition of Social Emotional Learning." *Virginia Department of Education.* Accessed on March 2, 2023. https://www.doe.virginia .gov/programs-services/student-services/integrated-student-supports/social -emotional-learning-sel.

38. Personal communication.

39. Hegseth, Pete. *Battle for the American Mind: Uprooting a Century of Miseducation* (New York: Broadside Books, 2022), 80.

40. Morton, Neal. "Washington Was One of the Last States to Require High School-Exit Exams. Now Seniors Can Apply for a Waiver to Graduate on Time," *Seattle Times.* June 3, 2019. https://www.seattletimes.com/education-lab/washington -was-one-of-the-last-states-to-require-high-school-exit-exams-now-seniors -can-apply-for-a-waiver-to-graduate-on-time/.

41. "Preserving a Constitution Designed for a Moral and Religious People." *Center for Christian Thought Action.* August 3, 2020. https://ccta.regent.edu/2020/08/03 /preserving-a-constitution-designed-for-a-moral-and-religious-people/.

Notes

42. Stanley-Becker, Isaac. "Susan E. Rice's Son Is a Trump-Loving Republican. He Says a Stanford Classmate Assaulted Him at Pro-Kavanaugh Event." *Washington Post.* October 15, 2018. https://www.washingtonpost.com/news/morning-mix/wp/2018/10/15/susan-rices-son-is-a-trump-loving-republican-he-says-a-stanford-classmate-assaulted-him-at-pro-kavanaugh-event/.

43. Kennedy, Dana. "Mount Holyoke Grad Deprogrammed from Women-Only Woke Culture." *New York Post.* November 26, 2022. https://nypost.com/2022/11/26/mount-holyoke-grad-deprogrammed-from-women-only-woke-culture/.

Epilogue: A Warning

1. "Full Text of Clinton's Speech on China Trade Bill." *Institute for Agriculture and Trade Policy.* March 9, 2000. https://www.iatp.org/sites/default/files/Full_Text_of_Clintons_Speech_on_China_Trade_Bi.htm.

2. Branigan, Tania. "Xi Jinping Vows to Fight 'Tigers' and 'Flies' in Anti-Corruption Drive." *The Guardian.* January 22, 2013. https://www.theguardian.com/world/2013/jan/22/xi-jinping-tigers-flies-corruption.

3. "The Degeneration of the CPSU Is the Fundamental Reason for the Disintegration of the Soviet Union." *Shenzhen Academy of Social Sciences.* October 9, 2021. http://www.szass.com/szskzk/zlk/llyd/xsyj/content/post_737441.html.

4. Eckardt, Andy and Marie Brockling. "97-Year-Old Former Secretary at a Nazi Death Camp Is Convicted by German Court." *NBC News.* December 20, 2022. https://www.nbcnews.com/news/world/97-year-old-secretary-nazi-stutthof-camp-convicted-german-court-rcna62519.

5. Nerozzi, Timothy. "Sen. Blumenthal Expresses Regret for Attending Communist Awards Show." *Fox News.* December 18, 2021. https://www.foxnews.com/politics/sen-blumenthal-expresses-regret-attending-communist-awards-show.

6. "Communism Killed over 100 Million." Victims of Communism Memorial Foundation. Accessed April 29, 2023. https://victimsofcommunism.org/.

7. Ocasio, Bianca Padró. "DeSantis Signs Bill Mandating School Lesson on Communism." *Miami Herald.* May 9, 2022. https://www.miamiherald.com/news/politics-government/article261246872.html#:~:text=DeSantis%20signs%20bill%20mandating%20communism,as%20GOP%20leans%20on%20education&text=Public%20school%20teachers%20in%20Florida,people%20suffered%20under%20those%20regimes.

INDEX

Index

Index

Index

Frankfurt School, 79–83, 88, 253–54, 257
Franklin, Benjamin, 77
"free love," 83–84
free market, 72, 81, 86, 90, 270–71
free speech, 13, 14, 87, 125, 126, 140, 142, 144, 150, 178
Free Speech Movement, 139
Freire, Paolo, 249–50, 255
Freud, Sigmund, 171
Friedan, Betty, 84

gang violence, 153
Garland, Merrick, 258
Garza, Alicia, 88, 145, 147
gender (gender identity), 110, 179–81
Gender Queer: A Memoir (Kobabe), 178
Georgetown University, 107
German Communist Party, 150
Germany, 77, 79, 83, 137, 189, 274. *See also* Nazism
Gingrich, Newt, 20
Ginsberg, Allen, 83
Gipe, Gabriel, 255–56
Gittings, John, 135
Global Times, 147, 191
globalism, 71, 90
God, 18, 87, 174–75, 217, 224–25, 227, 229, 236, 256
Golden Globes, 109
Goldenberg, Ashley Rae, 152
Gonzales, Mike, 145, 147
Gorsuch, Neil, 231
Goya Foods, 181–82
Graham, Billy, 208
Gramsci, Antonio, 78–80, 83, 92, 227
Great Britain, 73
Great Famine, 74, 198
Great Leap Forward, 73, 133, 198
Great Proletarian Cultural Revolution. *See* Chinese Cultural Revolution
Great Society, 202–3
Griffin, Kathy, 116
Guangdong Province, 221
Guangzhou, 54, 217
Guevara, Che, 254–55

hairstyles, 166
Han Chinese, 163
Hanks, Tom, 182
Hannah-Jones, Nikole, 22, 258
Hannity, Sean, 17–19
Harbin, 218
Harris, Kamala, 112, 151
Harris, Sam, 236–37
Harry Potter books, 182
Harvard University, 262
Hegseth, Pete, 263
Henan Province, 195
Heritage Action Sentinels, 20
Heritage Foundation, 145, 200
heterosexuals, 109
Heywood, Andrew, 78
Hinton, William, 135
Hitler, Adolf, 79, 116, 136, 273
Hollywood, 232
Home Raid, 164–65, 183
homosexuals, 110
Hong Kong, 53–54, 166–67, 195
Hoover Institution, 141
Horkheimer, Max, 79
House of Representatives, 5, 149
How to Be an Antiracist (Kendi), 107–8, 182
Huang, Teacher, 28–29
Huang Cheng Ba (Chengdu), 162
HuffPost, 66, 227, 236
Hui, 163
Humboldt University, 88
Hunter, Edward, 246
"Hypocrisy of American Civil Rights" (article), 147

identity Marxism, 105–6, 181, 231
immigrants and immigration, 51, 57–58, 77, 111, 183
In Defense of Looting (Osterweil), 148–49
An Inconvenient Minority (Xu), 263
Independent Women's Forum, 20
India, 211, 225, 226
individualism, 89, 173, 202, 242
indoctrination, 15, 91, 132, 191, 194, 204–7, 240–46, 252, 253, 257,

Index

Index

"loyalists," 129, 134
Luce, Henry, 212

Macquarie Dictionary, 158
Madison, James, 265
Maher, Bill, 92
The Man Who Stayed Behind
  (Rittenberg), 125
Manchuria, 241
Manhattan Institute, 185
Mao, Madame, 167
Mao Zedong, vii–ix, 3–5, 8, 10, 11, 14,
  25, 26, 29, 31, 32, 34–39, 42, 43,
  70–76, 81–83, 85–87, 92, 94–100,
  102–9, 113, 115, 117, 119–38, 144,
  145, 147, 150, 151, 155, 158, 159,
  162, 165, 167–72, 174, 181–83, 185,
  188–94, 196–98, 203, 210, 212–15,
  218, 223, 226, 234–35, 240–41,
  243–44, 246–52, 254, 256, 260,
  262–64, 269–75
Mao Zedong Thought, 35, 38, 82, 162,
  240–42, 248–52, 270
Maoism, 3, 32, 76, 92, 108, 125, 145, 147,
  159, 219, 234–35, 260, 269
Maoism Middle School (Beijing), 166
Mao's Iron Girls, 167
Marcuse, Herbert, 83, 88
Martin, Trayvon, 145–46
Marx, Karl, 77, 128, 168, 171, 175, 188,
  199, 225, 271
The Marxification of Education
  (Lindsay), 81
Marxism-Leninism, xiii, 75, 242, 270
Marxists and Marxism, viii, 4–6, 8,
  11, 13, 22–23, 35, 64, 70, 76, 77,
  86–92, 94, 96–97, 105–10, 113–18,
  120, 128, 139, 143, 146, 148, 150,
  158, 159, 163, 171–72, 175, 176,
  188, 190, 199–202, 208, 211, 215,
  226, 229–32, 237, 244, 246, 249,
  254–57, 259, 260, 262–64, 272–73,
  275. *See also* Communists and
  Communism; cultural Marxism
Mason, Eric, 233
Mason, George, 177

mass shooters, 203
May Fourth Movement, 189
May 16 Notification, 74
McCarthy, Joseph, 139–40
McCarthyism, 139–40
McPhelin, Michael, 140–42
McWhorter, John, 235
Medical News Today, 110
Mendez, Jessica, 15
meritocracy, 251, 262–63
Messing, Debra, 108
Metaxas, Eric, 233–34
Middlebury College, 143
Ming dynasty, 162, 168
Minneapolis, Minn., 12
Moms for America, 20
Mongolia, 213
Moore, Julianne, 108
moral relativism, 235–37
Morrison, Robert, 216
Mount Holyoke College, 266
mRNA COVID vaccines, 112
MSNBC, 107
Muhammad, Elijah, 229
Murray, Charles, 143
Murray, Douglas, 173, 183–84
Musk, Elon, 81, 91, 206
Muslims, 163, 211, 214, 218, 230, 231.
  See also Islam
Mussolini, Benito, 79

NAACP, 108, 117
Nadler, Jerome, 149
The Naked Communist (Skousen), 256
Nation of Islam, 229
National Education Association, 252,
  253
National Lawyers Guild, 152
National Museum of African American
  History and Culture, 173–74
National Public Radio (NPR), 149, 182
National School Boards
  Association, 20
nationalism, 90
Nationalists. *See* Kuomintang
Nave, Pat, 51, 52, 210

Index

propaganda teams, 101, 123
propaganda vehicles, 126
public schools, 2, 16, 177, 180, 204, 229, 232, 253–54, 256
Pulitzer Prize, 258
Puyi, 241–43

Qin, Emperor, 171
Qing dynasty, 168
Qingdao, 189
Qinghai, 218
Qinghua University. *See* Tsinghua University

Race Marxism (Lindsay), 81, 106
racism, 2, 3, 15, 17, 60–63, 65, 66, 80, 89, 106–8, 115, 174, 178, 182, 235
radio, 39, 50
Rampton, Martha, 200–201
Reagan, Ronald, 208
Real News Network, 146
rebirth, 243
Red Army, 83, 170, 219
Red August, 130–31
Red Class, 99, 104–5
Red Flag magazine, 196
Red Guard Cemetery, 135–36
The Red Guard Generation and Political Activism in China (Yang Guobin), 136
Red Guards, 10, 31–33, 41, 94–95, 116, 119–39, 143–45, 148–51, 153, 155, 157–66, 168–69, 171, 176, 177, 183, 185, 191, 193, 201, 214, 217, 218, 230, 243, 244, 247, 264
"Red Intellectuals," 251–52
Red Star over China (Snow), 103
Red Terror, 148
Red Virtue: Human Relationships in the New Russia (Winter), 202
reeducation, 38, 42, 129, 137, 198, 241, 242. *See also* Thought Reform
Reffitt, Guy W., 205
Reffitt, Jackson, 205
Reid, Jen, 176–77
Reid, Joy, 107

The ReidOut (TV show), 107
Reimagine Monument Avenue (Richmond), 176
religion, 110, 210–12, 221, 223–25, 228–29, 234–37, 256. *See also specific religions*
"Remember the Bitterness," 36
Republican Party, 14–16, 64, 111, 116, 177, 180, 182, 187, 266
Rice, Susan, 266
Rice-Cameron, John David, 266
Richmond, Va., 176
riots, 2, 12–14, 77, 134, 148, 151, 204
Rittenberg, Sidney, 125, 130
Robinson Crusoe (Defoe), 55
Rockefeller Foundation, 160
Rockwell, Annabella, 266
Roe v. Wade, 84, 88, 232
Romania, 19
Roosevelt, Teddy, 176
Rowling, J. K., 182
Rubin, Jerry, 83, 88, 139
Rufo, Christopher, 153, 260
rule of law, 89
RuPaul, 178
Russia (including Soviet Union), 19, 36, 72, 73, 75, 77, 175, 188, 198, 202, 206, 213, 272–73

San Francisco, Calif., 84, 147
Sanders, Bernie, 98, 109
Sanford, Fla., 146
Sarachild, Kathie, 201
Saraswati, Raquel Evita, 230–31
Sarsour, Linda, 230
Sears, Winsome, 107
Seattle, Wash., 12, 152
Second Amendment, 13
second-wave feminism, 84, 200–202
self-criticism, 31, 35, 242
Serbia, 19
Seuss, Dr., 178
sex and sexuality, 83–85, 109–10, 179–83. *See also* transgender (transgender ideology)
Shaanxi, 83

Index

ABOUT THE AUTHOR

Xi Van Fleet describes herself as "Chinese by birth, American by choice, survivor of Mao's Cultural Revolution, defender of liberty." She was born in China, lived through the Cultural Revolution, and was sent to work in the countryside at the age of sixteen to receive her re-education. After Mao's death, she was able to go to college to study English and has lived in the United States since 1986. In 2021, she delivered a school board speech in Loudoun County, Virginia, against critical race theory that went viral and ignited national conservative media attention. She now devotes her time and energy full-time to warning about the parallels between Mao's Cultural Revolution in China and what's unfolding in America today. Since going public with her message, Xi Van Fleet has appeared on Fox News, Newsmax, and radio shows and podcasts across the country.